Plain Pursuit

A Daughters of the Promise Novel

BETH WISEMAN

THOMAS NELSON
Since 1798

NASHVILLE   DALLAS   MEXICO CITY   RIO DE JANEIRO   BEIJING

Published in Nashville, Tennessee. Thomas Nelson is a registered trademark of Thomas Nelson, Inc.

Thomas Nelson, Inc., books may be purchased in bulk for educational, business, fund-raising, or sales promotional use. For information, please e-mail SpecialMarkets@ThomasNelson.com.

Scriptures taken from the King James Version of the Bible.

Publisher's Note: This novel is a work of fiction. Names, characters, places, and incidents are either products of the author's imagination or used fictitiously. All characters are fictional, and any similarity to people living or dead is purely coincidental.

Library of Congress Cataloging-in-Publication Data

Wiseman, Beth, 1962–
   Plain pursuit : a Daughters of the promise novel / Beth Wiseman.
     p. cm.
   ISBN 978-1-59554-719-4 (pbk.)
I. Amish—Fiction. I. Title.
   PS3623.I83P58 2009
   813'.6—dc22

                          2009009227

Printed in the United States of America

09 10 11 12 13 RRD 5 4

To my mother, Pat Isley

Glossary

ach: oh

Aemen: Amen

baremlich: terrible

boppli: baby or babies

bruder: brother

daadi: grandfather

daed: dad

danki: thanks

die weibsleit gwilde bis in die nacht: the women quilt long into the night

Deitschi wege: Dutch ways

dippy eggs: eggs cooked over easy

Englisch or *Englischer*: a non-Amish person

es dutt mir leed: I am sorry

fraa: wife

guder mariye: good morning

gut: good

hatt: hard

haus: house

in lieb: in love

kaffi: coffee

Kapp: prayer covering or cap

katzhaarich: short-haired

kinner: child

maeds: girls

make wet: rain

mamm: mom

mammi: grandmother

mei: my

naerfich: nervous

onkel: uncle

Ordnung: the written and unwritten rules of the Amish; the understood order by which the Amish are expected to live, passed down from generation to generation. Most Amish know the rules by heart.

outten the lights: turn off the lights

Pennsylvania *Deitsch*: Pennsylvania German, the language most commonly used by the Amish

rumschpringe: running-around period when a teenager turns sixteen years old

schnuppich: snoopy

schtinkich: smelly

sell is es bescht vun allem: that is the best of all

streng meiding: strong shunning

ummieglich: impossible

wunderbaar: wonderful

ya: yes

1

LUNCH WITH HER EDITOR USUALLY MEANT ONE THING. Trouble.

Carley couldn't think of anything she'd done to warrant the meeting. Granted, she hadn't written any award-winning stories for the newspaper lately, but she'd held her own. Every deadline had been met. The stories had been newsworthy. But something was clearly on Matt's mind. His forehead creased with concern as they took their seats at a small deli near the office.

"They have good burgers here," Matt said, scanning the menu.

He was stalling.

"I'm just going to have a salad." Closing the menu, she folded her hands and waited. It was straight-up noon, and the harried waitress was taking orders several tables over. Carley was glad to see her favorite sandwich shop back in business and full of hungry patrons. It had taken months for Houston to recover from the devastating effects of the hurricane, but life had obviously returned to normal.

Normal. Such a loose term, she thought, waiting for Matt to drop whatever news had prompted the lunch.

Matt finally closed his menu and sighed. "Carley, you're a good reporter . . ." The lines above his bushy brows became more prominent. She waited for the *but*. He cleared his throat instead, and she took the opportunity to remind him of her tenure.

"I've been with the paper four years. I'd like to think I've done a good job." He nodded his agreement, although his expression remained solemn. "What's wrong, Matt?"

She searched his face, her heart rate kicking up. Matt had been her editor at the paper since she started, and they'd been to lunch only twice. Once as a celebration of sorts when she won a prestigious award, and once when Matt felt an article she wrote had crossed the journalistic line.

She hadn't won any awards lately.

"Carley, you've got plenty of unused vacation. Why haven't you taken any?" His eyes cut to the jagged scar spanning three inches across her left forearm. Instinctively, her right hand covered the evidence of the event that had forever altered her life.

"I took two weeks off when Mom died." *Where is he going with this? It's been six months since the accident.*

"Carley," he grumbled, "that wasn't a vacation, and part of that time you were in the hospital yourself." He shook his head as the waitress approached.

"I'll have the grilled chicken salad," Carley said after Matt ordered his burger and fries. She immediately regretted her decision. What was the point? You couldn't live forever. She bet her mother would have loaded up with an extra helping of pie on Christmas Day if she'd known it was her last day on earth.

"No, wait. I change my mind. I'll have a burger and fries too."

"Good girl," Matt said after the waitress scurried away. "You're too thin as it is."

"Now what were you saying, Matt?" She'd rather get this over with and salvage her appetite.

"I want you to take some vacation time."

Although his tone left little room for argument, she quickly countered. "I don't need a vacation."

"If you don't see it, then I'll just come out and say it: you aren't at the top of your game. You're a far cry from it, Carley. Your stories lack the zing they used to have. The facts are there, but they're lacking . . . What's the word I'm looking for?"

"I have no idea." She folded her arms across her chest.

"Emotional capacity," he continued. "You used to weave emotion into your stories—just enough to spruce up the article." He shrugged, and she saw the pity in his eyes as they locked with hers. "The intensity of your writing just isn't there anymore."

"I—I didn't realize that." She fought the sudden tremor in her voice. "I'll work harder."

When it appeared Matt was going to argue, she dug deep for the truth. "I need to work, Matt. It's all I have."

She dropped her gaze, hating the vulnerability she knew her expression revealed. *Matt has to understand. I can't take any time off. What would I do?* Until six months ago, her leisure time had been divided among her mother, her boyfriend, and her friends. Now her mom was gone, and Dalton had broken off their three-year relationship. And after one too many declines, her few girlfriends quit asking her to participate in their activities.

She had nothing but work.

"That's what I mean, Carley," Matt urged. "You are a beautiful woman with no relationships or interests outside of work.

You're slowly withdrawing from life, and it's noticeable in your writing." He leaned over the table. "Carley, on a personal note, we're worried about you."

"Who is *we*?" She knew the answer. "Katrina?"

Her reporting rival had bumped up a notch to assistant editor awhile back and now latched onto every opportunity to remind Carley of her position.

"Yes, Katrina and I discussed it, Carley, but—"

"She doesn't like me, Matt."

Right away she realized the comment sounded childish.

"Not true." Matt shook his head and pushed an envelope in Carley's direction. "This is a month's vacation pay. You've accumulated a lot more than that. Take a month off, Carley. Come back refreshed. You should have taken more time off after the accident."

Carley peered at the envelope on the table as the waitress returned with their lunches and offers of ketchup and extra napkins. "I'm not taking a vacation, Matt. Why should I be forced to use my time right now?"

"Because you wouldn't like the alternative." He wrapped his mouth around his burger.

Carley wasn't hungry for anything except Katrina Peighton's hide. This was her doing, not Matt's.

"So let me get this straight. Either I go on vacation or I'm fired?"

"Don't look at it that way, Carley," Matt said between bites. "Take advantage of this. I would."

Her thoughts churned. *What will I do? Sit around my big empty house?*

No. Too much time to think.

She bargained. "I'll take a week off."

"A month, Carley. We will welcome you back with open arms in one month."

By the end of the meal, she'd reluctantly accepted the envelope. Not that she had any choice in the matter. Matt made it quite clear her vacation started directly after lunch.

2

CARLEY TRIED TO KEEP HER EYES ON THE ROAD AS SHE
studied the map laid out beside her on the car seat. She'd never
been to Lancaster County, Pennsylvania, but a sign flashed by,
indicating twenty-six miles to the town of Paradise. Good. She
was on the right track.

She watched the farmland scrolling by and thought about
seeing Lillian. Her friend had fled the craziness of Houston a
year and a half ago, moved in with her Amish grandparents, married an Amish man, and now happily resided in the town of
Paradise with her new family. Carley couldn't help but wonder
how much her friend might have changed. From her initial letters
Carley knew Lillian's grandparents' farm in Paradise had provided Lillian with a safe haven where she could get her life
together. But when Lillian wrote to say she had converted and
was staying—that was a lot to swallow. Carley couldn't get past
the lack of electricity, much less the fact that Lillian had married
Amish widower Samuel Stoltzfus, become a stepmother to his
thirteen-year-old son, and now had a baby of her own.

Of course, Carley knew she had changed too. Everything had
changed last Christmas Day . . .

According to Lillian's letters, she had been baptized in the

Amish faith—a required step toward marrying an Amish man. Her friend also adhered to all their Plain customs, including the wardrobe. It was an unbelievable transformation. No television, makeup, jewelry. No computer.

Hmm. Carley eyed her laptop on the floorboard of the rental car. How was she going to charge the battery?

One thing shone through in all Lillian's letters: she was happy. As a writer, Carley excelled at reading between the lines. She had looked for clues that perhaps Lillian wasn't as content as she let on. She couldn't find one. Lillian's destination seemed to have brought her the peace Carley knew Lillian longed for.

Carley felt like she was still wandering, her own destination unknown.

Which brought her to her current situation. In her last letter to Lillian, Carley had asked her friend if she might come for a visit and do an article about the Amish ways. Lillian quickly responded with an invitation—which Carley accepted the day her forced vacation began. She would put her leave to good use. Even better, she would incorporate work into her trip.

Work would keep her sane.

Lillian popped a loaf of bread into the gas oven. Carley would be hungry when she arrived. Hopefully her friend would like the meatloaf and baked corn casserole she had prepared, along with the chocolate shoofly pie for dessert. If she hurried, she could have the meal ready before Anna woke up for her feeding.

She scanned the wooden table in the middle of the kitchen. It was covered with a variety of jellies and applesauce and some pickled red beets. For a moment she pondered whether she should have tackled the sauerbraten recipe instead. But the meatloaf was a lot less work, and Anna had been fussy all afternoon. She'd fallen behind on the household chores.

Maybe she should have baked a peach pie instead of the rich shoofly with its filling of molasses and brown sugar.

Or *maybe* she should stop worrying so much about Carley's arrival. But she couldn't help it. Their last time together, Lillian had sported blue jeans, a name-brand blouse, stilettos, full makeup and silver jewelry, and a designer handbag.

She tucked a loose strand of hair beneath her white *Kapp*, glancing down at her blue linen dress covered by a black apron. Her plain black leather shoes were a far cry from the spiked heels of her past.

The screen door slammed shut behind her. Samuel.

"It smells *gut* in here," he said, kissing her smile before tossing his hat onto the rack in the den.

"*Danki.* I hope it's *gut.*" She breathed in the aroma of baking bread while she mixed the sauce that would go on top of the meatloaf. "I hope Carley likes it."

"Your friend will be here soon, no?"

Lillian knew Samuel worried about her *Englisch* friend coming to visit. They had discussed it, and although Samuel assured her it was fine for Carley to stay with them for the month of May, Lillian also knew Carley's visit was an exception to an unspoken rule: *no outsiders allowed.* But it wasn't that long ago *she'd* been the outsider in the Old Order Amish district. How quickly a year and a half had gone by.

"She should be here any minute," Lillian informed Samuel.

"It's almost four thirty, and I know you must be hungry. David should be home soon too. He's at *Mamm's* doing some yard work." She stirred the sauce atop the gas range. "I think you'll like Carley, Samuel. And she promised me the story she writes for her newspaper will include only things we're comfortable with."

She caught the uncertainty on Samuel's face, which he quickly hid with a half smile. "*Ya*, I know," he replied.

"You said there are a lot of misconceptions written about the way we live. Wouldn't it be nice for someone to get it right in print?" She challenged his skepticism with a playful wink, hoping to alleviate some of his fear.

"*Ya*, it's just that . . ." He hesitated, grimacing.

"What?" She turned the fire down under the sauce and slid in beside him at the kitchen table.

"I'm sure everything will be fine, Lillian. I just don't trust those who print words about our lives, and I don't know this *Englisch* woman."

Lillian grasped his hand. "But I do. And I trust her, Samuel."

"Then I will trust her too." He gave her hand a squeeze. "Now where's my little *boppli*?"

"Anna should be waking up hungry any minute. I was just trying to finish supper before Carley gets here." She returned to the sauce, and Samuel stood. "Carley is a *gut* person, Samuel. Try not to worry."

As his arms wrapped tightly around her waist, Samuel nuzzled the back of her neck. "*You* are a *gut* person, Lillian. Besides, worry is a sin."

"*Ya*, it is," she whispered as she tried to push aside her own worries over Carley's arrival.

Carley pulled into the dirt driveway off Black Horse Road. In the distance, she could see two gray buggies parked beside a white farmhouse surrounded by colorful foliage. Two crimson barns stood off to one side. Drawing closer, she noticed two horses peeking out the window of the smaller structure. The place was incredibly manicured—neatly trimmed grass in the yard, and the fields freshly cut as well. She could already picture herself watching the sunset from one of the wooden rockers on the large wraparound porch. It would be like living in a postcard.

She continued to scan her surroundings as she parked the white Ford alongside one of the buggies. When she stepped out of the car, she poked her head inside one of the boxlike transports. Black leather seats and room enough for four. She couldn't wait to go for a ride.

The squeak of a screen door drew her attention toward the house. The woman running down the porch steps—in a blue dress with a black apron, white cap, and black shoes—might have been hard to recognize on the street. But Lillian's full smile and bubbly bounce gave her away instantly. That was how Carley remembered Lillian, and she was glad to see some things hadn't changed.

"Lillian!" She hurried across the yard, greeting her friend with a hug. "You look great!" It was true. Her friend's transformation into an Amish woman worked for her. Dressed in her Plain clothes, devoid of makeup and the accessories of the past, her face gleamed. Carley could only assume it was the peacefulness Lillian had spoken of in her letters.

Carley needed a dose of that.

"I look a lot different than the last time you saw me." Lillian's voice sounded uncertain.

"Yes, you do. You look happy. And I'm so glad for you. Where's the baby?" She couldn't wait to get her hands on little Anna.

"Inside with Samuel. Come in, come in." Lillian grabbed Carley's hand and tugged her toward the house with the enthusiasm she was known for. "You look great, too, Carley. You really do."

It was a sweet thing to say. And Lillian tried to sound convincing. But Carley knew she didn't look great. The past six months had taken their toll.

Forcing the thought aside, she clomped up the porch steps behind Lillian. When they reached the top, Lillian stopped and eyed Carley's shoes. "I'll tell you a secret," she whispered. "I miss fancy shoes."

Carley looked down at her friend's feet. "You always did have a thing for shoes. But I bet those are a lot more comfortable than these." She pointed to her brown, pointy-toed pumps.

"Oh, I'm sure they are. But if you catch me trying on your shoes while you're here, don't tell anyone."

"It'll be our secret."

The two of them giggled like schoolgirls. It felt good. As Lillian ushered her into the house, Carley wondered if Matt had been right. Maybe she did need a vacation. Being around Lillian might provide a much-needed reprieve from the grief that had blanketed her in Houston.

They entered the house through the kitchen. Backless benches on each side of a wooden table stretched long enough to seat at least ten people. While there were no ornate carvings on the table or benches, the colorful display of various foods complemented it.

Plain whitewashed walls and white countertops were enhanced by vibrant blooms on each of the three windowsills. No microwave or electrical gadgets. With the exception of a large rack holding various pots and pans next to the stove, there were no wall hangings. The room was functional yet charming.

Carley glanced up at the lantern dangling from the ceiling above the middle of the table. "Wow."

Lillian stood at a gas range against the far wall, swirling a spoon in a large pot. Wonderful aromas emanated from that part of the room. "It's a lot different from the kitchen I had in Houston," she said sheepishly as she set the spoon on the countertop and motioned for Carley to join her at the kitchen table. "But you know how much I like to cook. And one thing is for certain: Samuel and David like to eat."

"Do you miss it—your life before, I mean? The modern conveniences?"

"Nope," Lillian said without reservation, then paused with a twinkle in her eye. "Only the shoes."

Carley heard footsteps approaching. Lillian jumped up. "Be right back," she chirped and headed toward the other room.

It was only a few seconds before she returned holding a baby, with a man by her side. "This is Anna and my husband, Samuel."

Carley stood up and moved toward them. Samuel met her with a handshake and greeting, but it was the beautiful bundle in Lillian's arms that Carley homed in on.

"Oh, Lillian. She's beautiful. May I?" Carley extended her arms.

"This is a dear friend of mine, Anna," Lillian whispered. She placed the baby in Carley's arms.

"Look at you," Carley cooed, snuggling Anna closer.

"Our *boppli* will be six months old on Tuesday," Lillian said, pride evident in her tone.

"*Ya*, I reckon she'll be baking bread and canning vegetables before we know it," Samuel added.

Lillian nudged him. "Let's don't rush it."

Anna's bright blue eyes fused with Carley's. She squirmed. "Oh dear. She isn't going to cry, is she?" Carley looked up at Lillian.

"If she does, it's because it's near feeding time," Lillian assured her, reaching down to softly stroke Anna's head. "Such a gift from God," she whispered.

"Yes," Carley agreed. She squelched the thought of having her own child.

The screen door slammed, and they all turned their attention to a smaller version of Samuel walking into the room. The boy had the same solid build, bright blue eyes, and square jawline as his dad, minus the full beard.

"Well, hello there," Lillian said. "Carley, this is our son, David. David, this is my friend Carley I told you about." Lillian reached down to take Anna. "I'm going to feed Anna so we can all sit down and eat in peace. It won't take long. Help yourselves to what's on the table. I'll be right back to serve supper."

Reluctantly Carley gave up the soft bundle then extended her hand to David. "Nice to meet you."

"*Gut* to meet you too," the boy answered, removing the straw hat from his head. His bobbed haircut was similar to his father's, but a lighter shade of brown. Both father and son wore black pants, dark blue shirts, and suspenders. They had each put in a hard day's work as evidenced by the stains on their clothes.

Samuel and David both sat on the bench across from Carley. "Lillian has been lookin' forward to your visit," Samuel said.

"Thank you for having me in your home." Carley knew it was uncommon for the Amish to host an outsider. She wondered how Samuel truly felt about it, particularly since she was there in part to write an article about the Plain ways.

Samuel nodded in acknowledgment before turning to his son. "How are *Daadi* Jonas and *Mammi* Sarah Jane?"

"Today was a *gut* day for *Daadi* Jonas, *Mammi* said."

Before Samuel could reply, Lillian reentered the room. "Back already. Would you believe Anna fell asleep again, so I'm going to let her lie while we eat. David, did you say Grandpa had a *gut* day? And *mei mamm* is okay too?"

David nodded.

Lillian placed a loaf of freshly baked bread on the table and turned her attention to Carley. "Remember I told you that my mom moved in with my grandpa? Well, David goes over there every day and helps with the chores. It works out well during the summer, but when David goes back to school, it will be a challenge. There's a lot to do at both households, and David can only go after school. Thank goodness this next year will be his last." She paused. "Here in the district, children attend school through the eighth grade."

She placed a pan of meatloaf on the table, followed by a casserole and several other side dishes.

"Lillian, this all looks great. You shouldn't have gone to so much trouble." Carley inventoried the table.

"*Ach*, it may look like a lot. But trust me, it takes a lot to feed these two."

Again Lillian smiled at Samuel with a warmth Carley found endearing. Maybe someday she would find that kind of love. Although after the way Dalton had dumped her, she'd lost her faith in relationships.

Besides, what man would want her?

All heads bowed in silent prayer. Carley discreetly glanced around at each of them.

What a lovely family.

───────

"Your friend went to bed early," Samuel said to Lillian when they dressed for bed. "Being from the city, I would expect her to stay up past eight thirty. We're used to going to bed early and getting up early. I reckon she's not."

"She said she was tired from the trip," Lillian answered, pulling a floor-length white nightgown over her head. "Besides, we'll have lots of time to catch up."

"*Ya*, a whole *month.*" Samuel grinned at her.

She poked him. "It will be fine, Samuel," she said as she slid into bed beside him. Grabbing her book off the nightstand, she dimmed the lantern and pulled it closer to the edge of the table. "I'm going to read for a little while."

Samuel didn't fall asleep right away as he normally did. She'd barely finished a page when he propped himself up on one elbow and turned to face her. "She sure is *katzhaarich.*"

Lillian turned to her husband, whose face was drawn down in disapproval. "*Ya*, she is short-haired. But it's considered very stylish by the *Englisch.*"

Samuel reached over and ran his hand through Lillian's brown

waves, which now cascaded well past her shoulders. She hadn't cut
her hair since her arrival to the district. "Your friend's hair barely
covers her ears," he said, his eyes narrowing. "It isn't right. 'But if
a woman have long hair, it is a glory to her: for her hair is given
her for a covering.'"

"Good thing I didn't have short hair when I met you," Lillian
teased, closing her book. She turned to face him.

"I would have loved you anyway," he assured her.

He wrapped his arms around her and snuggled closer. Lillian
closed her eyes and reveled in the comfort of her husband's
embrace, silently thanking God for the wonderful family He had
bestowed on her.

Carley quietly maneuvered her way down the stairs, easing up on
her weight each time one of the wooden steps creaked. It was
completely dark as she shone the light from her cell phone on
the steps in front of her. She had slept a whopping three hours
before a horrible leg cramp thrust her out of a sound and much-
needed sleep.

She tiptoed her way into the kitchen and scanned the countertops. A partial loaf of homemade bread was wrapped in foil inside
a clear bag. *Yum.* The warm bread with butter had been so tasty
at supper.

Her cell phone offered a dim ray of light, enough for her to
fumble the bag open and retrieve one of the precut slices. Then she
glanced around the room, blinking at the darkness. *Ah, of course—no
electricity, no microwave.*

She placed the bread on a napkin on the table, stepped toward
the propane-fueled refrigerator, and pulled the door open. She

squinted as the contents lit up, and selected a pitcher of sweet tea and a tub of butter.

Just a little tea and some bread. Then maybe she could go back to sleep.

Unsure how to light the overhead lantern and unwilling to wake anyone up, she kept her cell phone propped up on the table. The digital clock on the screen read 11:40. Too late to call Adam. He might be awake, but she was sure Cindy and the kids were asleep.

Carley felt bad about her last conversation with her brother. Adam had agreed she needed a vacation, but didn't think she should spend a month so far from home. Even after explaining the purpose of her trip, he hadn't let up, and the conversation quickly deteriorated. Both said some things they didn't really mean, and Carley ended it by hanging up on him.

Adam, her older brother and only sibling, was overprotective. He'd been that way since their father died when she was seven. However, he'd gotten worse over the six months following the accident. When Carley gave up her apartment and moved into their mother's house, Adam and Cindy moved from across town to right down the street from her. It was too close for comfort, and Carley told them so. But Adam was insistent. And the ever-protective hovering grew worse.

She rubbed her temples. As always when she allowed herself to think of the accident, her mind filled with images. The haunting flashbacks were always the same—the red Chevy pickup barreling into the driver's side of Mom's tan Toyota; her mother's face covered in blood, resting against the steering wheel, eyes widened in horror . . .

Carley gulped down the piece of bread in her mouth and

grabbed at her side. The stabbing pain was a reminder of the spiked piece of lumber that had fallen from the truck and rocketed into her, grazing her forearm before implanting itself deep within her abdomen.

If only they hadn't decided to go to the movies that Christmas Day. If only she'd driven instead of her mother. If only . . .

With feverish intent, she sucked in a deep breath and attempted to visualize something soothing. The gentle swooshing of ocean waves usually helped clear the disturbing memories. She concentrated on recreating the sounds in her head.

I am okay. I will be okay.

She finally calmed down, but she felt drained. Maybe now she'd be able to go back to sleep.

She put her glass in the sink, tossed the napkin into the trash container, and pointed her cell phone toward the stairs. She had only taken a couple of steps upward, when she heard a loud scramble and thud upstairs, followed seconds later by footsteps. Slowing her pace, she listened.

When she heard Lillian cry out, "Samuel! Help! Come quickly!" Carley bolted up the stairs two at a time.

3

CARLEY WATCHED LILLIAN AND SAMUEL HOVERING OVER David, who lay sprawled on the wooden floor of his bedroom. The dimly lit lantern shed enough light for Carley to see blood covering the teenager's face from his nose to his chin.

Samuel inspected his son's chin. "It's not as bad as it looks. You're gonna be fine, boy," he whispered to David. "But you will need a few stitches, looks like."

"I'm sorry, Pop." David winced in pain. "I don't know what happened. I got up to go to the bathroom, then everything started going gray. And then I woke up facedown on the floor."

After handing Samuel a wet rag, Lillian turned to Carley. "Can you drive us to the hospital?"

"Of course," Carley answered. She'd planned never to set foot in a hospital again. But David's injuries didn't look too bad. Hopefully they would get in and out in a hurry.

"Pop, I'm real sorry," David repeated, flinching when his father applied pressure with the wet towel.

Samuel spoke softly in Pennsylvania *Deitsch* to his son. Carley didn't understand a thing he said, but his tone was sympathetic and comforting.

After changing out of their nightclothes, they all met

downstairs in the kitchen. Samuel sat on the bench next to his son. He removed the blood-soaked rag and placed a clean wet towel against David's chin.

"We better get going, no?" Lillian asked as she joined them with Anna in her arms.

Carley couldn't quite get used to Lillian's new way of speaking. She was impressed by how easily Lillian had adapted to this community, especially the language.

"How far is the hospital?" Carley asked.

"It's about sixteen miles to Lancaster General," Lillian said, retrieving a bottle for Anna from the refrigerator. "I've already installed the base of the baby carrier in your car. But I'm wondering if we're all going to fit."

"It'll be tight with the car seat, but we'll make it work." Carley closed the door behind them all as they made their way to the car. She'd planned to return the rental car after a few days, but now she wasn't sure she wanted to rely solely on buggy transportation for the next month.

The familiar scent of "hospital" hit Carley the moment the double doors into the ER swung open. The waiting room was filled to capacity.

"This is going to take forever," Lillian whispered to Carley, her face reflecting the worry in her heart.

I hope not, Carley thought as she struggled to cast aside the creeping visions of her own hospital memories. She blew out a breath and took a seat, holding Anna while Lillian filled out the appropriate paperwork. Samuel was having another look at David's chin. Poor David was pale as a ghost, and Carley wondered if he'd ever been inside a hospital before. In addition to the pain he was in, the kid looked scared to death.

Carley noticed the curious stares all around them. Samuel and Lillian pretended not to notice. Maybe they were used to it, but Carley thought it was rude. With so many Amish in the area, she'd assumed their Plain clothes wouldn't draw attention.

"What do you think happened?" Carley asked Lillian when she saw she was finished with the paperwork.

"I don't know. From what David said, it sounds like he fainted. He doesn't remember his face hitting the floor."

"Has he ever fainted before?"

"No, never." Lillian stood. "I'm going to go turn in this paperwork. Then I guess we just wait."

Carley gently rocked Anna while Lillian walked to the line at the receptionist's desk.

"Pop, I'm not feeling so *gut*." David bent forward in his chair.

Samuel placed his hand on his son's back. "I know. Keep the rag on your chin so as not to start up the bleeding again."

"It's not my chin, Pop," David stammered. "I feel . . . I don't know . . . I feel funny. I . . ."

Samuel grabbed for David's suspenders just as David fell forward in his chair. "David!" He pulled him back to a sitting position.

"Should I get help?" Carley asked as she stood with Anna in her arms.

"David!" Samuel bellowed again when it appeared David was losing consciousness.

Lillian pushed her way to the front of the line, threw the paperwork on the desk, and ran back to her family. "David!"

All the commotion caught the attention of a doctor coming

out of the emergency room. The man walked briskly in their direction.

"What's the problem?" he asked, squatting down in front of David, who slumped in his chair, barely able to keep from falling off.

Disheveled was the first word that came to Carley's mind as she watched the doctor examine David. The man wore a white coat with the requisite stethoscope dangling around his neck. But his shirt was wrinkled and one shirttail protruded from his pants, also in need of a hot iron. His name was printed across a name tag hanging crookedly on the right side of his coat. *Dr. Noah.* Wavy dark hair, uncharacteristically long for a doctor, framed his face.

Carley and Lillian waited for Samuel to respond. Nothing. Instead, he eyed the doctor with what could only be described as . . . contempt.

Carley could relate—she'd rather be anywhere else than in a hospital. People died in hospitals. She still recalled the way the doctor had delivered the news of her mother's death. Distant. Cold. Just a day on the job for him. Then he had returned the next day with the same detached expression and delivered Carley more bad news—this time about her own health. He'd mechanically spewed out words that would change her life forever, and did so without an ounce of compassion.

Samuel's eyes narrowed, his chin lifting as he stiffened.

When David flinched from the doctor's touch, Samuel leaned forward. "Don't—" He drew a breath, released it slowly. Pressing his lips together, stifling his words, he locked eyes with the doctor, who was waiting for an answer—from someone.

Lillian glanced at her husband and waited for a response before turning toward the doctor. "He fell and hit his chin at home," she said when Samuel didn't say anything. "We think he fainted. Now he seems like he might pass out again."

"Can you hear me?" Dr. Noah asked David.

David nodded. About the same time, a nurse approached, pushing a wheelchair. "Here you go, Doctor," she offered.

"I don't need a wheelchair," David argued. He stood up, his legs wobbly.

"David, maybe you should sit and—," Lillian pleaded.

David just shook his head. "I can walk."

"All right, then. Come with me," the doctor said to David.

He ushered David down the hallway, bypassing the evaluation rooms and heading right to the main emergency room. When he pushed the round button on the wall, the large double doors swung open. He motioned for David to walk ahead of him then turned to face Carley, Samuel, and Lillian, who was now toting Anna.

"Just Samuel for now," Dr. Noah instructed, pointing. He held the door open for Samuel to follow him.

Carley watched Lillian give her husband a questioning look, obviously surprised the doctor knew Samuel's name.

———

Noah's mind kept darting back to the past. His training taught him to push personal issues aside and focus, but as he gazed at the boy, Noah noticed immediately how much he looked like his father.

As the nurse helped David onto the bed, Noah prompted her to start an intravenous line. He wasn't sure if the boy needed any pain medication. More worrisome was how pale David looked. Best to be prepared.

Noah motioned for Samuel to step away from the bed so he could have a look at David's chin. "Hang tough, buddy," he said soothingly, pulling back the bloody towel. After a brief examination, he turned toward Samuel. "Yes, he's going to need some stitches."

Samuel fumbled with his straw hat, twirling it in his hands. He grimaced when David groaned at Noah's touch.

"He's going to be fine," Noah assured Samuel. "About three stitches should fix him up." He turned back to David. "You might have a little scar on your chin for a while, but that's kinda cool for a guy your age, huh?"

As if Noah weren't in the room, Samuel addressed his son. "Did you hear, David? A few stitches and we will go to the *haus*."

"*Ya*, Pop."

About twenty minutes later, Noah had David's chin fixed up. But he knew something much bigger was going on than a cut on the kid's chin. The boy's blood pressure was high, which Noah knew could be from the pain or the fear from being at the hospital. But he was extremely pale, and something had caused him to pass out and slam to the floor.

Noah motioned for Samuel to follow him outside the door.

"He's a handsome kid," Noah said cautiously.

"*Ya*. He is a *gut* boy."

"Samuel, David is very pale. Has he fainted like this before?"

Samuel dangled the straw hat in one hand, scratched his forehead with the other. "No. He's a healthy boy."

Before Noah could say anything else, Samuel turned back into David's room. Noah followed. Again pushing his personal demons aside, he said, "Samuel, I had the nurse get a urine sample and draw some blood. There are some tests I'd like to run—"

Samuel shook his head, just as Noah expected. "We will take him to Dr. Reynolds for a checkup."

"David doesn't need any of Dr. Reynolds' herbal treatments. He doesn't need a natural doctor, Samuel. I'd like to do some tests." Noah glanced at David, unwilling to worry the boy. "Just to be sure that—"

"When can I take David home?" Samuel interrupted. His tone was familiar—distant and laced with resentment.

Noah decided not to argue. He already had David's blood and urine, and he was going to run the tests regardless.

He turned to David. "David, have you been feeling bad lately? I'm just wondering why you fainted. Has this ever happened before?"

"No," David responded. "But . . ." The boy glanced at his father, worry in his eyes.

"What, David? It's important to tell me if you've been feeling bad," Noah pushed.

"I throw up a lot."

"What?" Samuel asked, taken aback. "When?"

David shrugged. "I reckon mostly after supper. Sometimes after breakfast."

"I will mention this to Dr. Reynolds," Samuel said.

Noah rolled his eyes. He knew it was pointless to argue with Samuel any further. He would wait for the test results.

"I guess there's no reason why you can't take David home. You'll need to have those stitches taken out in about ten days," he instructed.

Samuel nodded.

"Is that your wife and baby outside?" Noah asked.

"*Ya.*" Nothing more.

"I was sorry to hear about Rachel. She was a good woman." Noah hesitated. "From what I heard."

He shouldn't have added the last part, but his own resentment tended to spill over from time to time. But as was the Amish way, Samuel avoided confrontation and didn't reply.

"Well, it looks like you've started a new life. You have a lovely family."

Samuel nodded, refusing to make eye contact.

"Who's the other woman?" Noah helped David sit on the side of the bed.

"Lillian's friend from the city. From Texas. She's staying with us for a month and writing a story about our ways."

"Oh, really," Noah said with sarcasm. He knew he should keep his mouth shut. "Guess times have changed if you allow an *Englischer* into your home to write a story about your ways."

"Lillian trusts her to write a story that rightly talks about our beliefs and way of life."

Noah grunted, and Samuel's eyes glassed over with barely contained rage. Noah knew Samuel would hold back, though. No one practiced the Amish beliefs more stoutly than this man. And as he suspected, Samuel took a breath and refocused on his son.

"Things could have been different, Samuel," Noah said with regret. "I'll leave you with David, and I'll have the nurse get the paperwork so you can go home. David, have your pop call me if you start feeling bad or—"

"The boy will be fine," Samuel snapped.

Sighing, Noah headed out of the room. Neither father nor son noticed as Noah paused to take a final look at them.

Carley leaned down to retrieve Anna's pacifier, which had plopped out of her mouth. She handed it to Lillian. The baby was fast asleep in the carrier on the floor between them.

Lillian's expression puckered. "I wonder how that doctor knows Samuel." She crossed her legs and folded her arms. "Did you hear him call Samuel by name?"

Carley nodded. "Samuel looked pretty tense. You said his wife died of cancer. Was she in this hospital before she died? Maybe that's how they know each other."

"*Ya.* That could be. Samuel told me Rachel spent a lot of time in this hospital before she died. Actually, she passed here. I suspect it's weighing heavily on both Samuel's and David's minds."

Carley sat up a little straighter. "There's the doctor now." She pointed down the hall. "Maybe he's coming to tell us about David."

The doctor headed toward them.

"How's David?" Lillian asked.

"He's going to be fine." He squatted, resting his arms on his knees. "He needed a few stitches on his chin."

"Thank goodness," Carley said, and Lillian sighed with relief.

Carley's response drew a look from the doctor. Their eyes connected and held—so long she blushed and broke the gaze. She
didn't care too much for doctors. Not even handsome ones.

He reached toward Anna, gently touching the child's arm.
"And who is this beautiful girl?"

"This is Anna." Lillian leaned down and admired her little
one.

"And you must be Lillian?" Dr. Noah looked up and extended
his hand.

Lillian returned the greeting, then turned toward Carley. "And
this is my friend Carley."

"Nice to meet you, Carley," he responded, taking hold of
Carley's hand. Once again his dark brown eyes held hers. His
grip was firm. Too firm. She wriggled free of his grasp.

"Hello."

"Do you know my husband?" Lillian asked.

Instantly Dr. Noah's attention returned to Lillian. He smiled,
but it was clearly forced.

"Yes, I do." He stood. "I'd better go. I have patients. Nice to
meet you both."

And he was gone.

"That was odd," Lillian said once he was out of earshot.
"Don't you think so?"

"Yeah, it was rather strange."

"Hmm. I'll have to remember to ask Samuel about it."

It was three o'clock in the morning when Samuel joined Carley
and Lillian at the kitchen table for a cup of tea.

"David is finally asleep, and I just checked on Anna," he said, scooting in beside Lillian on the wooden bench.

"You look so tired, Samuel." Lillian lovingly caressed her husband's arm.

Samuel took a sip of his tea. "I reckon you ladies are mighty tired too." He looked up at Carley. "I'm real sorry about this, Carley. Not the best way to begin your vacation."

"No, no . . ." She shook her head. "There's no need to apologize, Samuel. I'm just glad David's all right."

"The doctor at the hospital called you by name," Lillian interjected. "How do you know him?"

Samuel's expression soured at the mention of the doctor. He shrugged.

Lillian looked hesitant to quiz him further, but after waiting a reasonable amount of time, she pushed on. "Was he Rachel's doctor?"

"No," Samuel said, taking another sip of his tea. It didn't appear he was going to elaborate.

Carley and Lillian exchanged questioning looks. Lillian evidently found his lack of communication bothersome and appeared to think carefully about her next statement. Nervously twirling a loose strand of hair dangling from underneath her prayer cap, she said, "He seemed to take a keen interest in Anna."

This caught Samuel's attention. "What do you mean?"

Lillian was caught off guard by his tone. "Maybe he just likes babies."

Carley had noticed it too—the tender way Dr. Noah doted on Anna. "I wonder if Noah is his first or last name."

"It's his first name," Samuel said matter-of-factly as he

stood up and walked toward the sink. Placing his cup there, he turned off the last of the lanterns on the counter, dimming the light considerably. "I'm off to bed." He leaned down to kiss Lillian on the cheek. "Going to be a long day tomorrow. We're all gonna be tired."

"What time do you want breakfast, Samuel?" Lillian asked, before turning to Carley. "Normally we eat around four thirty."

Carley almost choked. It was close to three thirty now. "Every day?" She heard the surprise in her own voice.

Lillian smiled in sympathy. "I'm afraid so." She glanced at Samuel. "But since it's almost three thirty, maybe we should make an exception tomorrow, no?"

Samuel rubbed his eyes. "*Ya*, we all need a little sleep. Seven o'clock should be fit for breakfast."

As he walked out of the kitchen, Lillian said, "Samuel?"

"*Ya?*" He poked his head back around the corner.

"Does David need a follow-up visit with Dr. Noah?"

Carley could tell that Samuel's evasiveness regarding the doctor bothered Lillian.

"No, we'll cart him to Dr. Reynolds when it's time to take out the stitches."

Lillian waited until she heard Samuel close the bedroom door upstairs. One brow inched upward as she twisted her mouth into a scowl. "I wonder why my Samuel doesn't want to say how he and Dr. Noah are acquainted."

"Men. No telling," Carley mumbled, stifling a yawn.

"This is not like Samuel to be so evasive about something." Lillian rubbed her chin. "We talk about everything." She paused,

looking sternly at Carley. "But he was very firm about not wanting to share information."

"Yes, he was," Carley agreed.

She recalled the awkward way she and the handsome doctor
had locked eyes, along with the lengthy handshake they'd shared.

And now that she thought about it, he had attempted to defy
her stereotype of his profession for a moment—taking the time
to speak with Lillian, doting on Anna, almost as if he . . . cared.

At least he took the time to pretend; she'd give him that.

4

CARLEY AWOKE TO HER CELL PHONE ALARM CHIRPING AT seven o'clock. She grabbed it from the nightstand, silenced it, and noticed only one bar of battery power left. She'd need to remember to charge it in the car later. She was already exhausted from her travels. Functioning on so little sleep was going to be a challenge.

As she stretched beneath the cotton sheet, she realized she'd kicked the quilt to the bottom of the bed during the night. She sat up to fetch it, blinking her eyes into focus and surveying her small room. Simple but nice—and spotless. A two-tiered nightstand stood beside the bed with a lantern, Bible, and box of tissue on top. An oak chest with four drawers rested against the far wall, and a wooden rocker sat in the corner. Unlike the plain furniture downstairs, the chest had discreet carvings etched along the top and bottom. A small mirror was suspended by a silver chain on the wall to her left. And a thick, dark green blind was partially drawn over the window, which she had opened the night before. Otherwise, the walls were bare.

The focal point in the room was the large white vase on the chest filled with vibrant blossoms, presumably from Lillian's flower beds in the front yard. She wondered if Lillian had gone to extra effort, if perhaps Lillian had been nervous for Carley to see her new look and way of life.

She tucked the quilt around her waist, afraid that if she lay down again she'd fall back asleep. Studying the intricate designs and bold colors, she was reminded of the quilt her mother used to wrap up in on cold nights. Her grandmother had made the quilt, and this one shared similar colors and designs.

She ran her hand along the stitching, the hearts bursting with red, yellow, and blue flowers. Leafy greenery joined the emblems together in a fabulous pattern.

"I miss you, Mom," she sighed.

As if hearing her, a cow offered acknowledgment in the distance. A breeze blew through the open window and swirled around the room—the smell of freshly cut grass commingled with a hint of manure. Delicate rays of light were streaming onto the wood-plank floor as the sun began its ascent.

Her surroundings invoked a sense of calm—a feeling she hadn't had in a long time.

Rustling noises from downstairs brought her out of her musing, along with the aroma of cooking bacon. She edged out of bed and grabbed her red suitcase from the corner, pulling out a pair of white tennis shoes, blue jeans, and a pink T-shirt. Forgoing her normal makeup routine, she was ready in about ten minutes.

"Good morning," she announced downstairs, entering the kitchen.

"*Guder mariye* to you." Lillian continued to stir the eggs as she motioned to her right. "There's hot coffee or there's milk and juice in the refrigerator. Help yourself to anything."

Carley made her way toward the coffee and noticed Lillian was dressed almost exactly the same as the day before, the only difference being a deep purple dress instead of a blue one. Her hair was tucked neatly beneath the white cap on her head, and black socks were pushed down toward her black shoes. And despite the events of the night before, Lillian glowed.

"Where's Samuel?" Carley added some milk to her coffee. "And how's David this morning?"

"Samuel went to work in the fields about an hour ago. I made him a little breakfast early when I heard him get up. He's a hard worker. I had doubts he would sleep until seven this morning. And David is still sleeping, so I'll take him some breakfast upstairs in a little while. I imagine he needs the rest."

"But Samuel didn't get to sleep until almost four." *Only two and a half hours of sleep at most.*

Lillian just twisted around and grinned.

Carley watched her shuffle back and forth between the stove and refrigerator, putting jellies on the table in between stirring the eggs. "Can I help you with anything?"

"Nope. Almost done. Anna's sleeping too. This will give us some time to talk." She scooped eggs onto a plate in front of Carley and then took a seat across from her at the table and pushed the bacon and biscuits over. "I ate earlier with Samuel," she said affectionately.

Carley looked at the food lined across the table in front of her. "Lillian, you shouldn't have made all this for me. I don't want you to treat me as a guest. I could have eaten a bowl of cereal or something."

Grinning, Lillian shushed her. "Carley, I'm so glad you're here." Sincerity rang in her tone.

"Me too." Carley swiped rhubarb jam onto a homemade biscuit. "Thank you for letting me come and for agreeing to let me do a story about the Amish lifestyle." She studied her friend. "Lillian, you look so happy."

"I am." Lillian rested her elbows on the table and propped her chin in her hands. "I have an amazing life, and I'm so blessed. God showed me the way. I wasn't listening at first. But once I turned my life over to Him, things began to change for me. And everything just keeps getting better."

It was odd to hear Lillian speak of God. It was an area they had never covered during their friendship, and Carley wasn't sure how to respond. As a confirmed Catholic, she'd done the church thing until she was out of high school. But then there was college, work, and a ton of other reasons why it didn't fit into her schedule. She thought about it from time to time. But even when she attended church, something was always amiss. It was a ritual she'd tired of and become too busy for.

Maybe that was why God had punished her—for turning away from Him.

She'd begged Him to spare her mother's life. No deal. She'd pleaded with Him to heal her own body. Again, no deal.

Talking about God wasn't a conversation she was comfortable with. She changed the subject. "So is Dr. Reynolds your family doctor?"

"He's a natural doctor. In our district, we tend to seek out natural doctors prior to utilizing conventional medicine."

Carley nodded, helping herself to another biscuit.

"I'm so sorry about your mother, Carley. I wanted to travel to the funeral, but I was very pregnant at the time. Samuel was worried for me to go."

"And he should have been. It wouldn't have been good to travel that far from home so far into your pregnancy."

"And are you doing okay?" Lillian knew Carley had suffered some serious injuries.

"Yeah, I'm doing well," Carley lied. The red Chevy came blazing through her mind, then her mom's face, the wooden spike impaling Carley's stomach—

She took a deep breath.

"Are you all right?" Lillian leaned toward her.

"I guess things have been a little rough. I really miss Mom." She drew in another breath and fought the knot building in her throat.

"I can't even imagine, Carley. I'm so sorry." Lillian sat up a little straighter. "*Ach*, I hear Anna. I'll be right back."

A few minutes later Lillian returned holding Anna, with David trailing behind her.

"David, how are you this morning?"

"I'm all right." He winced. "*Mei* chin hurts though."

"Just going to take some time to heal," Lillian said. She placed Anna in the high chair and began to prepare a plate of breakfast for David.

Carley leaned toward Anna, taking in the aroma of lotion and baby powder. *So precious.*

"On Wednesdays *mei Englisch* friend, Barbie Beiler, picks me up and takes me to the farmers' market in the town of Bird-in-Hand.

I can take the buggy, but I always purchase so many things. I like spending the day with her, so she takes me in her car. She'll be here in about thirty minutes. You'll like her." Lillian paused, giving Carley a sympathetic look. "You look pooped, Carley. If you'd rather not go with us, you're welcome to stay here and enjoy some peace and quiet. I know you must be tired from your trip, plus very little sleep last night. It's completely up to you."

"So let me get this straight," Carley began. "You can't own a car, but you can ride in one? Even when it's not an emergency like last night?"

"*Ya.* There are so many different types of cars. To own one would cause competitiveness and vanity. The bishops in most districts would never hear of owning a car, certainly not in an Old Order Amish district. But we are allowed to ride in cars."

Carley suppressed a yawn. As much as she'd like to take a trip to town, jet lag was settling in. "Are you sure you don't mind if I just hang around here today?"

"Absolutely not," Lillian answered.

"And feel free to leave this precious bundle with me, if you want." Carley reached over and stroked Anna's soft skin. She'd forgo sleep to take care of little Anna.

Lillian's face lit up with surprise. "I wouldn't know how to act if I wasn't carting Anna. It's not too often I have an opportunity to go to market on my own." She pondered the offer. "Are you sure? I mean, Anna would probably take a nap with you later this morning. And we won't be gone too terribly long."

"I would love to stay here with Anna, and you enjoy some time by yourself," Carley assured her.

"Are you sure?"

"Quite sure. Me and Anna will just laze around this morning."

"Deal." Lillian sounded thrilled. "And David will be here too. But Samuel is expecting him back on the plow tomorrow, so I imagine he'll catch up on his sleep today."

Carley nodded. "It'll be fine. You go and have a good time."

Noah pulled out of the hospital parking lot, thankful his shift was finally over. Despite his exhaustion, he couldn't stop thinking about Samuel and his family—and the reporter they were allowing into their lives when he was not welcome himself. Attractive, yes. But her presence in Samuel's house brought on pangs of resentment, no matter how misdirected.

And Samuel's allowing her to write about them? Incredible.

He deviated from his normal route home and headed down Lincoln Highway toward Paradise, knowing it was probably a mistake but compelled to do so just the same.

He could gather his thoughts on the way to Samuel's place.

Prior to yesterday, it had been sixteen years since he had seen Samuel, who seemed to have it all now. A beautiful wife. Beautiful children.

But Noah knew it all came with a price. Losing his first wife to cancer had to have been quite a blow. He recalled a letter from Mary Ellen about Samuel's wife's death. The letter hadn't arrived in time for Noah to attend the funeral.

As bitterness crept in, Noah wondered if moving back to Lancaster County two months ago had been a mistake. And yet, ignoring his internal warnings, he turned right off of Lincoln Highway and onto Black Horse Road.

A nap was exactly what Carley needed. Curled up with Anna on the couch in the den, they both slept for over an hour, only stirring when Anna voiced her hunger.

Carley fed Anna some peas, carrots, and applesauce that Lillian had prepared before she left. Then she lifted Anna's bottle from the bowl of hot water on the counter and squirted a tiny amount of the white liquid on her finger to check the temperature. "Perfect," she whispered to Anna, offering her the bottle.

David was still upstairs. Carley headed to the front porch and took a seat in one of the wooden rockers. It felt good to go barefoot, her toes free to wriggle as she pushed against the porch floor until the rocker began to glide. She could see Samuel far off in the pasture, four mules pulling him and a plow across a flat surface. *Amazing that with all the modern technology, it's still done this way.*

Closing her eyes and resting her head against the back of the rocker, she breathed in the fresh country air. "It's peaceful here, Anna," she whispered. "And beautiful—just like you." She leaned forward and kissed the baby on her forehead.

In addition to the picturesque scenery, Carley liked the way things smelled here. Inside Lillian's house, the pleasant aroma of freshly baked cookies and bread lingered. Outside, the smell of freshly cut grass and mowed fields brought on a sense of tranquillity. It was all very simple.

There wasn't a cloud in the sky, and a light breeze sailed across the porch. Carley felt like she could sit here forever.

She lifted her head to the sound of car tires rolling against the dirt driveway. As the white car neared, she sat up a little straighter and strained to see who was driving.

"Company, Anna," she whispered, standing. "I wonder—"

Dr. Noah stepped out of the car.

"Uh-oh." Without her even realizing it, Carley's hand crept up to her scraggly slept-on hair.

"Hello," the doctor said as he walked toward the porch. "I came to check on David."

Gamely trying to ignore the fact that she had not a scrap of makeup on, Carley watched the doctor approach. His shirttail was still out, he looked like he'd slept in his clothes, and his nametag was hanging sideways. She felt marginally better about her own appearance. This doctor was a mess.

It seemed odd that an ER doctor would make a house call over a few stitches on David's chin. "I think David is resting upstairs. But he seems fine."

He stopped in front of her and leaned in, smiling at Anna. His smile certainly made up for his lack of grooming efforts.

"She is a beautiful baby," he said.

"Yes, she is."

He ogled Anna for a few more seconds then straightened. "I suppose that's Samuel over there?" He nodded toward the field.

"Yes. He's been out there since early this morning." A breeze carried his scent—day-old cologne with a dash of antiseptic. Something inside her twisted.

He stepped back and squinted into the sun's glare toward Samuel, the tiny lines around his dark eyes becoming more distinct. "I need to talk to Samuel and Lillian."

"Lillian went to town with a friend. And, as you can see, Samuel is plowing. Can I help you with something?"

"No, thanks." He placed his hand in a salute over his eyes, blocking the sun as he stared at the field, obviously hoping Samuel would notice he was there.

As they waited to see if Samuel headed toward them, Carley fished for a conversation starter. "Samuel mentioned Noah is your first name. Why don't you use your last name?" She'd been curious about that.

"My last name is hard to pronounce and stirs up a lot of questions I'd rather not deal with."

"What is it?"

Noah ignored her question, let out an exasperated sigh, and then reached into the inner pocket of his white coat and pulled out a card. "I need to talk to Samuel. Here's my number." He handed the card to Carley. "It's very important that he or Lillian call me."

Carley accepted the card and watched him walk down the stairs and across the front yard toward his white Lexus. She couldn't help but wonder how many times the good doctor had delivered news such as she'd received about her own health and the death of her mother. *And does he do it with ease and a lack of compassion like the others?*

Which led to another thought.

"Wait!" she yelled.

He spun around.

"Is something wrong?" Carley headed carefully down the porch steps with Anna. There had been a sense of urgency in his tone.

"It's about David. They need to call me."

"Do you want to come in and see David?"

"No, I don't think Samuel would want me going inside." He nodded at the card. "Just have him call me."

She watched him slide into his car and head back down the dirt drive. She climbed back up the porch steps with Anna.

About David? The boy had a nasty cut on his chin. What could Dr. Noah need to talk to Samuel and Lillian about? And why wouldn't Samuel want him in the house?

Dr. Noah had barely made the turn onto Black Horse Road when Carley saw Samuel come blazing across the pasture with the mules. She waited.

Samuel briskly strode across the front yard and up the porch steps. "What did *he* want?" he huffed when he hit the porch. "That was Noah, wasn't it?"

Carley offered him the card. "Yes, it was. He said it's important that you or Lillian call him."

Samuel pushed back his straw hat and stared at the card, almost in disbelief. Then he grunted, wadded up the card, and threw it down on the porch. "My brother has no business here," he spat, thrusting himself back down the porch steps two by two and back toward the fields.

"Your *brother?*" Carley knew her eyes were wide with wonder, but Samuel just walked away.

Carley waited until Samuel was actively plowing before she reached down and retrieved the business card. Flattening out the crumpled white paper, she read the name.

Noah Stoltzfus, MD.

5

CARLEY LAID ANNA IN THE CRIB IN LILLIAN AND SAMUEL'S room later that afternoon while pondering how Lillian could have not known about Samuel's brother. They were married. Wouldn't that have come up in general conversation? She began walking down the stairs but slowed her descent when she heard voices.

"I don't understand," she heard Lillian say.

"I reckon we can talk about it more after supper." Carley glimpsed Samuel's backside as he made the statement and headed out the door of the den.

It was obvious to Carley what had caused Lillian and David's dumbstruck expressions. Samuel had revealed how he knew Dr. Noah. Carley hadn't broached the subject with Lillian earlier. She wanted to give Samuel a chance to offer up the news he had so abruptly shared with her earlier. She was glad he'd finally done so. It had been hard not to say anything to Lillian.

Carley came the rest of the way down. "Everything okay?" She could see the wheels churning in Lillian's head.

Lillian shrugged in frustration then slapped her hands to her sides. "Samuel was just telling David and me that Noah is his brother."

Carley wasn't sure what to say. Maybe she should have told Lillian, softened the way for Samuel—for all of them. She took a seat beside David on the couch as Lillian began to pace.

"Samuel has two sisters and one brother," Lillian said. "Well, make that two brothers. Samuel said Noah was shunned."

"But wouldn't he have mentioned Noah to you, even if he was shunned?" Carley posed the question to both Lillian and David.

"Evidently not," Lillian said.

David shook his head. "When a *streng meiding* happens, we don't talk of it. That person has to leave their family, friends, and life behind."

Lillian sat down on the couch on the other side of David. "I know, David. But I'm just surprised your pop didn't tell us about Noah. That's all." She patted him on the leg, then leaned toward Carley. "Did Anna do all right?"

"She was perfect," Carley said, hoping to lighten Lillian's mood.

David appeared disinclined to end the discussion about Noah. "I wonder what Noah did to get shunned."

"Well, he's a doctor." Lillian stood and resumed her pacing. "He would have been baptized and then chose to leave afterwards, presumably to further his education and become a doctor. That would never be allowed."

"I've heard about shunning," Carley began, "but it just seems cruel to oust your own like that. I mean, to never see that person again seems awfully harsh."

Lillian's short time in the Amish faith left her dependent on David. She turned to him. "Maybe you can explain this to Carley better than I can."

"Folks are warned before they're banned," he said with conviction. "We know what will happen if we choose baptism and then break our baptismal vows."

Lillian seemed more bothered by the fact that her husband hadn't told her about his brother. "I don't know why Samuel didn't mention Noah," she said, disappointed. "I still have a lot to learn. But for now, I guess I'd better go check on Anna before I hang the clothes on the line."

Carley followed Lillian up the stairs and waited until they were out of earshot from David before she offered Lillian the business card.

"Noah said it's very important that you or Samuel call him. It's about David, Lillian."

Lillian stared blankly at the card. "Oh no." Then she looked up at Carley and handed the card back. "Can you please call him and tell him we will be taking David to Dr. Reynolds next week?"

"But, Lillian, it sounded urgent. Are you sure you shouldn't call him?"

Lillian shook her head. "Samuel said we are not calling him. I don't want to go against Samuel's wishes."

Carley kept the card and didn't push the subject. Having grown up in another world than this, Carley knew it was hard for Lillian to be so submissive, even though Samuel was a wonderful man who made Lillian happy.

But regardless, someone needed to call Noah.

Noah opened the front door of his three-bedroom house and greeted the same mess he'd left. He flung his white coat onto the tan leather couch amid a growing pile of laundry. Pulling a seventy-two hour shift had been unavoidable when Frank's wife went into labor early. Dr. Frank Overton had covered for him on several occasions, and Noah wasn't about to let him miss the birth of his first child.

"Come on, Chloe," he hollered out to the backyard. His yellow Labrador ran in through the kitchen door, panting with excitement. He'd need to remember to pay the kid next door for feeding her while he pulled the extra shift.

Five minutes later he was dragging himself into the king-size bed and giving a nod for Chloe to do the same. As the Lab got comfortable at the foot of the bed, Noah closed his eyes. He should have been out instantly, but his mind was awhirl with thoughts of Samuel and his family. And the reporter. He still found it unbelievable that Samuel would allow her to do a story about the Amish. Samuel's new wife must have convinced him to allow it. The Samuel he knew wouldn't have heard of such a thing.

There it was again—the familiar bitterness creeping into his heart like an old friend who continued to betray him over and over again.

It had been hours since he left word for Samuel or Lillian to call him. If they didn't, he'd be forced to go over there again. His news couldn't wait much longer.

Suppertime passed awkwardly, with no mention of Noah. After helping Lillian clean the supper dishes, Carley excused herself and took a drive. Maybe Lillian, Samuel, and David needed some time alone.

The towns of Bird-in-Hand, Intercourse, and Paradise are within a ten-minute drive of one another. As she slowed and passed the numerous buggies on the highways and back roads, she thought about how far she was from Texas. While the dipping, curving roads were similar to those in the Hill Country of central Texas, several things distinguished Lancaster County from her home state. Every half mile or so, Amish men plowed fields with antiquated equipment. In addition to buggies, Plain people used foot scooters for transportation. Here men and women sailed along the country roads, carting goods in the metal baskets on the front of the scooters.

The farmsteads were fairly uniform in this part of Amish Dutch Country. Usually a large two-story house, painted white, with a spacious front porch. Two or more outbuildings, mostly stained a dark crimson, although some were weathered natural wood. And one or two buggies were parked near the houses.

Almost every house had a clothesline running from an upstairs window down to a tree below. Hanging from the lines were dark-colored dresses like Lillian wore, blue and brown slacks, dark-colored shirts, and lots of black socks.

Each farm had a silo for housing feed—another distinction from Texas spreads, where most farmers utilized a nearby feed mill, picking up large bags as needed.

Although sharing likenesses in layout, each homestead still boasted character and individuality.

She turned her attention from the scenery to the problem at hand, reached around to her left back pocket, and pulled out Noah's business card. *Someone* needed to call him. A courtesy call, at the very least.

"Yes, hi. Dr. Stoltzfus?" she asked when he answered the phone. "This is Carley Marek, Lillian and Samuel's friend."

"Just Noah," he quickly said. "Samuel's not going to call, is he? And he probably instructed his wife not to call either."

"That's correct."

A heavy sigh came from Noah's end. "That's what I figured."

"I . . . was surprised to hear that you're Samuel's brother." Carley hesitated. "And, uh, Lillian and David were shocked as well."

"It was pretty obvious at the hospital that they didn't know who I am."

"I think they were fairly . . . surprised." She didn't want to say too much on Lillian's or David's behalf.

"So will you be including information about shunning in your article now?"

"I hadn't really thought about it. But I have to tell you, the practice seems cruel to me."

"We all know going in what can happen if we don't adhere to church laws."

"Sounds like you're defending it."

"No, not defending it. Just explaining it. Where are you?"

His abrupt change of subject caught her off guard. "Just driving around. I'm in Bird-in-Hand right now."

"I thought it sounded like you were driving. Listen, I was getting ready to head out for some supper. Any interest in joining me? I'm about twenty minutes from Bird-in-Hand, but I can head your direction since you're not familiar with the area." When she hesitated, he added, "It would be unethical for me to discuss David with you. I just thought maybe we could talk. Maybe convince you to have Samuel or Lillian call me."

"I ate already."

"Yeah, I suppose four thirty is still the supper hour. And we're almost two hours past that. What about a cup of coffee?"

He's being pushy. "I'd better get back. It's only my second night here. I was just trying to give Samuel and Lillian some time alone to talk about . . ."

"Me?" He laughed. "Trust me. It will be a short conversation. What about dinner tomorrow night? There's a café off the main drag in Paradise."

"I don't know." His persistence was starting to make her uncomfortable.

"Or just a cup of coffee."

Just as she opened her mouth to firmly decline, the good doctor threw her a temptation the reporter in her couldn't resist.

"We can even chat about the story you're writing. I can give you some insight about shunnings. Don't all good reporters cover things objectively?"

Darn. He was feeding her journalistic drive. It *would* be nice to hear his side of the story.

"Maybe just coffee," she said, relenting.

"Great. I'll meet you at the Dutch Bakery on Lincoln Highway at six o'clock. Just turn left off of Black Horse Road and it's on the right. Is that time okay?"

"I guess so."

"And, Carley—it would be good if you could convince Lillian to call me before then."

After Carley agreed, she closed the cell phone. She wasn't stupid. If she did convince Lillian to call him before then, Noah wouldn't have any reason to keep the coffee date. And she'd never get his side of the story about the shunning. But, she reminded herself, David was the issue here.

David was back in the fields with Samuel the next morning, so Carley tried to talk Lillian into calling Noah. It was the right thing to do. If Noah chose to cancel the coffee date, so be it. She'd make do without his input for her story. Doctors weren't high on her list of people to socialize with anyway, she reminded herself.

"He looks fine," Lillian said. "A few stitches aren't keeping him from work. He has an appointment with Dr. Reynolds next week to see if the stitches can come out. And I'm sure if anything is wrong, Dr. Reynolds will find it."

Lillian's tone indicated she didn't want to talk about it anymore. She changed the subject and explained that several women were getting together for an occasion they referred to as Sisters' Day. Lillian's friend Sadie was hosting the event, usually held once a month. According to Lillian, Sisters' Day was a gathering of women, not necessarily sisters, who spent the day together doing a preplanned task—quilting, canning, baking, sewing, or even cleaning house for a sick friend. All the women looked forward to the monthly get-together.

"And it's a gossip fest," Lillian said. Then she tapped her finger to her chin and corrected herself. "Actually, gossip is a sin, so let me say it another way—things are discussed about the community and the people within the community." She smiled, as if that justified any potential wrongdoing.

After cleaning the breakfast dishes, Lillian readied the buggy and she, Carley, and Anna left for Sisters' Day. Carley was glad to see Lillian put Anna in a child carrier in the backseat of the buggy. She'd noticed during her drive the afternoon before that some of the Amish women carried their babies in their laps, and the practice made Carley incredibly nervous.

"This is your first buggy ride, no?" Lillian asked as they turned out of the driveway onto Black Horse Road.

The *clippity-clop* of hooves hitting the pavement, the way the horse followed Lillian's every command, the breeze in her face— it was wonderful. But Carley had one concern. "Yes. And I was wondering—will we be going on the highway where all the cars are? This road is fine, but I'd be a little nervous on the highway."

A huge understatement. Watching cars quickly swerve around the buggy was bound to bring thoughts of the red Chevy into play. It had taken her long enough to get back into a car and drive again after the accident. Unprotected in a buggy amid the traffic—she wasn't ready for that.

"I was *naerfich* at first too," Lillian recalled. "But I got used to it. And no, Sadie lives two turns up on the right. We don't have to get on the highway."

"Did it take you long to learn the language?"

"Actually, it's a German dialect with some English mixed in. And I still have a lot to learn."

Carley was unsure whether to broach the subject of Noah, since Lillian hadn't, but her curiosity won out. "Did you and Samuel have a chance to talk about Noah?"

Lillian's twinkling eyes darkened. "We talked about it a little, but Samuel made it clear to both David and me that Noah was not a part of our lives and that it should not be discussed."

"Isn't that odd, though?" Carley was quick to ask. "I know you've only been Amish for a short time, but don't you think that totally cutting off a family member is extreme?"

Lillian deliberated before answering, pursing her lips. "I guess it must seem that way. But when a person is baptized, they promise to abide by all the church laws. Like Samuel said, Noah knew what he was doing. He knew that if he left the Order, he would be shunned—for life."

"It just seems so sad to me." Carley wondered how Lillian would feel about her having coffee with Noah that evening.

"Carley, it might be best if we don't bring up Noah anymore, especially around Samuel. It's an unfortunate situation, but I don't think we will be seeing Dr. Noah again. Samuel said there's probably nothing wrong with David. Noah is just trying to find a way back into Samuel's life, and Samuel wants no part of it."

Carley opened her mouth to clarify, but before she could speak, Lillian surprised her with some new information.

"Evidently there's much more to the story." Her gaze met Carley's, almost daring her to speculate.

"Like what?"

"Well," Lillian said, taking a breath, "breaking his vows wasn't the only thing Noah did. It was bad enough that he chose to leave the district, go to college, and become a doctor. But there's something else."

"What?" Carley searched Lillian's face for a clue. "What did he do?"

Lillian shrugged and shot her a dead-end look. "I have no idea. Samuel wouldn't say."

What? "He told you Noah did something else, but he won't tell you what it is? But he's your husband."

"*Ya*, and I must respect his privacy. He's the head of the household."

"Wait a minute. This doesn't sound like the Lillian I know. Don't you feel like Samuel should tell you? And what's this about him being the head of the household?"

"I knew that when I married him, Carley. Things are different here. Samuel and I have a wonderful relationship, but some things aren't pushed." Lillian sighed. "Sometimes I press Samuel when I shouldn't. It's not easy for me to just let things go. Especially if I feel strongly about it." She lowered her chin, cutting her eyes toward Carley. "Or if he's not telling me something."

Carley was surprised that Lillian accepted Samuel's refusal to speak about the shunning. But knowing Lillian, she had probably forced the issue a tad. She just lost the argument in the end. Carley reminded herself how different Lillian was now, and how much happier she was because of her new life. Maybe sacrificing in some areas was worth it.

"There's Sadie's place." Lillian pointed to her right. "You'll like Sadie. And there will be several other ladies here too. Oh! And don't mention Noah. Samuel's two sisters will be here also."

Carley nodded as Lillian went on. "We're going to tag the quilts for the mud sale this Saturday. A mud sale is held at the firehouse. They call it that because the fields outside the firehouse are almost always muddy from rain this time of year. Thankfully it's been dry around here lately. The one we're going to is in Penryn, about thirty minutes from here. You'll love it. It's a huge auction with mostly Amish men, women, and children running it. They'll auction all kinds of farm equipment, housewares, and trinkets. But the biggest-selling items will be the quilts. Our district has two hundred and forty quilts to auction. And I'm in charge of the quilt sale this year." She beamed with excitement.

"I've heard the quilts are very expensive—that they can cost over a thousand dollars. I want to go to the shops in town and get one, but I need one that isn't quite so expensive."

"No, no," Lillian said. "If you want a quilt, buy one at the auction. They'll cost less. Not by much, but it will save you a little money."

Carley's stomach flipped a bit when they pulled up near the other buggies at Sadie's farm. She wondered how she would be accepted by the other women. Her bout of nerves worsened at the thought of meeting Noah for coffee later that evening. She'd already made up her mind not to mention the date to Lillian. Even the thought made her uncomfortable.

But more unsettling was wondering what Noah had done to be so severely shunned by his own blood.

Following nearly twelve hours of sleep, Noah felt rejuvenated— and anxious about his coffee date with Carley later that night. Not only did he need her to convince Samuel or Lillian to call him, but his anticipation was magnified by the prospect of hearing about Samuel and his family. Of all his siblings, he missed Samuel the most.

For the first time since moving back, he felt motivated to clean and organize the house. Blaming it on his schedule at the hospital had been convenient, but with the next four days off, he had no excuse not to tidy up a little. For starters, he'd open the windows and air the place out.

He traveled from room to room, winding his way around boxes he still needed to unpack. When he reached the middle bedroom, he hesitated, then forced himself to twist the doorknob. Inside was a lone blue crate, which he stared at for a long moment. Then he shook his head, determined he would not think about it. Not now.

With care, he eased around the crate to the window, flung it open, and welcomed the fresh breeze. The room smelled as stale as the memories housed within the oblong box behind him. He knew he would have to open the crate at some point. But not today. Today he would spend cleaning and looking forward to his coffee date with Carley.

He'd face the demons from his past another day.

Lillian introduced Carley to seven other women, including Sadie. Two of them were Samuel's sisters, Mary Ellen and Rebecca. Katie Ann, Samuel's sister-in-law, was also there, along with Sarah Jane, Lillian's mother. Lillian explained that Samuel's mother, Esther, was down with a cold and wouldn't be attending.

Last came Linda and Miriam, Samuel's nieces. Both of the preteen girls took turns coddling Anna, thrilled at the opportunity to participate in this sale.

The women were pleasant enough, but guarded. Sadie was by far the friendliest of the bunch. She was a tall woman with fire red hair, striking sky blue eyes, and ivory skin—an appearance unique among the women around her, who all had dark or sandy-blonde hair and olive complexions.

Carley couldn't get over the work that must have gone into each quilt present. One had such vibrant colors. The women busied themselves organizing the counterpanes, then passed them along to Linda and Miriam for a tag. Carley walked to the far wall and squatted down to inspect a pile of folded quilts. She studied the top quilt—a brilliant display of maroon and pink roses connected by a spiraling, leafy green vine. The one underneath included a design of large dark blue circles with touches of a lighter blue woven throughout. Each circle connected to the next, with large yellow diamonds and sprinkles of pink filling the centers.

Carley joined the women in the middle of the room. "How long does it take to make a quilt?"

The women glanced blankly at one another. Finally, Sadie pumped out a hearty, "I don't think anyone knows."

"Hundreds of hours." Katie Ann sighed. *"Die weibsleit gwilde bis in die nacht."*

"The women quilt long into the night," Lillian's mother translated for Carley.

"I think Morning Glory will bring over a thousand dollars," Linda squealed, pinning an auction number on a quilt.

"I reckon Summer Bride will bring a *gut* amount too," Miriam chimed in.

"This will be the first mud sale for the *maeds*," Mary Ellen explained. "I hope it doesn't make wet at the auction."

Carley tried to make a mental note for her article of the way the women spoke. She could only assume "make wet" meant rain.

"God bless our handiwork," Rebecca offered as the women bowed their heads in silent prayer.

Carley lowered her head, waited a moment, then raised a brow to see if the women were done. They all nodded with an *"Aemen."*

As Linda and Miriam continued to speculate how much each quilt might bring at the auction, Carley flipped through the tags still waiting to be pinned on the quilts. *Sunshine Sweetheart, Country Charm, Red Rose of Sharon, Ocean Wave.*

"Lone Star quilt," she exclaimed when she saw the tag. "Maybe I'll bid on this one. Which is it?"

Linda jumped up and down. *"Sell is es bescht vun allem!"*

"What'd she say?" Carley whispered to Sarah Jane, who was sitting next to her on the floor.

Sarah Jane smiled. "She said that is the best of all."

Linda found the quilt that matched the Lone Star tag and held it up for Carley to see. Trimmed in navy blue, the counterpane featured one star in the middle that elegantly spiked outward, its points meeting a thick blue border about six inches from the delicate lace along the bottom. Various shades of blue and green filled the star, along with discreet splashes of red and yellow.

"I love it." Carley pictured how good it would look on her bed at home. Maybe she would splurge and buy the quilt.

Once the quilts were all tagged, Sadie offered up an enormous display of refreshments. As Lillian had predicted, the women began to chat about who might be courting whom, how many acres a neighboring farmer was giving to his son as a wedding present, and whether or not all the celery planted at the Lapp farm meant a wedding was forthcoming. The women explained that celery was used in various Amish dishes traditionally served at weddings. They also told Carley that weddings were held in November and December after the harvest was complete.

Carley's favorite moment was when Rebecca chimed in. "John Petersheim, Abner's boy, seen fit to race his buggy down Leaman Road goin' much too fast. I seen it happening," she gasped. "He's in his *rumschpringe*. I heard the *Englisch* policeman wrote a warning on a pink slip of paper for him to slow down."

Kids would be kids, Carley assumed, Amish or otherwise. And these women weren't so different, either. Mothers, daughters, friends—kindred spirits with a united faith.

A silent blessing ended the festivities, and the women began to say their good-byes. As each woman extended a hand to Carley on her way out, she felt her emotions slip. She missed her mother, missed the closeness of good friends. How had her life gotten so far off track? The warmth in the room reminded her of time spent with girls in her youth group at church when she was young. What had happened to all those girls?

Lillian toted Anna out to the buggy. "What did you think?"

"I loved it, Lillian. Your friends are wonderful. I had a great time."

"Surprised, aren't you?" Lillian teased. "You thought they would be different, didn't you?"

"Maybe just a little," Carley confessed, her cheeks warming.

"I thought maybe tonight after supper, we could sit down and I'll explain some things I've learned about the *Ordnung*, which is the order of conduct for the Amish. We can start working on information for your article."

Carley wanted to tell her about her coffee date with Noah, but the words wouldn't come. Instead, she nodded in agreement.

Noah headed down the highway toward the bakery to meet Carley, wondering what Samuel might have said to her. He wanted to start out with her on neutral ground, not have to rehash things best left in the past. He'd made some mistakes for sure. But being a Christian, no matter what faith you adhered to, included forgiving. And yet Samuel was as unforgiving a man as he had ever known.

Noah swerved around a buggy and recalled his days behind the reins. They'd been good days. But when his calling became too strong to ignore, he knew being baptized had been a terrible mistake. He took his eighth-grade education and left to further his knowledge in an unfamiliar world. He had almost no money, few friends, and no family to support him. Lucky for him, Doc Eddington took him in and let him sleep on his couch. As Doc mentored Noah, the calling to become a doctor strengthened.

However, some of his decisions in those days continued to haunt him, particularly the way he paid for his college education.

He longed for a renewed relationship with his family, and seeing Samuel's family at the hospital—especially David and Anna—fueled his hope for some sort of reconciliation. Noah knew he should have tried harder to communicate with Samuel in recent years. But pride and bitterness often took the lead, and months without communication turned into years.

He was jolted back to the present when his cell phone rang. He didn't recognize the number at first, but then remembered the out-of-state area code Carley had called from earlier.

"I'm sorry to have to cancel so late," she whispered when he answered. "I'm not going to be able to make it."

"I'm almost there," Noah responded, not bothering to hide his disappointment.

"I meant to call earlier, but the time got away from me."

"Why are you whispering?" He was right. They'd gotten to her.

"I'm in the bathroom."

"Hiding?"

"Sort of," she responded. "Listen, there seems to be some major tension between you and Samuel. Maybe our meeting isn't such a good idea. I don't want to lie to Lillian about where I'm going, and I don't think she or Samuel would be very happy about me meeting you."

"It's just coffee, Carley."

"I know," she said defensively. "Anyway, I'm sorry for the late notice."

He sensed she might be about to end the call. "Wait, wait. Don't hang up." A lot was at stake, plus she was his only link to an inside glimpse at Samuel's life. He didn't have time for her fickle behavior. "What about your article? I think I could contribute a lot to that, and—"

"I can't, Noah. Not tonight. I'm so sorry that you drove all this way."

She's going to hang up. "Wait," he said again. "Did you convince Lillian to call me?" He needed to know that much, at least.

"I tried, Noah. But they're going to take David to Dr. Reynolds. I'm sorry. I have to go."

The connection clicked off.

Noah slammed his cell phone closed. He passed the Dutch Bakery on his left and kept going. Black Horse Road was only a few blocks up the highway.

Forget her. I'll go straight to the source.

6

AFTER CALLING NOAH, CARLEY HELPED LILLIAN TAKE THE laundry off the line. "I hate to sound like a broken record," Carley began, "but don't you miss having a washer and dryer?"

"Nope." Lillian gave one end of a bedsheet to Carley and backed away from her. They folded inward, meeting at the edges.

"It's just such a huge change for you." Carley was quite sure she couldn't have made the transformation herself.

Lillian took the sheet and gave it a final fold. "It was a big change." She held the sheet up toward Carley. "But smell this. All our clothes have this freshness after being hung outside."

Carley smelled the clean sheet. "You're right," she conceded. "But still . . ."

As they continued unpinning sheets and towels from the line, they heard a car coming up the driveway.

"*Ach*, I wonder who's here. I don't recognize the car," Lillian said.

"I do," Carley mumbled.

"Really? Who is it?" Lillian left the basket and began walking across the yard.

Carley stayed by her side. "It's Noah."

Lillian halted. "Uh-oh. I don't think Samuel wants him here."

Knowing it was none of her business, Carley said, "At least hear what he has to say about David." She paused. "Maybe it would be best if the two of them reconciled."

Lillian shot her a surprised look. "It's not that easy. Besides, we don't know exactly what Noah has done. He left the district after he was baptized, which is bad enough. But remember, Samuel said there's more."

Carley decided not to comment on Samuel's refusal to share information with his wife. Maybe he had his own good reasons. Either way, Noah was stepping out of the car. Carley wished she'd just met him for coffee. His coming here might be far worse than the upset her coffee date would have caused.

The doctor cleaned up well. He was freshly shaven, with starched blue jeans and a yellow golf shirt. His brown loafers looked brand new. Even his dark, unruly hair was neatly parted to one side.

"Hello, ladies." He walked toward them in the yard, thumbs hooked in his back pockets.

Lillian forced a smile. "Hello." Carley watched Lillian glance down the driveway before adding, "Samuel will be home any minute."

Noah didn't seem fazed by Lillian's warning.

"I won't be staying." He faced Lillian and got straight to the point. "Lillian, when David was in the hospital, we drew blood and got a urine sample. Since David had fainted and looked so pale, I ran some tests." He reached into his pocket and offered Lillian another business card. "You need to make an appointment right away for David to see Dr. Ken Bolton. Tell him I sent you. Otherwise, you'll be waiting weeks for an appointment. Ken is a nephrologist."

Lillian took a deep breath and then accepted the card. "What is a nephrologist?"

"A physician who specializes in kidney disorders."

"Does David have a kidney infection?" Lillian asked. She looked confused.

Carley suspected that whatever was wrong with David was much worse than a kidney infection if Noah was suggesting a nephrologist.

"No, I don't think so," Noah responded. "David is very anemic, Lillian. He also said he's been vomiting and—"

"Vomiting?" Lillian asked, surprised.

"Yes. Anyway, I ran some kidney function tests." Noah rubbed his forehead. "Lillian, the test results were not good. David's kidneys are having trouble functioning. It's not my area of expertise, though. Dr. Bolton is the best nephrologist I know. It's important you get David an appointment right away."

"I will," Lillian said. "Should we be scared?"

"*Scared* isn't a good word. *Concerned* would be better. But you should get the appointment soon, Lillian."

"Are you okay?" Carley asked her friend.

Lillian nodded.

With a final nod, Noah turned his attention to Carley, sizing her up. "Reconsider our coffee date."

How dare he? "I told you—" Carley stopped when she heard the *clippity-clop* of hooves. Samuel rounded the corner and headed up the driveway. Carley's eyes shot to Lillian—who looked both worried about a confrontation between the brothers and confused that Carley may have considered a date with the wayward brother.

"He asked me for coffee, but I thought it wouldn't be a good idea," Carley confessed to Lillian, shaking her head.

"No, no," Lillian quickly responded. "Please go. It would be good for you to *go*." Her eyes pleaded with Carley to do whatever it took to get Noah to leave.

"But, Lillian, I don't think—"

Noah inched forward. "It's just coffee."

I don't care what it is. I said no. "Maybe another time." Carley stood firm, her eyes locked with his in defiance.

Samuel's buggy neared the car. Lillian placed her hand on Carley's arm. "You two go and have coffee," she instructed. "It'll be fine."

She pulled Carley in the direction of Noah's car. Noah strode ahead and opened the front passenger door.

"I'd rather not," Carley whispered to Lillian, keeping her eyes on Noah.

Samuel was pulling the buggy to a stop alongside the car. "Please," Lillian begged. "We'll talk tomorrow." She gently nudged Carley until it became impossible for her to do anything other than take a seat in the car.

"Okay, fine," she conceded a tad ungraciously as she plopped down on the seat.

Once she was settled, Noah closed the door and walked around toward the driver's side. Samuel met him at the back bumper, and

Carley watched in the side mirror as words were exchanged. Neither man looked too happy. Less than a minute later, Noah lowered himself into the driver's seat, started the car, and headed down the driveway. He looked at Carley.

"I told you I couldn't go," she huffed. "I don't know what's going on with you and Samuel. And I don't understand how the whole shunning thing works, but you put me in an awkward situation with Lillian." She paused, her tone softening. "But at least you got to talk to Lillian about David."

"I'm going to meet with Dr. Bolton about David's test results. But be sure Lillian gets David to his office soon."

Carley nodded, realizing he'd ignored the first part of her statement.

"So Samuel mentioned the shunning?" he finally asked after a few moments of silence.

"Not to me. He talked to Lillian and David."

His expression soured. "What did he tell them?"

"I don't know. I wasn't there. Lillian just told me that you were shunned and . . ." She paused, hesitant to go on but too curious not to. "And that you did something else too."

"Did he say what that was?"

"No, I don't think Samuel told her." She crossed her legs and folded her arms across her chest. "So—what did you do?"

"Do you mind if we go to the café up the road instead of the bakery? I know you probably already ate supper, but I'm starving. Not much in the way of supper selections at the bakery."

"That's fine." She waited for an answer to her question. And waited. "You're avoiding my question. You must have done something really *bad*."

Carley could see from Noah's expression that she'd gone too far.

"I'm sorry," she offered softly. "I . . . didn't mean to make light of your situation."

He didn't acknowledge her apology and instead steered the car into a parking lot on the right. "This café isn't anything fancy, but the food is good. So is the pie if you're interested."

Inside, the hostess motioned them to a table for two in the corner. She handed them each a menu and promised to return shortly. Carley scanned the pie selections but allowed her eyes to drift up and over the edge of the menu to discreetly observe her dinner partner.

Noah caught her off guard when he slapped his menu closed. "How's your story coming?"

"There's been so much going on, I haven't started. Actually, Lillian said we would spend some time tonight going over parts of the *Ordnung*." She glanced at her watch. "We'll see, though. They all go to bed early."

"Ah, yes. Early to bed, early to rise." He sighed and seemed lost in his thoughts.

After an awkward minute of silence, Carley got down to business. "So you said you'd give me info for my article. What can you tell me about some of the Amish practices?" She couldn't figure out why he'd pushed the coffee date since he'd already told Lillian about David.

"Do you know much about the Amish faith?"

"A little." She glanced around at the women waiting on the tables, clothed in Plain dresses and white aprons, with white caps on their heads.

"Besides the obvious."

"Of course I know the Amish people ride in buggies, dress like that . . ." She nodded toward the approaching waitress. "And that they have a very strong faith."

After Noah ordered the chicken special and she the shoofly pie, she went on. "I know the Amish adhere to the rules of the *Ordnung*, the order of conduct. Oh, and I know you get shunned if you're baptized and then leave the community." Leaning back against her chair, she sipped her coffee. There. She had given him an opening to discuss the shunning.

At first she didn't think he was going to bite, but after a few seconds, he said, "I left because I was called by God to do something else."

"I see." She set her cup on the table and began tapping the rim with her finger. "And I suppose this calling was to become a doctor."

"You say the word *calling* as if you might not believe such a thing exists."

"I guess I've just never gotten the call." She eyed him cautiously, knowing her comment might spark a debate.

Noah studied her. "Maybe you will."

"Maybe." She shrugged, then waited for the waitress to place their food on the table before going on. "I don't expect to 'get the call.' I'm already doing what I'm meant to do." *Except for the family I'll never have.*

"Is that what you think you're meant to do—just be a reporter?"

"There are worse professions. I like my job." She took a

bite of pie. "What do you mean '*just* a reporter'? What's wrong with that?"

He lifted his shoulders, dropped them, and said, "Nothing's wrong with it. I just thought maybe you utilized your talent to serve Him in some way."

"Who?"

His fork halted halfway to his mouth. "God." He seemed surprised at the question.

Carley thought about his answer. "Reporting is a service to God. I report the truth to people." Maybe her voice was a little defensive, but who was Noah to judge her?

"I guess it depends on what you're reporting." His eyes held hers. She looked away.

"Back to my original question. Do you have anything to contribute to my article?"

"Shunning is supposed to keep others in the district from following in brazen footsteps and to keep the church pure. However, it's not necessarily issued with the type of resentment my brother has displayed over the years." He paused. "Is that what you had in mind?"

"Yes, I'd like to include information about shunning. I don't think people really understand it—at least the *why* of it. So whatever you'd like to tell me would be great." She reached into her purse and pulled out a small pad and pen.

"Granted, the Lutheran religion I'm part of now is a far cry from my Amish upbringing, but I've never regretted my calling." Now it was Noah who sounded defensive. "I've saved dozens, if not hundreds, of lives over the years. And I've made mistakes." A sigh escaped, but regret was quickly replaced with resentment. "But why can't Samuel see past the rigid ways of the Amish and try to understand and forgive me?"

She scribbled information on the small pad, hoping he would continue.

"Samuel was the most distraught about my decision to leave the district," he went on. "He and I are the youngest out of the five of us and the closest in age. When I left at eighteen, Samuel took it the hardest. He was seventeen at the time."

Carley sensed it was difficult for Noah to talk about this, but her reporter instincts prevented her from offering a way out of the conversation. She continued, "And . . ."

"Ivan, Mary Ellen, Rebecca, and even *Mamm* sent letters while I was living in the city of Lancaster. Even after I moved to Minnesota to do my residency, they kept me apprised of events in Lancaster County—the births of my nieces and nephews and deaths of those I cared about. The bishop allows letters to be written to those who are shunned, so Samuel could have written, but he practiced the shunning to the fullest extent, refusing to answer even one of the letters I mailed him over the years."

It was a few seconds before Carley realized she had stopped writing. Her reporter zeal had momentarily shifted into neutral as she listened with empathy to Noah's story—a story laced with heartache. She couldn't imagine not having her family. Not by choice, anyway. It would be unnatural for him not to harbor resentment at the way the Old Order operated, she surmised.

"Most of the time, I'm able to put them all out of my mind. But seeing Samuel and his family brought everything back to the forefront."

The depth of his loss was mapped across his face. His heart was laid out before her, his usual arrogance gone.

"But you said it yourself," she consoled, leaning in. "You've saved so many lives. How can that be wrong?"

His eyes lightened, but she sensed his heart was heavy, in spite of his attempt to mask his emotions. "I don't think it's wrong. I just have a difficult time accepting a practice that excludes me from the love of my family." He shrugged. "But I knew the rules when I got baptized."

"Well, I think the rules are cruel and uncalled-for. And I just might put that in my article."

I must be crazy, Noah thought. Airing his bitterness to her would only further alienate him from his family. If she printed it. Of course, if she did, he'd have no one to blame but himself. He'd bribed her, more or less. *Come have coffee with me and I'll tell you about my Amish upbringing.* No matter that the real reason for the meeting was his desire to hear about his family.

He'd missed so much. Samuel, his kid brother—now a father. Noah recalled his and Samuel's relationship with their own father, long deceased now. He hoped to have that kind of father-son bond someday—the kind he'd had with his father and the kind Samuel seemed to have with David.

The thought warmed his heart, but then he recalled the harsh words Samuel had used earlier, outside of his car. *"You are not my brother."* The sting remained.

Noah wouldn't turn back this time without a fight. Somehow he'd make things right.

"Carley, I hope you won't use my name in the article. I'm just trying to give you some insight into what shunning is all about."

She looked disappointed. "But your name would give the article credibility."

"And it would cause even more discord with Samuel and our family if he knew I discussed our situation with you—and you printed it." He pushed his plate to one side and leaned back in his chair.

"Well, I don't want to print anything that might hurt Lillian and her family," Carley said, chagrined. "But I'm getting mixed signals from you. You're bitter about the shunning but admit it's an accepted practice that you understood before you left the community. What are you hoping for—a renewed relationship with your brother?"

He should have just given her the facts and not gotten so caught up in his own pool of self-pity. He knew God didn't approve of this attitude.

He mulled it over for a few seconds and chose his words carefully. "I understand the practice of shunning. And yes—I am bitter about it. But to answer your question, it's important to me that my family understand my calling and somehow still be a part of my life."

Her eyebrows furrowed. "So are you hoping I'll talk to Lillian and soften the way for you to make peace with Samuel?"

She was intuitive. "Would you? Soften the way, that is?"

"I don't know Samuel at all," she was quick to say. "Lillian and I were good friends before she moved here. She's completely changed her life and seems really happy, and I'm glad for her.

But honestly, Samuel doesn't seem to want to talk about you or have you around his family."

"Ouch." She was blunt. And it stung.

"I'm not telling you anything you don't already know." She sat up a little straighter, her look challenging him. "And I see the purpose of the coffee date. I've been wondering why you were so insistent after you had already told Lillian about David. Now I see. You want me to play go-between for you and Samuel."

"Well, I was hoping for that, but it's not like you haven't gotten anything out of the deal. I've shared a lot of personal details." *Way more than I intended.* "Spend the day with me tomorrow. I'll show you around. I can fill you in more about the Amish lifestyle. And maybe you'll see that I'm not such a bad guy."

"I don't think you're a bad guy. But aside from that, I'm just not sure that I can help you smooth things over with Samuel. I'd hate for you to waste your time."

"Somehow I don't think getting to know you would be a waste of my time." She was beautiful. And interesting. Not to mention a potential key to unlocking Samuel's heart. Even if the latter didn't pan out, the thought of spending more time with her appealed to him.

Lillian won't like it, Carley thought, although Lillian was the one who'd pushed her into this in the first place.

It sure seemed that the handsome doctor was only using her to try to get in good with Samuel. But hey—if he was willing to share information about the Amish faith, maybe she would consider it research.

Although when she thought about it, she wasn't sure it was worth it. She'd seen a softer side of him, but it didn't change the core of who he was. A doctor. She was willing to acknowledge the goodness of the profession, but it was the lack of compassion by those in the white coats that she had a problem with. She couldn't imagine delivering bad news with such detachment as she had witnessed in the hospital. Yet it seemed to come so easy for them. *How can you trust someone who refuses to acknowledge human suffering with some level of sympathy? Do they have no emotions, or just a grand ability to mask them?* Either way, she had trust issues with doctors.

"I'm sure I can learn whatever I need to know about the Amish from Lillian and Samuel."

"But will it include a scenic drive through the country? And—if you're nice—maybe even a trip to the river."

"If I'm nice?" He might be arrogant, but he was also charming.

"Dr. Noah! Dr. Noah!" a tiny voice belted from the far side of the restaurant. Carley and Noah turned their attention toward the small bundle of energy bouncing their way. The little girl looked about four or five. She had flowing blonde ringlets down to her waist, blue eyes wide with wonder, and a smile that could have turned the hardest of souls to mush. The girl was dressed in a pink frock with matching shoes and short white socks. A doll with similar attire was tucked underneath her arm.

The child dropped the doll on the floor, jumped into Noah's lap, and threw her arms around his neck.

"My sweet Jenna, how are you?" Noah kissed her warmly

on the cheek, seeming equally pleased to see her. "Where's your sister?"

"Dana's over there." Jenna pointed across the room to a young woman sitting down at a table for two. She was a very young woman, possibly a teenager.

Repositioning her pointed finger toward Carley, the girl asked, "Is this your girlfriend?"

"No, no," Carley quickly replied. "I'm a friend. My name is Carley."

"She's pretty." Jenna leaned her head on Noah's shoulder.

"Yes, she is very pretty." Noah smiled at the girl before he glanced across the table at Carley.

"I have to go back now," Jenna said. She scooted off Noah's lap and collected her doll. "Bye." She planted a kiss on his cheek and waved to Carley.

"Sorry about that," Noah said when the child was out of earshot.

"Don't be." She was surprised he felt the need to apologize. Clearly the child adored him, which only lent credibility to his "I'm not such a bad guy" statement. "How do you know her? Is she a patient of yours?" Carley glanced at Jenna's sister. A pretty girl with flowing brown hair—and a huge scowl on her face. Carley quickly looked away.

"No," he said without elaborating, quickly getting back to the subject at hand. "Now what about spending the day with me tomorrow?"

"I'm pretty sure Lillian and Samuel would not approve of us spending time together, and I'm a guest in their home."

He gazed at her a moment then shrugged. "I understand."

Whoa, is the good doctor giving up so easily? She should be glad about that. This man had issues—issues she had no business burdening herself with. She had her own problems.

But . . . something inside her twitched and the words just spewed out. "I'll tell you what," she began cautiously. "Why don't you tell me what you did that Samuel seems to think is so bad? Then I'll go with you tomorrow."

"Ah, a negotiator." He avoided her eyes, a solemn expression on his face. Then he looked back up at her and turned the tables. "I'll counter that. You go with me tomorrow, and I'll tell you my dirty little secret then." He extended his hand across the table in an optimistic gesture he seemed to hope would seal the deal.

I hope I don't regret this.

She reached across the table and grasped his hand. "Deal."

7

JUST A FEW MORE MINUTES, CARLEY THOUGHT WHEN HER cell phone alarm went off at four fifteen. She'd been allowing herself fifteen minutes to get dressed and be downstairs for breakfast, but was thinking maybe she could do it in five. Why things had to get started so early around here, she still wasn't sure. If they'd sleep in another couple of hours, then they'd be able to stay up until nine or ten. Carley couldn't get her body, or her mind, adjusted to the schedule. And why was it that she looked like something the cat dragged in each morning while Lillian simply glowed? Maybe happiness did that to a person.

As it turned out, no one was glowing this morning.

Samuel didn't say much during breakfast. Carley suspected Lillian had told him about David's test results. She wondered if she and Noah had been the topic of conversation the night before as well. There hadn't been an opportunity to talk to Lillian privately, so she was anxious for Samuel to be on his way this morning. It was five o'clock when he kissed his wife and headed out the door. David finished his breakfast while Carley helped Lillian clean the kitchen.

"David is going to do some light work around here today instead of working the fields with Samuel," Lillian told Carley.

She placed two plates in the sink before turning to face David. "You're sure you feel up to it?"

"*Ya*, I feel *gut*." He reached for another piece of toast before he stood up and headed toward the back door. "I don't know why I can't go work the fields, but I'll go tend to the cows."

The door had barely closed when Lillian turned to face Carley. "I'm so worried about David. Did Noah offer up any more details about what might be wrong with him?"

"I don't think he knows. That's why he's sending him to a specialist."

Lillian shook her head. "I don't understand. I mean, look at David. He seems fine. *Ya*, his color isn't so *gut*. But otherwise he doesn't seem to feel bad. I'm going to need to borrow your cell phone in a little while to make an appointment with Dr. Bolton. Samuel and I discussed it, and Samuel realizes this isn't a matter for our natural doctor."

"Of course you can use my phone, and I agree with you about bypassing the natural doctor and going straight to a specialist."

"I'm so sorry I pushed you to go have coffee with Noah last night," Lillian said. "Samuel isn't an aggressive man, and he's obedient to the teachings of the *Ordnung*. But I don't know Noah, and I feared what would be said between the two of them. And despite my efforts, they still traded words. Samuel didn't say what transpired." Lillian sighed heavily. "Samuel retreats when Noah is mentioned. He doesn't like to talk about him, and . . ." She stopped. "I'm sorry."

"It wasn't so bad."

Lillian handed her a rinsed dish. "Does he seem like a nice man?"

Carley dried the plate and placed it in the cabinet. "He's pushy. He shouldn't have shown up the way he did. But thank goodness he did. At least you know about David now." Lillian handed her a clean bowl to dry. "And to answer your question, he did seem nice. A bit arrogant, but nice."

"What did he say about Samuel?"

"He said Samuel is the only sibling who didn't keep in contact with him in some way. Evidently Samuel's sisters and other brother exchanged letters with Noah. Even their mother stayed in contact with him."

"Really?" Lillian motioned for Carley to take a seat across from her at the kitchen table. "Anna will wake up soon. So tell me everything."

"As we suspected, Noah was shunned for leaving to become a doctor. He said it was his calling and that he feels Samuel should be more understanding of that. He said writing letters is accepted by the bishop, but Samuel chose not to write Noah. Noah wrote to Samuel, but the letters were returned."

"What about the other thing? Did he tell you what else he did?" Lillian planted her elbows on the table, rested her chin in her hands, and leaned forward.

"No." Carley sighed, too nervous to mention her plans for the day.

"Hmm. I just can't imagine."

"Noah did say Samuel took it the hardest when he left." Carley paused, unable to stifle her own curiosity. "Lillian, I have a terrible time understanding why Samuel won't talk to you about this. He's your husband. That just seems odd to me."

Pondering her response, Lillian shrugged. "It's more of a respect issue than anything. Samuel and I are very close. Whatever happened pains him a lot. I know he'll tell me in his own good time. Amish men rule the roost, so to speak. I know it must seem incredibly old-fashioned. It did to me too. But I try to live the *Deitschi wege* as if I have always been Amish. Samuel will tell me when he is ready."

"Well, you may not have to wait that long." Carley twisted her mouth to one side. "I'm spending the day with Noah. It's research for my article. And he said he would tell me what he did that has Samuel so upset."

Lillian's expression plummeted. "Samuel won't like this," she asserted. "He won't like it at all."

"Lillian, I won't go if you don't want me to." Carley wondered if Lillian could hear the regret in her voice. "Or maybe just don't tell Samuel?" She heard herself suggest the lie—and cringed.

"*Ach*, no. I don't keep anything from Samuel."

But he's sure keeping something from you, Carley thought. Pushing judgment aside, she added, "When Noah was talking about Samuel and the shunning, it was clear that he's still very hurt."

She'd no sooner said it when she realized her preconceived thoughts about Noah might be *off* more than she wanted to admit.

"I had a hard time accepting the shunning issue," Lillian sympathized. "But it's an accepted practice, and the Old Order Amish adhere to it. So what time is he picking you up?"

"I'm supposed to meet him in town. I didn't want to cause a problem for Samuel by having him come here. But, Lillian, if you don't want me to go, I won't. I'm a guest here. I don't want to do anything to cause problems or upset Samuel."

"No, you go spend the day with Noah. You're a grown woman, and it's not our place to tell you who to spend time with."

Despite her words, Carley knew Lillian hoped she'd stay home. Instead, she nodded. "Okay."

Lillian's eyes widened, and Carley waited for her to confess her disappointment, but all she said was, "I'll expect you to tell me later what Noah did that has Samuel so upset."

"I will."

Carley found the white Lexus right away in the parking lot of the farmers' market in Bird-in-Hand. Noah was just getting out of the car with a beautiful yellow Lab when she walked up.

"This is Chloe," he said. "I hope you don't mind. Poor girl has been cooped up in the backyard while I've pulled extra shifts at the hospital."

Carley covered her surprise. She wouldn't have thought a busy doctor would have time for an animal. She squatted down to meet Chloe eye-to-eye. "Look at you," she said as the dog lavished her with sloppy affection. "You're beautiful!"

"She loves to go anywhere, and she's a good car rider." Noah released his tight hold on the leash. "She sure likes you."

"That's because she knows I'm a dog lover. She can sense that." She continued to scratch Chloe behind the ears, receiving another round of wet kisses.

"Well, what's your pleasure, Miss Carley?" Noah asked when she stood up. "We can do the tourist thing and drive around Bird-in-Hand and then through the town of Intercourse, or we can get off the beaten path and do a little cross-country traveling. You'd probably see a couple of covered bridges, Amish farms and schoolhouses, and there are shops here and there along the way."

"I can do the touristy thing anytime. Let's take the cross-country tour."

"Your chariot awaits." He opened the passenger door for her before stowing Chloe in the backseat.

"How old is Chloe?" She buckled up as they pulled out of the parking lot.

"She's two and just now starting to get out of the puppy stage. I'm not kidding you—this dog used to eat anything and everything. About six months ago, I made the mistake of leaving her in the house while I went to work for about four hours. By the time I got home, she'd destroyed a pair of tennis shoes, chewed a hole in my couch, and eaten through two throw pillows."

He smiled affectionately.

"Well, she's lovely." Carley turned around in her seat and stroked Chloe's head.

"I've got a fairly good-sized backyard, but she likes to get out and about. I was really hoping you wouldn't mind."

"I bet she loves the water."

"Oh yeah. If we go to the river, she'll jump right in." Noah waited on two buggies to cross in front of him before making a left turn. "I thought we'd head toward Ronks. It's a pretty drive, and there's a covered bridge on the way." He eyed Carley. "So tell me about yourself, Carley. What brings you all the way to Lancaster County for a story? I know Lillian is a friend of yours, but you're a long way from Texas."

"I had vacation time, and I missed Lillian. But it's hard for me not to work. I guess it's a combination of work and play."

"What do you think so far?"

She gazed out the car window. "It's very pretty here."

"May is a great time of year to come. It's starting to get warm, though." Grinning, he added, "So how's the lack of electricity working for you? Particularly the lack of air-conditioning?"

"It's a little warmer than I care for, but it's cool at night. Nothing like the heat in Texas, though. There's just not as much humidity here." She paused. "But honestly, it's not as primitive as I thought it would be. I mean, Lillian and Samuel have a refrigerator powered by propane, a gas stove, and modern plumbing."

Chloe offered up a loud bark, as if to remind them she was still there. Noah twisted his head around. "Hey, girl. I still love you." He smiled in Carley's direction. "Guess she's used to having me all to herself."

Carley found that hard to believe. Surely the doctor had a steady supply of lady friends.

"Anyway," she went on, "I'm having trouble with their schedule. I don't see why everything has to begin so early in the morning. I seem to start off tired in the morning, stay tired all day, and still have trouble falling asleep at eight or nine o'clock. Then it starts all over at four thirty or five the next morning."

"The Amish are the most hardworking people on the planet." His pride was evident.

"I don't know how Lillian does it. I try to help, but I need a nap around two or three."

"That's why you're not falling asleep at night."

"I guess." She wondered if she was pulling her weight. She often left Lillian to finish the ironing, fold the clothes, or handle one of the many other chores that her friend tackled daily—while she was off catnapping. But it was her *vacation*.

"How long are you staying?"

"A month."

"I'm sure you'll find lots to do while you're here."

Vacation or not, she was feeling guilty. Maybe she'd start doing more to help her friend. "Lillian's day is full. She takes care of the baby, tends to the garden, bakes pies, washes clothes, hangs them to dry, prepares three full meals . . . and her house is in perfect order." She shook her head. "And Lillian is the happiest I've ever seen her."

"It's the way of life and strong faith in God. That brings peace."

"But you left. Did you have that same peaceful feeling before you got your . . ."

"Calling? Yes, I did. But when God called, I knew there was something else for me. During our *rumschpringe*, all my friends from Paradise spent their time going to Lancaster, watching movies and drinking beer." He grinned. "All the things expected of teenage boys at that age. But I spent my time at Lancaster General Hospital. A non-Amish friend in Paradise was a resident at Lancaster General. Doc Eddington would take me to town in his car and let me hang out at the hospital. I read as many medical books as I could get my hands on. I just knew that I was meant to be a doctor. Later when I left the community, it was Doc who let me sleep on his couch and helped me get on my feet."

"Most people believe it to be such an honorable profession. I would think they would make an exception to the shunning."

There. She'd opened it up. Maybe now he would offer details of his secret.

Noah couldn't seem to rid himself of the shame and guilt he'd felt over the years. In his heart, he knew God had forgiven him. He just needed to forgive himself. He had a plan that would offer some redemption. A plan he was already putting into play.

He decided he wasn't ready for that subject, so he changed it. "Do you mind my asking what religion you are? I was just wondering if your beliefs are similar to the Amish and if you're a Christian."

"I was raised Catholic. I don't really go to church these days, though."

He sensed bitterness in her tone. "I'm not sure you have to go to church to be a Christian and have a relationship with God."

She shrugged, then sat quietly.

"You don't like talking about God, do you?"

"You talk about Him a lot," she answered. "I would think you'd feel a little cheated by Him."

"Not at all."

"Your calling cost you your family. That doesn't seem Godly in my eyes."

"I won't deny that I've had my share of trouble coping with that. But to question God's will only sets you up to take your own path instead of the one He has planned for you. Once you know you are a child of God, you can trust Him to make the right decisions for you, even if you don't know it at the time."

"You know, you're right. I'm not really comfortable talking about God, Noah."

"Let's change the subject."

To his surprise, she continued the conversation. "I went to church the first part of my life. It was ingrained in me since I was a child that we were to act a certain way, go to church each Sunday, and say our prayers at night. I did all those things. I just didn't . . . get it. I still pray sometimes. I'm just not sure God is listening."

As much as Noah wanted to tell her God *was* listening, he wasn't sure this was the best topic of conversation. It seemed to be a touchy subject for her.

"Carley, I don't really know you. I shouldn't have brought it up. We can move on to something else."

But she continued.

"If He were listening, He would have heard my prayers about a couple of things very dear to me," she said.

"Sometimes we can't understand God's plan for us."

"You're right. I definitely don't understand His plan. My mother died about six months ago in an accident. I prayed really hard for her when she was in the hospital. She died anyway."

"I'm sorry, Carley." He hesitated, realizing he was treading on delicate ground. "I know it's hard to understand how something like that could be part of God's plan. Were you and your mother close?"

Her face lit up as she turned toward him. "Very. My dad died when I was young. My mom and I were very close. She was my best friend."

"So you're without much of a family?"

"I have a brother, Adam."

"That's a nice shop." Noah slowed the car and pointed to his left. "It's not owned by the Amish, but everything in there is handmade by the Amish. Do you want to stop?"

"That'd be great."

"Sorry, I didn't mean to interrupt you."

"That's okay. Not much else to tell."

Carley couldn't get over some of the prices on the quilts. "Look at this," she whispered to Noah, running her hand across the counterpane. "This quilt costs two thousand dollars."

"I know. It's amazing people pay that for a cover." He chuckled.

"It's not just a cover. Look at the intricate details, the fine stitching, and the coordination of colors. It's gorgeous."

"Buy it, then."

Trust the arrogant doc to speak so casually about such prices. "I don't have that kind of money." She pushed the quilt aside, moving along to the next one on the rack. "This one is only seven hundred. It's pretty too."

"Buy it," he repeated, grinning.

"You in a hurry?" She inched one brow playfully upward.

"No."

"Oh, I thought maybe you were worried about Chloe." They'd left her in the car with the windows down.

"Chloe's fine." Joining her search through the rack, he said, "Hey, now here's a bargain. Only four hundred dollars. Buy this one."

Carley shook her head. "You're such a *man*. Hurry, buy this one—buy that one. I'd have to see every single one of these before I bought anything. And there are at least a hundred here."

"I might have to go walk Chloe."

She smiled. "Don't worry. I'm not going to go through all

of them. I'm going to see if I can buy a quilt at the mud sale on Saturday."

"Where's the mud sale? I didn't know one was going on this weekend. Have you ever been to one? Do they have those in Texas?"

"Not that I'm aware of. I'd never heard of a mud sale till I got here. I'll get a better deal on a quilt there. It's in Penryn."

"Wow. You'll definitely be going off the beaten path. And you'll have a good time. It's run almost entirely by the Amish. The quilts will be the biggest-selling items."

"That's what Lillian said. Her nieces, Linda and Miriam, are so excited about the sale. Especially Linda. They are both darling girls, and Linda is so full of energy."

Continuing to flip through the quilts, she glanced at Noah. It took her a couple of seconds to notice his forlorn expression. She turned to face him. "I'm sorry. I wasn't thinking. They are *your* nieces too. Have you ever seen them?"

"No." He slid his hands into his pockets, his eyes veering to the far side of the store. "There're some more quilts over there."

"What about pictures? Have you seen pictures of any of your nieces and nephews?"

"No pictures. Remember, Amish don't take pictures or pose for pictures. No graven images."

"Oh." Carley tapped her finger to her chin and knew she might be suggesting something she'd later regret. "They'll all be at the mud sale. Everyone. Your sisters, both brothers, and all your nieces and nephews."

"I don't know . . . ," he said when he'd figured out what she was saying.

"It's a public event. You could at least see them from afar, if nothing else."

He considered the idea. "Maybe. I'll think about it."

"We'd better get back to Chloe." She maneuvered around the quilt rack and toward the exit. Noah followed but seemed a million miles away.

⁂

The covered bridge past Ronks made for a nice place to stop. Noah pulled the car off the road, and it wasn't long before Carley began to scurry around with Chloe, who was clearly thrilled with all the attention. He wasn't sure who had more energy—or who was having more fun—her or the dog. Dressed in blue jeans, a white cotton blouse, and white tennis shoes, Carley was an enchanting vision amid the colorful wildflowers. Her multi-layered blonde locks hit the base of her neck, lending her a sophisticated yet youthful look.

"She'll wear you out," he hollered, pointing to Chloe.

"She's great!" Carley ran in circles with the dog.

Noah watched them, surprised she hadn't hit him up yet about his secret. Actually, it was no secret at all. She was worldly enough to have already figured it out. Googling his name on the Internet would have quieted her curiosity.

Just the thought of his decision over a decade ago made him cringe.

"Whew!" Carley returned to Noah's side. "You were right. She wore me out." With an ear-to-ear grin, she bent down and scratched Chloe's ears. "But you are so much fun." She rose. "I just love her."

"Me too." Noah gave Chloe a pat on her head. "I hope to have a houseful of kids someday, but she'll have to do for now."

Carley's face tensed.

"Did I say something wrong?"

"No." She quickly turned to the structure on their right. "I love these covered bridges."

Looking at her, thinking of children, he voiced a question he'd tried to hold back. "Did Lillian get David an appointment with Dr. Bolton?"

"Yes. But it's not for two weeks."

"Did she give him my name? Two weeks is too long to wait." Noah sighed. "I'll call Ken tomorrow and talk to him."

"Wow. You're really worried. What do you think is wrong with David? He seems fine."

"I hope he is," Noah said. "I'll go over the test results with Ken and get him to bump up David's appointment." He smiled in her direction. "Let's don't worry about what we're not sure of."

The problem was that Noah was sure. He wanted to confirm with Ken, but he knew exactly what was wrong with David. He had seen it before. He just didn't want to be the one to tell Samuel his son was in end-stage renal failure.

8

NOAH COULD SENSE IT WAS COMING. THE QUESTION HE'D been dreading. And he was right.

She waited until they were at the river and had finished the sandwiches they'd picked up at the deli. As Chloe romped and played at the water's edge, occasionally jumping in, Carley hit him with it.

"So, Noah . . ." She stuffed her sandwich remains into the bag.

"Guess you're ready for me to fess up." He sighed. "And a deal's a deal."

Pulling her knees to her chest, she rested her chin on her hands. "You didn't murder anyone or anything, did you?"

It would have been funny if she didn't look so serious. "No. Of course not."

"Something illegal?"

"No, Carley. I'm afraid it's not anything near that juicy." He tried to avoid her questioning eyes. "But it's something I'm not proud of, either."

She didn't say anything, so he went on. "I was eighteen when I left the district. I slept on a friend's couch, passed the college entrance exam, and started taking basic classes. I had a little money I had earned selling birdhouses at the farmers' market.

91

When that ran out, I was determined to find a way to put myself through college and medical school. I worked two jobs for a while—at a drugstore in Paradise and part-time doing construction on the weekends—but I was barely getting by."

He paused and she nodded for him to continue.

"Anyway, I wrote a book." Here came the hard part. "About my family."

"But—" She was starting to get the point. "Ahh. I'm assuming the book was not well received by your family?"

"That would be an understatement."

Why'd I ever agree to this? Because it could possibly help him make amends with Samuel, and she needed to know the issues. "I'm not proud of it, Carley. Every family, even Amish families, has things they don't want the general public—or even their neighbors—to know." He thought about the blue crate in his extra bedroom, filled with books and other memories from his old life, and shook his head. "It might not have been well received by my family, but the public loved it. I was twenty when I wrote it. Young and stupid. A friend who was a journalism major showed it to his professor, who edited it for me and showed me how to submit it to publishers. To my surprise, it sold—and I got an advance big enough to get me through the next semester."

"What was it called?" She eyed him cautiously, for the moment keeping her opinions to herself.

"When you hear the book title, you'll understand why Samuel can't seem to get past his resentment. I was bitter at the time. The shunning was worse than I imagined. Somewhere in the back of my mind, I thought my family would make an exception for my choices and that I'd still have them in my life. I was taught to know otherwise, but still . . ."

He watched a mix of curiosity and pity flash across her face. "Don't feel sorry for me, Carley. I know you think shunning is cruel, but I knew the choice I was making. And regardless of my family's reaction, what I did was wrong. Divulging personal aspects of their lives was—is—unforgivable."

"What's the name of the book? Maybe you're being too hard on yourself."

Strange. He felt he hadn't been hard enough on himself. "Would you have written a book about your family, spilling all the personal details?" The question was rhetorical. "The name of the book is *Banned by Blood: An Amish Shunning.*"

Whatever family issues Noah had offered up in the book, one thing was certain—he was remorseful. "Noah, it was a crummy thing to do. But you said yourself, you were young. And it's clear to me that you're sorry. Part of being Christian is forgiving, right? God forgave you, and you have to forgive yourself." She gave him no chance to respond. "There's a lot I don't get about the Amish faith. Like I told you before, this whole shunning thing is a cruel process I have a hard time understanding. But forgiveness should be adhered to as a Christian way to live. I would think even more so in such a religious community."

"Careful, Carley. You're diving into a conversation about God, and you said you're not comfortable with that."

"I believe in God." She knew her tone was defensive, but it was true. "I believe in heaven and hell, the forgiveness of sins—all of it. I'm just not usually comfortable talking about it, because there's something missing in my relationship with Him. As for the book you wrote, it's done, it's over. Time for everyone to move on. Forgive yourself, Noah. I'm sure God has forgiven you."

"I think God has forgiven me. As for it being done and over—I'm reminded of the error of my ways in the form of a quarterly royalty check. Don't get me wrong, it's no huge sum of money. But evidently people are interested in an insider's look at shunning. And all the little details of my childhood." He grimaced.

"Has everyone in your family read the book?"

"I don't know. Like I told you, my sisters, Ivan, and my mother responded to my letters over the years. None of them mentioned the book. In my letters, I apologized repeatedly for writing it. But as is their way, it just wasn't brought up. There weren't a lot of letters. A couple of dozen or so through the years to all of them. Samuel never responded." He paused. "And there are several stories about Samuel in the book."

"Like what?" Carley was trying to envision how she would feel about Adam if he had written a book about their family. While she couldn't think of anything overly interesting about her family, she supposed she would feel betrayed just the same.

Noah rubbed his forehead. "There were some great stories in the book that I was proud to share." He smiled slightly. But only for a moment. "And then there were other stories I had no business making public."

Carley waited.

"Samuel and I saw something that we shouldn't have when we

were kids. Samuel was twelve. I was thirteen. We were somewhere we weren't supposed to be." He glanced in her direction then out toward the road. "We made a pact that we'd never tell a soul."

"And you included that story in the book?"

He ran his hands through his hair and blew out a hard breath. "Yeah, I did."

She leaned back on her elbows, crossed her ankles.

Noah struggled. He kept opening his mouth to speak then stopping to shake his head. Maybe she should let him off the hook.

But she didn't.

"We snuck out of the house late one night," he began, avoiding eye contact. "It was on a Saturday. I remember that because I'll never forget how I felt at church service the next day."

He seemed hesitant to continue and lost in recollections. But after a break, he went on.

"Anyway, we took off on foot across the pasture, carrying a flashlight, heading to the Lapp farm. We were scared to walk down the road, afraid someone might see us. So instead we crossed three pastures to get there. We were supposed to meet Johnny Lapp in the barn. He was older than us—sixteen. And he was in his *rumschpringe*." He glanced again in Carley's direction. "Remember, that's a coming of age for the Amish, when they can run around. Parents tend to look the other way during that time in a kid's life."

Carley nodded.

"But Johnny wasn't there. Samuel and I snuck into the barn and waited. Johnny had promised us some cigarettes. We just wanted to feel grown up. We'd never done anything like that before. But after an hour, when Johnny never showed up, we assumed he couldn't get out of the house. Plus we were starting to get really nervous that Pop would realize we were gone.

"We had just started to tiptoe out of the barn when we heard a screen door slam. We took two steps backward into the barn and squatted down as fast as we could and turned off the flashlight. The moon was full that night. We watched through the slats in the barn as Johnny walked alongside his pop, across the yard, and over near the woodshed. Samuel and I tried not to breathe, but I swear I could hear Samuel's heartbeat."

Carley was thinking this type of thing would be common in the city—kids sneaking out behind their parents' backs. She wasn't sure what all the fuss was about. In her later years, she shared with her mother some of the things she and her girlfriends had done when they were young.

"Jake Lapp started taking a strap to Johnny. In a different way than Pop had ever taken a strap to any of us." Noah shook his head. "He beat that boy silly. Over and over. And Samuel and I just watched, peeking through the slats in the barn. Although if the truth be told, I closed my eyes after I watched Johnny fall to the ground."

They sat in silence for a few seconds. Carley wasn't sure what to say. What started as an innocent story had turned into something horrible. She was sickened, and she regretted ever pushing Noah to tell it to her.

"Samuel wet himself," Noah went on. "It felt like forever before Johnny's pop walked back into the house. Johnny stood up and looked toward the barn. He probably figured we were in there. That we saw everything. We watched him limp across the yard and into the house. We waited about five minutes before we bolted out of the barn and headed toward home."

Carley swallowed hard.

"Please understand, Carley. That is not the way things are done in an Amish community. But I certainly exploited the rarity of that one situation in the book. Oh, I changed the names and everything. But to this day, I wonder if Johnny Lapp ever read the book. Or his pop, for that matter. I'm guessing Samuel did."

"That would be hard—to see something like that happen to a friend, especially at that age." Carley's parents had never laid a hand on her. She couldn't imagine. And this didn't sound like a bitter explosion on Noah's part. To Carley, it seemed like a childhood memory he needed somebody to hear.

Today she'd seen a vulnerable side of him. He was flawed yet admirable, his pushiness fueled by his own desire to right his wrongs.

"The next morning, church service was at a neighbor's house. Jake Lapp's voice seemed to rise above everyone else's as he sang 'Amazing Grace.' Johnny never looked at me or Samuel once. And Samuel and I vowed to never talk of it or tell anyone. For whatever reason," he said, pausing, "I shared it with the world, making all the Amish look like child abusers, and that is so far from the truth. These people are the most peaceful people in the world. I made them look ugly by highlighting that one rare incident." His face twisted in painful recollection.

"Noah, clearly what you saw had a profound effect on you."

"I should have kept that particular story to myself. I also probably could have left out the one about *Mamm* causing a small grease fire in the kitchen one day, or the one about Mary Ellen questioning where babies come from. But, Carley—"

The passion in his tone pulled her upright.

"I told some beautiful stories in the book. Tales I'm proud to have been a part of. But my bitterness was intertwined with the good stuff. And my family—this community in general—is so private. What I did was inexcusable."

"Noah," she said softly, "we don't have to talk about this anymore if you don't want to." If he was trying to pull at her heartstrings to get her to talk to Samuel, it was working. "I understand you're sorry for writing the book. I guess I'm wondering how you think I can soften this situation with Samuel. I don't know if I can do that. It sounds like he's been bitter about this for a long time. He didn't even tell his wife about the book. Or about you."

"He probably doesn't want her to read it. There are things in there I wouldn't want my wife to read."

Interesting. Carley wondered if he'd ever had a wife. "Have you ever been married?"

Noah looked nonplussed at the abrupt change in topic. "No. What about you?"

"Nope. Never married." She thought about Dalton and how they had been moving in that direction.

"How has someone as beautiful as you averted marriage all these years?" His tone was so sincere, her heart fluttered.

"Thank you for the compliment, but it's not like I'm that old," she said sheepishly. "Anyway, I know you're hoping I can help you with Samuel, but I don't see how."

"Maybe you can just talk to Lillian. She didn't grow up

Amish. Maybe she won't be as staunch in her views." Shifting his position in the grass next to her, Noah turned to face her. "I left Lancaster County to do my residency in Minnesota because I needed to get away from here. I thought some distance would be good. But there was no place far enough to run from the demons in my head. So I came back."

Carley was touched by Noah's emotion about his circumstances, but was it appropriate for her to try to sway Samuel via Lillian?

"Noah, I can see your regret. I can hear it in your voice. Naturally, you miss your family, but Lillian is my friend, and I don't want to abuse her hospitality by butting my nose in where it doesn't belong. Why don't you just tell Samuel all this? Maybe you don't need a liaison."

"Samuel wouldn't give me the time of day about this," he said with a sigh. "But, Carley—absolutely do not say anything that might put a strain on your friendship with Lillian." He shifted his weight and then plucked a blade of grass. "You know what? Never mind. You're right. I should talk to Samuel myself."

Is he getting a little edgy with me? "Are you getting mad at me?"

He looked up in surprise. "No. Not at all. I was just sitting here thinking how wimpy I must sound not to fight my own battles."

Carley read between the lines. It wasn't edginess; it was fear— Noah's fear that his brother would reject him again. "Noah, I still think you should consider going to the mud sale. Test the waters. All of your family will be there."

"They'll know you told me about it," he said. "They might not be too happy with you."

"I can live with that. And in the meantime, I'll just feel Lillian out about things."

Noah's expression took on a look of triumph, and it became clear there had been only one purpose to this day: despite Noah's charm and his heartfelt confessions, it seemed fairly obvious he'd been using her to get to Lillian. It was hard not to feel a level of disappointment. And, truth be told, a tinge of frustration.

But no sooner had the thought presented itself than Noah lifted his hand to her face. He brushed the tip of his finger lightly against her cheek and pulled back with a ladybug.

"Ladybugs are lucky," she said, embarrassed that his touch caused her to blush.

He smiled. "Maybe I should borrow this one." He studied the speckled insect crawling slowly across his finger. Then studied her.

She avoided his eyes, which seemed softer somehow, and instead looked toward Chloe. The dog was basking in the sun near the water, stretched out between two flattened rocks. "She looks all played out." Carley could feel Noah's eyes on her, but she kept focused on Chloe. "You know, after what you told me, I can't believe Samuel is allowing me to stay with them, much less do a story."

"Just be careful who you sell out. Once something is in print, you can't take it back." Noah placed the ladybug on a blade of grass.

"I'm not going to sell Lillian out. Or you, for that matter. If you don't want me to include any of this in the story, I won't."

"I don't want you to."

It took everything Carley had not to ask, *"Then what's in it for me?"* "Fine."

"There's something I want to show you. Are you up for another short road trip?" He stood up and offered her a hand.

Carley latched on, and he hoisted her up with little effort. She quickly pulled free of his grip and brushed the grass from her blue jeans. "I guess so. Where to?"

"About fifteen minutes from here, back toward Paradise."

Noah turned off of Lincoln Highway a few streets before Black Horse Road. After winding down the country road for about a mile, he pulled onto a dirt patch outside a one-story office building. The rundown building was oddly out of place. Acreage stretched as far as Carley could see, with no signs of life except for the cows grazing on the other side of the road. In the far distance, a silo rose from the horizon with no homestead visible.

The red brick building had clearly been abandoned for a long time. Spidery cracks lined the windows that spanned the front of the structure. The words *Stonewall Insurance* were chipped and barely visible in red lettering. Five round stepping-stones led the way to a small concrete porch with a large wooden door.

"I promise, it looks much better inside," Noah said as they made their way up the steps and to the front door.

"What is this place?" Carley glanced around while Noah fumbled with the key to the door. Abandoned flower beds were laced with tall straggly weeds on each side of the entrance.

"George Meyers ran an insurance company here for years, until he died when I was a kid. The building has just been sitting here ever since." Noah twisted the knob and motioned Carley inside. "It's safe. I promise." He grinned when she hesitated.

Her fears were unfounded. "This is a far cry from the out-side," she exclaimed upon entering, examining what looked like a new tile floor. The smell of fresh paint hit her instantly, along with a powerful aroma she couldn't quite decipher. "What's that smell?" she asked as Noah stepped ahead of her and flipped on a light switch on the far wall.

"A combination of about four different cleaning solvents. I've been scrubbing the place since I bought it, about a month ago. I was on a roll until I had to put in some extra time at the hospital, and I fell a little behind schedule."

"This is your place? What are you doing with it?" She followed him through another door and down a hallway with freshly painted white walls on each side.

"I plan to keep it plain and simple." He opened a door to his right. "I'll have four examining rooms, an office, a lab, and a small area for the receptionist. This is the only examining room I have finished." He swung the door wide and hit the light switch.

The room was patient-ready with an examining table, two chairs against the wall, a sink, and a small desk and stool. Clean and fresh. Plain and simple.

"Are you leaving your position at the hospital to have your own practice here?"

"I gave notice at the hospital last week." He walked down the hall, and Carley followed. When he flung open another door, the crispness hit her. "The plumber will be here next week to put sinks in the last three rooms. And the rest of the equipment will be delivered soon."

"Noah, I think this is great," she said. "But . . . you're certainly off the beaten path. This place is in the middle of nowhere.

Do you think it will be hard to draw in patients, or have you already established a following in the short time you've been back in Lancaster County?"

"The patients will come." He glowed with an excitement Carley hadn't seen since she met him. "Amish patients."

"What?"

"Well, not just Amish patients. Anyone is welcome, of course." He motioned her out of the room and down the hall. "All the Amish families near here have to get rides from the *Englisch* to their doctor appointments. There's nothing close enough that they can travel by horse and buggy. This location can serve a huge portion of the Amish community. I hope to be up and running within a month."

Carley was speechless.

"Here's my office," he said. The room at the far end of the hallway was completely furnished with an oak desk, matching hutch, and high-backed tan leather chair. Two small matching chairs faced the large desk.

He appeared to be waiting for a response.

"Noah, it's lovely. But . . ." What exactly made him think the Amish would come to him for medical care? She was very confused.

"But what?"

Was he kidding? Carley stood in Noah's soon-to-be office and clasped her hands together. "Noah, you were shunned. What makes you think these people will come to you for medical treatment?" She hesitated, waiting for the lightbulb in his head to click on. "Please forgive this comment, but won't they avoid you? You were banned from the community, wrote the book . . ."

His expression grew guarded. "These are my roots, Carley. I'm going to make this work. I will provide a convenient service, and I understand these people. I'm not naïve. I know it's going to take some time. I'll have to earn their trust. It's not up to me. It's up to God. But my shunning happened a long time ago."

"And is evidently still very fresh in some of their minds."

"I'll talk to the bishop if I have to," he said, undeterred, motioning her out the door. "I'll show you the rest."

Heading back down the hall toward the waiting room, he pointed to his right. "This is where the receptionist will sit. I'll need to hire a nurse too. But that's it, I'm keeping it small."

Carley leaned across the receptionist's desk and through a hollow window into the waiting area. "Do you have chairs ordered for that room?"

"They'll be here next week too. I have someone coming to work on the outside—to replace the glass and clean things up."

"Sounds like you've thought of everything."

He smiled at her skepticism. "I'm sure I haven't, but it's a start." He pushed open the door to the waiting room and waited for Carley to walk ahead of him. "I guess this is my way of trying to give back to the community something I took—their privacy. I want them to have a doctor they can trust, who understands them."

"Noah, forgive me again, but why should these people trust you? I would think you'd have better luck establishing patients who are not Amish."

"Ouch." He flinched.

"I'm sorry, Noah. I just thought that once you were shunned, it's a done deal." She paused. "Or can you say you're sorry or something?"

"I'm not sorry about choosing to leave. I'm sorry I wrote the book. To be reconsidered as an actual member of the Amish community, I'd have to be sorry I left, become reestablished in the faith, talk with the bishop, and get rebaptized. I'm not looking to do that. I just want Samuel and everyone here to know I'm trying to make a difference. A positive difference."

Closing the front door behind them, he turned the key and headed to a nearby tree where he had tied Chloe's lead rope. "I know the outside looks rough. But it will look better in the next couple of weeks."

"I hope it all goes well for you, Noah. And I will talk to Lillian. I don't know that it will do any good, but I respect what you're trying to do here."

"Like I said, don't jeopardize your friendship with Lillian on my behalf." He opened the passenger door for Carley and headed around to the driver's side.

She waited until they were back on the main road before she suggested that Noah take her home. "We've been gone most of the day. I guess I'd better get back to Lillian's." She retrieved her cell phone from her purse and noticed she had missed three calls—two from Matt and one from Adam. Deciding it would be rude to check the messages right then, she put the phone back in her purse.

"Everyone looking for you?" Noah smiled in a way that made her forget Lillian or anyone else.

"Just my editor at the paper and my brother. I'll call them both back later. My editor is probably checking on the progress of the story. My brother, Adam, is just checking on me because that's what he does—*all* the time."

"You sound irritated about that." Noah slowed the car to pull around a buggy in front of them.

"He's been overprotective since our dad died years ago, but since the accident, he hovers even more. He worries way too much."

"Was it a car accident?"

Carley recalled telling him her mother had died in an accident, but she hadn't elaborated. "Yes. My mom and I were in a wreck. That's how my mom died, and I spent awhile in the hospital." She smiled in his direction, seeing the concerned look on his face. "But I'm much better now."

"Oh, man." Noah's eyes met hers, questioning her bravado. "I'm sorry, Carley."

She pulled from his gaze. She didn't want to talk about the accident. Noah seemed to pick up on that. He faced forward. Silence. Then he turned again. "I'm sure it takes a long time to heal from something like that."

I'm never going to be healed.

She didn't say anything. She could feel his eyes on her and wished she could control the flush that colored her cheeks whenever he looked at her.

"What are you thinking about?"

She closed her eyes momentarily, fending off the red Chevy.

"Oh, I guess I was thinking about what I'd like to do with the rest of my life. You seem to have yours planned out." She shrugged.

"I don't know about that." His eyes shifted from the road back to her. "What do you want to do with the rest of your life?"

"I haven't a clue." She sighed. "Sad, huh?"

Noah's faith was intact, despite everything he'd been through. Why couldn't she have that kind of faith? He knew what he wanted and had plans for how to accomplish his goals. She, on the other hand, couldn't seem to focus on anything but the present. The future was too grim anyway.

"You'll figure it out." He tapped his fingers on the steering wheel. "Hey, I was supposed to have four days off this week, but it never seems to work out that way. I got called in to work the next two days. But I was wondering if you might want to do this again on Saturday—spend the day together."

Carley briefly considered his offer. "I can't. It's the mud sale."

Noah nodded. "Ah, that's right."

He looked pensive, and she wondered if he'd take her advice and show up, see all his nieces and nephews.

They turned into the parking lot at the farmers' market, and Noah pulled up next to Carley's car.

"So maybe I *am* meant to go." He shifted the car into Park as he turned to face her. "I'd be lying if I didn't admit that I'm nervous to see my family after all this time."

"You wouldn't be normal if you weren't nervous."

Driving her car back to the farmhouse, Carley kept thinking that Noah might be setting himself up for heartache—in several areas. But his passion about the clinic and his hopes for the future seemed to be Christ-driven. She couldn't help but wonder if turning her own life over to God might give her some relief from all that plagued her. Being mad at Him didn't seem to be working.

The familiar bitterness rose to the surface. *Why me? Why did You allow these things to happen to me?*

But no, that wasn't fair. Noah hadn't been dealt the best of hands either. Yet he kept God in his court. Maybe—

The sight of dozens of buggies parked around and in front of Lillian's house interrupted her thoughts. She didn't remember Lillian mentioning anything about having visitors today. And this was a *lot* of visitors.

9

CARLEY HEARD VOICES AS SHE WALKED UP THE PORCH
steps—a soft murmur and one deep voice that was louder than
the others. She pulled back on the screen door that led to the
kitchen, careful not to let it slam behind her. Just as she prepared
to round the corner and make herself known, she heard a man
say Noah's name. She held her position and listened.

"We cannot be of the type to use Noah Stoltzfus's services,"
the man said. "It is a *baremlich* thing when our *kinner* choose the
ways of the *Englisch* after baptism. Noah coming back after all
these years changes nothing. His *meiding* is to be upheld. Noah
will make *gut* with his *Englisch* patients. Our district must do no
business with him."

"Bishop Ebersol, it wonders me—if there is an emergency
problem that needs tendin' to for the *kinner*, is going to Noah
right?"

"I know he is your *bruder*, Mary Ellen," the same man responded,
"but you know what is right and wrong, no? Having said that, I
would think it right to say that *only* in emergencies should you take
yourselves or your *kinner* to Noah."

"*Ya.*" Mary Ellen sighed.

Noah was disillusioned if he thought this community was

going to bend the rules. He, of all people, should know that. Carley quietly adjusted her purse on her shoulder and leaned an ear toward the den.

"Samuel, you will now talk with the *Englisch* woman in your *haus* and tell her it is best that she not visit with Noah. We do not want her newspaper article filled with stories from the past."

"I will talk to her," Samuel answered.

There couldn't have been a worse time for Carley's cell phone to ring in her purse, the zingy music louder and more annoying than usual. She fumbled for the phone, which seemed to have an endless ringtone, flipped it open, and found the End button as fast as she could. She looked up to see Lillian standing in the entryway between the kitchen and the den, with several people peering over her shoulder.

"Sorry," Carley mumbled. She stuffed the phone back into her purse. "Sorry to interrupt your meeting."

Lillian quickly covered the space between them and turned to face the group gathering in the doorway, some straining to have a better look. "This is my friend Carley, visiting from Houston."

The guests began making their way through the kitchen and toward the back door, a few nodding in Carley's direction. Their expressions made Carley feel like she had committed some horrific crime. Only Mary Ellen and Rebecca smiled slightly at Carley while maneuvering through the room. Then along came Sadie.

"Hello, Carley," she said. "How nice to see you again." Sadie leaned in for a hug. "They are not as scary as they look." She pulled away with a wink before heading toward the door.

Carley tried to smile as the rest of the group trolled by, eyeing her with suspicion. Samuel was the last to come through the kitchen. After bidding farewell to the last person, he turned to face Carley and Lillian. "Can we sit down and talk?" He motioned the two women toward the benches at the kitchen table.

Lillian took a seat next to her husband, and Carley slid onto the bench across from them. Lillian fidgeted, obviously loath to look Carley in the eye.

"Carley, we are glad to have you here," Samuel said. He reached over and placed his hand on Lillian's. "Lillian has been lookin' forward to your visit."

"I'm happy to be here," Carley responded. Lillian continued to avoid eye contact, and Carley suspected it was difficult for her to bite her tongue and let Samuel have full control of the conversation. She wished she could tell her friend not to look so nervous. Carley didn't think any less of Lillian.

"The situation with *mei bruder* is causing a stir in the community. Noah comin' back is hard on my family, especially *mei mamm*." Samuel's tone was gentle, his eyes kind. "Did you know he is planning to open a doctor's office near here?"

"He told me today. Actually, he took me there to see it. It's going to be very nice."

Samuel drew in a breath. "Did he tell you about the book?"

Carley nodded and glanced at Lillian, who finally looked her in the eye. "Samuel told me about the book today," Lillian said.

"He really regrets writing the book, Samuel," Carley explained. "He said he was young and stupid. He wants to open the clinic as an effort to make up for his past mistakes."

"We will not be able to go to his doctor's office." Samuel's voice was firm but held a hint of regret.

"Noah said your mother, brother, and sisters have corresponded with him through the mail. Can't the shunning rules be bent somewhat?"

"Not for us, Carley." She saw Lillian squeeze Samuel's hand, as if knowing this was a difficult conversation for him. "I know it's hard for the *Englisch* to understand about shunning. Lillian thought it to be a *baremlich* thing in the beginning too—when she was studying the *Ordnung*—but now she understands it is to keep the church pure. And in keeping with that, I have to ask you not to put nothin' in your story about the book." His kind eyes were pleading with her.

"I'm not, Samuel. Please don't worry about that. Noah also asked me not to put in anything about the book."

Lillian squirmed, freed her hands from underneath Samuel's, and got to the point Samuel was trying to make. "Samuel would prefer it if you didn't spend any more time with Noah while you're here."

Samuel hung his head slightly while Lillian went on. "There's a lot of hurt and bitterness about what Noah did. He didn't just provide an inside look at the Amish lifestyle—he also divulged very personal things about the family and members of the community. He should have never done that to make a buck."

"He was hurt and embittered," Carley defended. "He had a calling from God to save lives, and his own family ousted him because of it. I don't understand how, as Christians, you can adhere to this shunning. It is the most un-Christian thing I've ever heard of." She glanced back and forth between the two of them. "I'm sorry, but that's how I feel. Noah is sorry. God forgives him. Why can't this district forgive him and give him an opportunity to redeem himself by helping those he loves?"

Samuel stood up from the table. "I'm going to let you and Lillian talk. David is upstairs with Anna. I'll go check on them before it's time to outten the lights."

Lillian waited until Samuel was out of earshot. "Carley, I hear what you're saying. I haven't always been Amish. Shunning is a touchy subject, but I have to support Samuel on this. Please tell me you won't spend any more time with Noah while you're here. Samuel is very worried about what kind of story you'll write for the newspaper, and now I understand why. He's already been burned."

"Lillian, I would never write anything to embarrass or shame you or Samuel. I think you know that."

"I know. But understandably, Samuel is worried. It would help ease the tension if you didn't spend time with Noah."

The thought of not seeing Noah again invoked regret, an emotion she hadn't expected to feel. But Lillian was her friend, and this was clearly important to her. Except . . . "Uh-oh. I think Noah might come to the mud sale on Saturday."

"Oh, Carley, call him and tell him not to! Please. Was he coming so that he could talk to Samuel?"

"I think he wants to see his whole family. Lillian, he's never seen his nieces or nephews. They are his blood." She shook her head. "I'm having a terrible time with all this, but I'll call him and let him know that it would be a bad idea to show up at the mud sale."

"Thank you, Carley. I promise I'll make this up to you somehow. I can tell that you like Noah, and I'm sorry to ask you to do this."

"He's nice enough. Honestly, I feel bad for him."

"I can tell that Samuel feels badly for him, too, even if he won't admit it," Lillian said as she stood up. "I'm going upstairs to check on everyone." She crossed the threshold from the kitchen to the den and then turned around. "There are all kinds of Christianity. Some people go to church every Sunday without a clue why they're there. Others never step foot in church but have a very spiritual connection with God. You have a relationship with God—I can hear in your voice. Please try not to think less of us because of the shunning."

"Where did that come from? I thought we were talking about Noah."

"I heard you loud and clear just now what you said about forgiveness. We're just trying to do the right thing."

Carley pondered Lillian's comments as she watched Lillian walk away. *Connection with God?* Carley didn't think so. She'd only recited what she had been taught in catechism. This relationship with God that everyone talked about eluded her.

And whose fault is that?

The thought hung over her. The answer came slowly.

"Mine," she said aloud.

She reached into her purse for her cell phone and sighed. She knew this conversation with Noah was going to be difficult. Not only did his family not want anything to do with him, but she was bailing on him also.

She opened the phone and stared at it. Then slowly closed her eyes. "Dear God . . . I . . . I pray that I handle this correctly," she whispered, "and that there will ultimately be some peace for this family."

Can You hear me?

Saturday morning, Carley watched Lillian bustle around the house—packing the diaper bag, making sure David fed the horses and milked the cows, and giving orders about what needed to be loaded in the car. All the while Carley repeatedly tried to call Noah. For two days she'd dialed his cell phone, only for it to go straight to voice mail. She had left two brief messages explaining that it would be best for him not to attend the mud sale and asking him to call her as soon as possible.

No return call.

Call me, Noah.

"I've got to help Samuel in the barn for a minute. He doesn't usually go to these things, but he has a few items he wants to auction. Did you ever get hold of Noah?" Lillian asked while handing Anna to Carley.

"Lillian, I haven't been able to get hold of him. I left messages, but I have no way of knowing if he got them. He very well could show up."

"Do you think he'll approach Samuel or any of the family?" Lillian tied her apron strings and headed toward the door.

Carley shrugged. "Maybe."

Noah tucked his blue shirt into his jeans and headed for the faucet. He filled up Chloe's water bowl and kicked himself for the umpteenth time for losing his cell phone. He hadn't a clue where it was, though he suspected it had gone missing at the hospital.

The problem was that he never wrote down phone numbers, only stored them in his phone—including Carley's. He hadn't had time to find her, either; his shift at the hospital had kept him too busy for anything but the endless stream of patients who came through the emergency room. He could only hope Carley had softened Samuel's heart and that his family would be happy to see him at the mud sale.

Although he shouldn't place all the pressure on Carley—it was his responsibility to remedy this situation.

Noah remembered attending the annual sale in Penryn when he was young. Members of the Old Order district ran the sale, and it was a time when both Amish and *Englisch* gathered together to bid on everything from farm equipment to household knickknacks.

He placed Chloe's water bowl next to her food bowl on the back porch and made note of the weather. God couldn't have blessed the event with a better day. The clear sky, sunshine, and wispy breeze left Noah feeling hopeful about the reunion with his kinfolk. And about seeing Carley again.

An hour later, Noah pulled into a parking spot near the Penryn Firehouse, thankful that he wouldn't have to take a shuttle bus from the church down the street. He walked toward the field and listened as the auctioneer accepted bids on a tractor—one of the many pieces of equipment to be sold. He continued across the dry pasture and lost himself in the crowd, thankful the sale wasn't living up to its name.

There was a fair mix of *Englisch* and Amish attendees. Amish men were running the outside auction. He knew the women would be inside readying the firehouse for the sale of quilts and housewares. The event was just how he remembered it. He drew in a deep breath in an effort to calm his rapid pulse.

He wondered, with guarded optimism, how his siblings would react to him after all these years. Time healed. It had been a long time. Would his mother embrace him as the prodigal son he was, or continue to shun him?

He felt despair at the possibility that Esther Stoltzfus might turn her back on him after all these years. That thought cast doubt that he should even be there, but he was resolved to make the attempt. It was all he could do.

Samuel, however, was his primary concern. He had to talk to Samuel whether or not he patched things up with the rest of them. He'd tackle Samuel to the ground if he had to. The situation with David had taken on a new sense of urgency following his conversation with Ken.

A soft voice—one he thought he recognized—interrupted his thoughts. "Noah, is that you?"

Mary Ellen. Her hair was pulled taut beneath her prayer covering and, of course, she didn't have a stitch of makeup on. Tiny freckles still spotted her cheeks like they did when she was a young girl. For a moment, Noah found himself back at the farm, scurrying around and playing hide-and-seek with Mary Ellen and the others, as if no time had passed.

Mary Ellen was lovelier than he remembered. He leaned in to hug his sister and tenderly wrapped his arms around her. "Oh, Mary Ellen. It's wonderful to see you."

Mary Ellen backed out of the hug almost instantly, void of the warmth he had hoped for. But it would have to be enough for now. Her eyes darted in every direction.

"Are these your children?" Noah asked. He motioned to a young girl on her left and two younger boys to her right. He extended his hand to the taller boy. "Hi, I'm—"

"Children," she snapped before Noah could say his name, "go inside and find your *daed*."

The two boys skipped away, but the older girl stayed put.

"Linda, go inside," Mary Ellen repeated sharply. "I will be inside soon."

Noah's heart ached with a vengeance.

"I want to stay, *Mamm*." The girl smiled at Noah.

"Go now!" Mary Ellen ordered.

After her daughter reluctantly walked away, Mary Ellen glanced to her left, then to her right. She forced a half smile. "Noah, it was *gut* to see you. I must go."

Noah called after her, but Mary Ellen never looked back.

Carley couldn't understand why she hadn't heard from Noah. Maybe he had gotten her messages and decided to just be done with all of them.

Lillian toted Anna and the diaper bag while Carley, Samuel, and David each carried a box of wares. Lillian wasn't too happy about being late. Anna wasn't happy in general. She'd fussed during most of the trip and continued to do so as they made the four-block trek from the car to the event.

"What if we missed the small housewares part of the auction?" Lillian zoomed ahead of the three of them. "We'll have to cart all these things back home again."

"They will auction some house goods early on, and then they

will auction the quilts," Samuel said. "After that, they will go back to auctioning everything else. It will all be mighty fine, Lillian."

Samuel turned toward Carley and grinned. "It is the first time she's brought some of her things to be sold. And it's her first time to be headin' up the quilt auction."

"And I hate to be late," Lillian sputtered. "I really do."

Carley enjoyed seeing Samuel smile. His mood had been lighter since everything got squared away the night of the meeting. She knew that would change if they ran into Noah.

"Hurry inside," Lillian instructed. "Everyone has worked so hard. Those quilts should each bring at least five hundred dollars, and some will bring as much as two thousand. Linda and Rachel, along with the other young girls, are so excited."

Samuel chuckled. "*Who* is excited, Lillian?" He turned toward Carley. "I believe *mei fraa* is the most excited."

"Oh no! Hurry!" Lillian groaned, pushing past the vendors selling hot dogs, pickles, and various snacks. "They're starting!"

Samuel good-heartedly shook his head as they followed Lillian into the firehouse.

Carley wondered if Noah was hidden somewhere in the crowd. The room was packed with several hundred people. In addition to the rows of occupied chairs in the middle of the room, people were standing along the walls. Around a hundred potential bidders were fortunate enough to have nabbed seats. Carley and her crew weren't so lucky.

"I'm going to head outside," Samuel said. "I think there is a plow with my name on it."

Lillian didn't respond. She was busy giving instructions to three young girls.

The auctioneer and his helpers took center stage. Two intricate quilts were stretched to capacity and hung from a contraption that was suspended from the ceiling. About a dozen young Amish girls stood nearby, ready to swap out the quilts after each one was auctioned.

"Do you want me to take Anna?" Carley offered. The baby was less agitated, but Lillian had plenty to handle without Anna in her arms.

"No, no," Lillian said. "Go get you an auction number and a list of quilts with their corresponding numbers. Find the one you said you wanted and bid on it. I bet you can get it for about six hundred dollars."

Wow. Six hundred dollars might be a good deal, but it was a lot of money for Carley. She'd have to see about that. But she had no chance of owning any of the quilts without a bidding number.

"Okay." She eased her way around Lillian and toward the office on the far side of the building. It was a good opportunity to look for Noah. If he was there, she needed to warn him that his family was not going to welcome him with open arms. *I should have never suggested he come here.*

There wasn't a line to get a number. Presumably, serious bidders had already been assigned one and were in place. Carley had never bid on anything in her life. She accepted her paddle with the number 468, rounded the corner, and began fighting her way through the crowd.

And—of all things—right into Noah's arms.

"Noah!"

"I've been looking for you. I lost my cell phone. Yes, stupid, I know." He shook his head, still holding her as people pushed their way past them. "Anyway, I ran into Mary Ellen."

"Oh no." Carley sighed. She suspected that couldn't have been good.

"What—has something happened?"

"Noah, there was a big meeting going on when I got home the other day. Bishop Ebersol was there, and he told everyone that your shunning must be upheld and that none of them are to visit your clinic." She searched his eyes for a reaction that wasn't coming. Then went on. "I'm so sorry, Noah."

Noah looked toward the ceiling and rubbed his chin. "I knew something was up when I saw Mary Ellen. She didn't even want me to meet her children."

"I'm sorry, Noah," she repeated, "but we knew this might happen."

"I suppose they're all going to go along with this?"

"Yes." She paused. "There's more . . . They are insisting that I not spend any more time with you while I'm here, Noah." She felt uncomfortable the minute she said it. Maybe it was presumptuous of her to assume he would even want to spend time with her. Perhaps she had exhausted her usefulness.

"That doesn't surprise me."

She waited for him to argue, to show remorse at not being able to see her. Something. He just stood there, staring at her.

"Well, I guess I'd better get back to Lillian before the auction starts."

"Wait," he said when she turned to leave.

He studied her face. She felt the blood creep into her cheeks. "What is it?"

"Carley"—the slow, steady way he said her name coaxed her eyes to his—"have dinner with me tonight."

A strange sense of relief that he wanted to see her again mixed with regret. "I can't, Noah. I told you, I'm not to see you. I'm sorry, but I'm a guest in their home. I tried to help you, and it didn't work. I sincerely hope things go well for you, but I think it's time we say good-bye." She started to turn away from him, but he gently grabbed her arm.

"Hold up a minute. Just like that? I'll never see you again?"

She was flattered by the intensity of his response, but she shook her head. "I can't go against Lillian's wishes while I'm here, Noah. It wouldn't be right."

"Okay, don't run off just yet. Carley . . ." He hesitated, moving closer. "I want to see you again." When she didn't respond, he went on. "I'll figure all this out, but first I have to find Samuel. It's very important that I talk to him."

"He doesn't want to see you, Noah. Give things some time. Maybe Samuel will come around. I don't think today is the day, though. This place is crowded, and there's a lot going on. Wait for a better time."

"It's important that I talk to Samuel today, Carley. What I have to say, he needs to hear from me. David is a very sick kid. I confirmed David's test results with Dr. Bolton. He wants David in his office tomorrow."

"On a Sunday?"

Noah nodded.

Carley's heart was already aching for both Lillian and Samuel.

"This is a big day for them. Can you wait until after the auction is over to talk with them?"

"Yeah. Just make sure they don't get away before I find them."

"Where've you been?" Lillian asked when Carley returned. "It took you forever."

"Noah's here."

Carley watched Lillian's face twist into a scowl. "Oh dear." She motioned to a girl up front. The auctioneer was starting the bidding on the first quilt.

"He said he must talk to Samuel today, Lillian."

Lillian let out a heavy sigh. "Did you tell him this is a bad time?"

"It's about David, Lillian."

Lillian turned toward her. "Did you tell him I made an appointment with Dr. Bolton?"

"Yes, but he said two weeks is too long to wait. Noah talked to Dr. Bolton, and he said he has to talk to you and Samuel immediately."

"David seems fine. If it was anything serious, don't you think he would be showing some symptoms?"

"He's awfully pale, Lillian."

Lillian folded her arms. "Samuel thinks Noah is exaggerating whatever might be wrong with David as a way to get close to the family."

"I don't think so, Lillian."

Lillian's expression grew solemn. "I'll make sure we talk to Noah today."

"Where's Anna?"

"Samuel's mother, Esther, is holding her. She's outside. Said it's too crowded in here for her." Lillian pointed toward the front of the room. "Look, they're starting."

"One hundred, one hundred, do I hear one hundred?" the auctioneer began.

"One hundred!" Carley turned her attention to the bidder in the third row. A woman in a red blouse held up her paddle.

"Do I hear one fifty? One fifty?"

Carley was standing to the side of those seated. She glanced up front toward Linda, who was beaming from ear to ear. She was holding on to the chain that would lower the quilt when it sold, with another quilt ready to heave upward. Carley waved at her. Linda's smile widened as she waved back. She quickly returned her hand to her side and attempted to stay composed, but her enthusiasm was hard to squelch.

"I've got one fifty. Do I hear two hundred? Do I hear two hundred?"

Carley glanced at the people who were sitting down. They all had pads of paper, pens, calculators, the list with the quilt names and numbers, and the same expressions of concentration on their faces.

A woman further back held up her paddle, indicating she would bid two hundred dollars.

"I've got two hundred, two hundred, two hundred . . ."

No one was bidding. Impossible. According to Lillian, the quilt was worth at least five or six hundred dollars. Carley looked at Linda, who was horror-struck.

Please, someone bid.

The auctioneer and two helpers, all Amish men, continued to scan the room, hoping to see a paddle. They gave ample time for anyone else to bid.

"Sold! Autumn Mist for two hundred dollars to the lady in the blue shirt."

"What?" Carley whispered.

The woman in the blue shirt turned in her chair, winked at a woman behind her, and looked forward again.

The next four quilts, each more elaborate than the first, sold for two hundred dollars apiece. Carley could tell that Linda, along with the rest of the girls up front, were fighting tears. The adult women were also visibly disappointed.

"We have over two hundred more quilts to auction," Lillian said in a panic. "Each one represent countless hours of work. This is just wrong!"

Linda and the other girls secured the next two quilts on the hooks and lifted them up. Pointing to the quilt on the left, the auctioneer began. Once again, the bidding stopped at two hundred dollars, with another woman smiling gleefully at her steal.

Sadie walked up to Carley and Lillian. "You see what's going on, don't you?"

Carley and Lillian looked at each other, and Lillian shook her head.

"The quilts are being stolen," Sadie cried, "by shop owners. And I would reckon to venture they will turn around and sell the quilts at much higher prices in their stores."

"The girls are so disappointed," Lillian said. "So am I."

"This is terrible," Carley added. "I'd try to up the bids, Lillian, but honestly, I can only afford one quilt, and I'd need to get one of the less elaborate ones. I'm afraid I'd up the bid and be stuck with a quilt I couldn't pay for."

"Don't you do that," Lillian said. "Because that could happen."

"I'll just wait until the Lone Star quilt comes up for auction. I want that one anyway."

The three women held their breath as the next quilt hit two hundred.

"Two hundred, going once, going— In the back! I have three hundred. Three hundred, three hundred. Do I hear three fifty?"

A woman in the front row groaned at being outbid but raised her paddle just the same,

"Three fifty. Do I hear four? Four hundred?" Only a moment later, the auctioneer yelled, "Five hundred! I've got five hundred in the back."

Another woman seated near the front hesitated, then lifted her paddle.

"We've got six hundred, six hundred, six hundred . . . Sold for six hundred dollars to the lady in the baseball cap midways back."

The next three quilts went for six hundred dollars, all thanks to bidder number 742 in the back, who continued to outbid the shopkeepers—even winning the bid on one of the quilts.

The bidding slowly began to edge upward. Carley knew she would be outbid on the Lone Star quilt.

"Here's your quilt," Lillian said excitedly. "Bid on it!"

"I can't afford over six hundred dollars, Lillian," she whispered, "as much as I'd love to have it. But I'll try."

"Just see. You might get lucky!" Sadie chimed in.

Carley went head-to-head with two different women, carrying her bid all the way to six hundred dollars, knowing she really couldn't afford even that much. But, suspended in all its glory, it was one of the most beautiful quilts she had ever seen. She wanted it more than ever.

"Six fifty!" the auctioneer yelled as he pointed at the woman in the blue blouse.

"I'm out." Carley sighed. Lillian patted Carley on the back but was focused on the continued bidding.

"It's up to nine hundred dollars!" Sadie yelped.

They watched the bid jump to twelve hundred then thirteen hundred.

"I knew it was a great quilt." Carley sighed again, shaking her head. She smiled up at Linda, who looked like she might burst at the seams.

"Fifteen hundred dollars! I have fifteen hundred dollars from the man in the back! Do I hear sixteen, sixteen, sixteen?" Pausing for a final look, the auctioneer yelled, "Sold! To the man in the back of the room. Number 742."

The bidding conspiracy had come to an end and the more elaborate quilts began to sell, the highest price hitting twenty-three hundred dollars.

Carley was bushed. They'd spent a busy few hours at the auction, followed by a check-in at housewares before picking up Samuel near the farm equipment. All around them, families carted wares toward buggies and cars.

Carley hefted her small box of affordable trinkets and smiled at Lillian. "Did you see Linda's face when the quilts started to sell for what they're worth?"

Lillian's face lit up. "*Ya*, I did. What a great day it turned out to be. A *wunderbaar* day!"

Carley glanced behind her where Samuel and David trailed, deep in conversation about farm machinery. "Did you talk to Samuel about speaking with Noah?" she whispered.

"No, I haven't had a chance." Lillian repositioned Anna in her arms. "I'm scared to hear what Noah will say."

Carley glanced back again. "I guess we're about to find out. Look who's following us."

Lillian spun around and stopped in her tracks. Samuel and David caught up with her.

"Why are you stopping?" Samuel asked.

Lillian pointed behind Samuel toward Noah.

When Noah caught up with them, Carley noticed the two quilts he had draped across his arm. One of them was *her* quilt. So he was the man in the back—number 742. The one who had saved the auction from bombing. She looked at him in wonder.

Noah stared hard at his brother. "Samuel, I have to talk to you."

"We have no business, Noah." Samuel turned toward his son. "David, go get yourself a soda."

"But I'm not thirsty, Pop."

Samuel fired David a stern look.

Once David was out of earshot, Noah said, "It's probably a good thing you sent him away, Samuel. I need to explain to you about—"

"You have no place in our family, Noah. It has been decided by Bishop Ebersol that—"

Noah interrupted, waving Samuel to silence. "I know all about that. Listen to me, Samuel. David is sick. Very sick. I reviewed his lab work with Dr. Bolton, and David has something called renal dysplasia. What you think about me had better take a backseat for now, because you need to hear me out."

There was no questioning the urgency in Noah's statement.

Samuel leaned toward Noah. "What?" His voice trembled. "What's wrong with my boy?"

10

THEY ALL HUNG ON NOAH'S EVERY WORD AS HE EXPLAINED that David had been born with kidneys that were too small.

"During puberty, the body grows. When a person has renal dysplasia, the kidneys remain small and can't keep up with the growth and eventually stop functioning. Since David is so pale and has been vomiting, we ran kidney function tests. David's kidneys are barely working, and he's severely anemic. I'm amazed he's getting around so well."

"What does this mean?" Samuel watched David returning with a soda.

"It means you need to meet with Dr. Bolton tomorrow. Even though it's a Sunday, he has agreed to see you and explain your options."

Samuel placed one hand on his hip and rubbed his forehead with the other. "Could he—?" His voice broke.

"We will get him well, Samuel."

Samuel looked intently at Noah. "Do not speak of this in front of the boy."

"All right."

When David rejoined them, Samuel motioned for his family to continue toward the car. Noah caught Carley's eye.

"I'll be there in a minute," Carley said to Lillian.

"Listen, I know it's taboo for us to be spending time together," Noah said once the family was out of earshot, "but please call me this evening. And, Carley, if David has any problems, take him straight to the emergency room."

"I will. I'd better go. I'll call you later."

"Oh, wait." He separated the two quilts. "One for you, one for me." He offered her the Lone Star quilt.

"No way," she argued. "You paid fifteen hundred dollars for that quilt. I'm not taking it. I can't afford to pay you—"

He shoved the quilt toward her, enough so that she had to accept it. Then he smiled. "What am I going to do with two quilts? I only have one bed." Continuing to grin, he turned away while she rambled on about how she couldn't accept it.

She gave up. Not that she minded. To the contrary—the thought of sleeping beneath Noah's quilt warmed Carley's insides.

They all watched Carley stow the quilt in the trunk. It was awkward, but no one said anything about it. Actually, no one said much of anything on the way home.

Lillian always made a grand meal, but for supper that evening she went the extra mile—baked chicken, mashed potatoes, green bean casserole, a broccoli and cauliflower salad, and raisin puffs for dessert.

"Raisin puffs are David's favorite," she had told Carley as she rolled the cookies in cinnamon and sugar before putting them in the oven.

But everyone just picked at the food. Even David, who

didn't know what was going on yet, pushed the food around on his plate.

Carley discreetly cut her eyes toward David, aware of the dark cloud hovering over all of them. He was paler than he had been, and how had she not noticed the dark circles under his eyes?

After they had picked at their food for long enough, Carley helped Lillian clean the supper dishes while Samuel and David retired to the den. Samuel carried Anna with him. Carley noticed he was staying particularly close to both his children.

"I need to go make some phone calls," Carley told Lillian when they finished cleaning. "I need to call my editor and my brother."

"And Noah, I suspect," Lillian said softly.

Carley watched as Lillian rested her hands on the edge of the sink and leaned over. As Lillian's shoulders began to gently rise and fall, Carley went to her side.

"Lillian, are you okay?"

Lillian was crying. The day's events had caught up with her friend. Carley knew Lillian had tried to hide her emotions from her family, but she was struggling to keep herself together.

It had been clear to Carley from the beginning that Lillian loved David as if he were her biological son, and she was reacting accordingly. Carley turned Lillian around and wrapped her arms around her friend. "I'm sure everything is going to be fine, Lillian."

"I'm sure it will be too." Lillian eased out of the embrace, wiped a tear, and stared hard into Carley's eyes. "It has to be."

Carley decided to wait to call Matt until business hours and dialed her brother's number instead. She stretched out on the Lone Star quilt she had spread across the bed and ran her hand along the intricate stitching.

Noah.

She couldn't help but smile as she recalled the way he forced the quilt on her.

"Hello, it's me," she said when Adam answered the phone.

"Carley, I was going to call you tonight if I didn't hear from you. How's everything going in Pennsylvania Dutch Country? Are you all right?"

"I'm fine. It's Samuel and Lillian's son. He's really sick. They just found out there's something seriously wrong with his kidneys. We're taking him to a specialist tomorrow." She paused. "And if that isn't enough, a long-lost shunned brother has entered the picture."

Adam listened as Carley went into further detail.

"You must be getting some good information for your article," he commented finally.

"You'd think so, wouldn't you?" The story had been the last thing on Carley's mind.

"You're sure you're okay, though?"

"Adam, I'm fine." She let out a sigh of frustration.

"Okay," Adam said as if he understood he didn't need to keep asking her. "So what's with the shunned brother?"

Noah's face kept flashing before her as she filled Adam in.

"Sounds like you've taken a keen interest in this man." Carley could tell that this concerned Adam.

"He's an interesting person," she said, choosing her words carefully. No need to fuel Adam's concern by discussing feelings she wasn't even sure about. "And he wants to have a relationship with his family. It's all very sad."

"Carley, it sounds like Lillian and her family have a lot of personal stuff going on. Maybe you should come home."

"No, I'm not coming home." She rolled her eyes. "Besides, I want to be here in case Lillian needs me."

"So you don't know yet if they'll put Lillian's son in the hospital?"

Carley took a deep breath. "No, I don't."

"Seems you wouldn't want to be involved in all that, Carley."

It would be fine with Carley if she never set foot in a hospital again. Just the trip to the emergency room with David conjured up vivid, painful recollections of her time in the hospital. "I wouldn't *want* to be involved, Adam, but if I'm needed . . ."

"Let me send you a ticket to come home, Carley. A month is too long for you to be away. And now with all this happening, I think you—"

"Adam—stop. I'm not coming home."

He continued to try to change her mind. He didn't.

Noah propped several pillows behind his back and motioned for Chloe to take her position at the foot of the bed. They settled in and he began flipping channels on the TV, not really noticing what was on. It was just something to do until Carley called. His mind was awhirl with thoughts of his family, and his heart was heavy.

Mary Ellen's rebuff—especially in regard to her children—replayed over and over again in his head. The way she withdrew from the hug and looked around to make sure no one saw her talking to him. That wasn't the Mary Ellen he remembered. The sister he had known was warm, affectionate, never met a stranger. Had she changed so much, or only with regard to him? Would Ivan and Rebecca respond with the same apathy?

And what about his mother? He wished he could have spotted her at the auction, but now worried her reaction might have mirrored Mary Ellen's. *Surely not.* She was his mother, for goodness' sake.

He crossed his legs, gave up on the channel surfing, and folded his hands behind his head. The image of his brother was clear in his mind. It had pained him to see such worry on Samuel's face at the mud sale, and the vision furthered his regret at not being around to know the man Samuel had become. Samuel was solid in his faith and stubborn as a mule. But one thing was certain—he loved his children.

The following day would be rough for all of them.

He grabbed the phone on the nightstand after only one ring.

"Hi, it's Carley. Are you sleeping?"

"No. Chloe and I are all tucked in. I was just waiting for you to call. How is everything over there?"

"No one said anything about David, but, Noah, I did notice he's really pale, and he has dark circles under his eyes. He didn't eat much either. Actually, no one did."

"I can't get that kid off my mind. As a doctor, we know how to distance ourselves. Clearly, this is different." Deciding to lighten the mood, he asked, "Are you tucked in under your new quilt?"

"Let's talk about this quilt," she said, indicating perhaps she *was* tucked beneath it. "I can't accept it, Noah. It costs too much."

"Consider it repayment for trying to ease the way for me and Samuel." Fifteen hundred dollars was nothing to him, and Carley sure seemed to want it. He had spied her bidding for it, then noticed she relinquished when the price hit six hundred dollars.

"I wouldn't say I eased the way very much at all."

Noah sighed. He didn't really want to talk about the events of the day. He didn't want to talk about David's grim outlook, either, but he should probably prepare her. "Carley, I think Ken—Dr. Bolton—will probably admit David into the hospital tomorrow."

"I was wondering about that." Carley sighed. "Lillian broke down tonight. She loves David like he's her own child."

"She seems like a good woman. Are they planning to have more children? Amish believe in big families. I guess that part of the culture remained with me, because I can't imagine not having a bunch of kids running around the house. What about you?"

"Lillian said they want more children. As for me, I don't think . . ." She stopped midsentence.

"Don't you want a bunch of little ones running around?" Noah asked.

"More than anything in the world," she said softly.

"I saw the way you are with Anna. I'm sure you'll be a great mom someday."

An awkward silence followed. He cleared his throat. "I'm sure this isn't how you envisioned your vacation."

"No, but I'm glad to be here for Lillian and Samuel. It's just that . . . I really hate hospitals."

"Hospitals are where lives are saved."

"Or where lives end."

The coldness in her tone silenced him for a moment. "Sometimes it's difficult to understand God's will."

"How right you are. I certainly don't understand it."

He knew that God was not her favorite subject, so he changed it. "Do they have you up at four thirty helping to milk the cows?"

"There is nothing about a sick child that is God's will," she said as if she hadn't heard him.

"Why is it, Carley, that you say you don't like talking about God, but every time I give you an opportunity to back out of a conversation about Him, you keep talking about Him?"

"Forget it," she huffed. "I don't want to talk about God."

"I think you do."

"I believe in God, Noah."

"I know. I never said you didn't."

This was heading down a bad path. Again he tried a new subject. "I'd like to meet you all at Ken's office tomorrow."

"Do you think that's a good idea? You know how Samuel feels, Noah."

"Right now there's a bigger issue to focus on than me and Samuel." *Besides, David is my nephew.*

"I know, but it might make things worse."

Her voice was sympathetic. He knew she was right, but he also knew he couldn't stay away. "I'll think on it tonight."

Noah heard her yawn and reluctantly told her good night.

He wanted to keep talking. He wanted her to listen. He wanted her to understand . . .

The phone clicked and he was alone again with his thoughts.

He flicked off the TV and his bedside lamp. Then he fluffed his pillow and got comfortable. But he couldn't stop thinking about Samuel, David, and what the next day might bring.

And he couldn't stop thinking about Carley.

Lillian knew that as worried as she was, Samuel was beside himself. She slid into bed next to her husband and rested her head on his shoulder. "I'm sure everything will be fine, Samuel." She leaned up and kissed him on the cheek.

"*Ya,*" he whispered as she repositioned his arm around her neck. He pulled her close. "I don't want Noah involved with my family."

"I know you don't, Samuel. But he was wise enough to recognize there was something seriously wrong with David. What if he hadn't diagnosed this?"

Samuel didn't say anything. They lay quietly for a few minutes.

Lillian tilted her chin upward and saw the whites of Samuel's eyes when a hint of moonlight streamed into the room. Normally her husband would be sound asleep by now. She draped her arm across his belly. "I love you, Samuel. And I know everything is going to be just fine."

Samuel stroked her tenderly. "Lillian . . ."

She propped herself up on one elbow and pulled herself closer to him. "*Ya?*"

Even in the darkness, Lillian could make out the distraught

expression on Samuel's face. "What is it, Samuel?" She felt his chest rising and falling beneath her arm. His breaths were long and labored.

"Why is Noah doing this? Why is he infecting our lives with all this sadness?"

Lillian knew Samuel well enough to know what was happening. Even though he believed with all his heart that all things were God's will, being human, he still needed someone to blame. "Samuel"—she reached for his hand and intertwined her fingers with his with a squeeze—"you know this is not Noah's fault. He didn't make David sick. He just diagnosed the problem."

"He was just a boy last time I saw him. Not much older than David."

Such regret in his voice. Lillian wished there was some way to ease her husband's suffering. "I know," she whispered.

Samuel turned toward her. With his face barely visible in the darkness, she reached up and touched his cheek. Her fingertips came away moist. "Samuel, my love . . ." She wrapped her arms around him.

"If anything were to happen to my boy—"

"David is going to be fine, Samuel." She squeezed him tighter.

"The good Lord took Rachel. You don't think He'd see fit to . . . to take David too?"

At a time like this, Lillian knew better than most how easy it was to question God's will. When her grandmother died, her faith had been shaken, but there was only one answer she was willing to give Samuel. "No, Samuel. God is not going to take David too."

It was one o'clock in the morning when Lillian awoke to a shuffling noise. She reached across the bed. No Samuel. Light from a lantern across the room drew her eyes to the wooden floor, where Samuel sat amid piles of papers. A wooden box was open next to him.

She sat up in the bed and brushed back tangled strands of hair. "Samuel, what are you doing?"

"I can't find the letter." His tone was frantic.

"What letter?"

"The letter from Noah." He continued to scramble through the papers on the floor, opening envelopes and tossing them to one side.

Lillian knew about the box Samuel stored under the bed—the keeper of his memories. She'd never looked in the box. He had told her once it housed important documents, deeds to the property, and . . . keepsakes from Rachel.

"What letter from Noah?" She was more curious than ever about what Samuel might have stashed in the box.

"I kept one letter." He scanned a piece of paper and set it aside. "I usually sent the letters back unopened or just threw them away." He shook his head and looked hard at Lillian. "But there was one letter Noah sent after Rachel died. I kept it and now I can't find it."

"Samuel . . ." She walked across the room and placed a hand on his shoulder. "It's one o'clock in the morning. Can this wait until later?"

He didn't answer but pulled another wad of papers from the box.

Lillian sighed. She knew they'd both be exhausted later in the day. "Do you want me to help you look?"

He answered quickly, "No."

"Then I'm going back to bed." She turned.

"Lillian."

"*Ya?*"

"I'm sorry I woke you. I just need to find the letter."

She nodded, unsure why a letter from Noah had suddenly become so important.

Carley wasn't surprised to see Noah in the waiting room of Dr. Bolton's office the following afternoon. Noah and a man she presumed was Dr. Bolton were deep in conversation.

Noah didn't offer an explanation about his being there. Instead, he dove right into introductions, beginning with Samuel. "Dr. Bolton, this is my brother Samuel."

Carley watched Samuel's eyes cut away as he took a deep, controlled breath and extended his hand to Dr. Bolton. "Hello."

Noah pointed to Lillian. "And this is his wife, Lillian."

"Thank you for coming in on a Sunday, Dr. Bolton," Lillian said in a shaky voice.

Dr. Bolton was considerably older than Noah. Carley figured late fifties. He was a short, stocky figure with hair arched above his ears. Gold-rimmed glasses sat low on his nose. Kind gray eyes smiled at Lillian when he extended his hand to her.

After exchanging introductions with Carley, Dr. Bolton turned to David. "And you must be the man of the hour." He offered his hand to David. "Did your parents explain to you what is going on?"

"Yes, sir." David stood a little taller as he shook the doctor's hand.

"Well, if it's all right with the rest of you, I'd like to examine David and ask him a few questions. When we get done, we can all sit down and see what we can do to get this young man back in tip-top shape." Dr. Bolton smiled as he motioned for David to walk ahead of him through the door leading to the examining rooms.

David looked at Lillian with fear in his eyes.

"It's okay," she whispered and nodded toward her stepson. "We'll be right here waiting for you."

Once David and Dr. Bolton were gone, Noah wasted no time addressing Samuel in a harsh tone. "I know you don't want me here, Samuel." There was no mistaking how Samuel glowered at Noah from the moment they arrived. "But like it or not, David is my nephew."

You're making a mistake, Carley thought. Way too harsh for beginning a conversation with Samuel.

Lillian stood up when Samuel did. "Samuel . . . ," she whispered when it appeared Samuel just might buck up to his brother.

Instead, Samuel took a deep breath and backed down.

They took their seats again. And waited. No one said anything else.

Carley caught Noah staring at her from time to time.

Twenty minutes later Dr. Bolton returned to the waiting room alone. Carley recognized right away the gravity of the situation. She had seen that look before when she and her mother were in the hospital. The first time was when they told her that her mother had died. The second time was when they delivered the news to Carley about her own grim future.

"After seeing his test results, I'm amazed that this boy is functioning at all," Dr. Bolton said. "And based on what he just told me, he's been feeling bad for a while. He's in the restroom right now, but David needs to go straight to the hospital. We need to get him started on dialysis right away." Dr. Bolton paused, giving Samuel and Lillian a strong version of "the look."

No, Carley thought, remembering back to her time in the hospital. *Please. Not bad news.*

"Samuel, Lillian, this is end-stage renal disease."

Lillian's eyes immediately filled with tears. Dr. Bolton knelt beside her and grasped her hand in his. "You keep your faith, Lillian." He glanced at Samuel and Carley and then back at Lillian. "Each of you needs to be very strong for this boy."

The tears continued to stream down Lillian's face, dripping onto her cotton dress. Anna began to wail, as if sensing the despair all around her, so Carley reached for the baby. She gently eased Anna into her arms before she stood to pace with the screaming little one. Lillian openly wept, and Samuel was trying to console her, but Carley knew his own heart was breaking.

The door flew open. David stood pale and wobbly in the doorway. "*Mamm*, why are you crying?" As if he knew, his bottom lip began to quiver. "I'm going to die, aren't I?" He walked toward them all and directed his attention first to Dr. Bolton and then to Noah. In a shaky voice he pleaded, "*Onkel* Noah, am I gonna die?"

Carley could see Noah's reaction to David calling him *uncle*. Noah struggled to say the right thing.

"Everything is going to be okay." Noah reached for David's arm. Samuel was quickly in between them.

"Everything is going to be fine," Lillian said, throwing her arms around David's neck.

"Why are you crying, then?" he demanded. "Someone tell me!"

They were all standing huddled together as Lillian tried to comfort David. "Everything is going to be just fine."

"That's right," Dr. Bolton added. He gave David a pat on the back.

"Everyone stop it! Stop treating me like a child! Tell me what's going to happen," he demanded further.

David began to rattle off a round of Pennsylvania *Deitsch* that Lillian didn't seem to understand. It was Noah who began to communicate with the boy. Carley had no idea what Noah said to him, but David grew calm. Samuel stood overwhelmed by everything, his feet rooted to the floor, his eyes glassy with worry.

David gathered himself and pulled away from Lillian. He looked long and hard at each of them, finally homing in on Noah. He hesitated, shifted. As David's eyes rolled back, Noah dove for him, softening his fall as they both went crashing to the floor.

"David!" Lillian yelled, rushing to his side.

Anna screamed louder. Samuel didn't move.

11

NOAH STOOD WITH SAMUEL OUTSIDE THE INTENSIVE CARE unit while Carley and Lillian sat with David in the room. Doctors and nurses moved quietly in and out, their unvoiced tension hanging in the air.

Fortunately David had regained consciousness quickly in Dr. Bolton's office. Noah had called ahead and made arrangements to get David admitted through the emergency room and then put into ICU. Renal dysplasia was confirmed following a renal ultrasound. Now they waited for the dialysis machine to be brought into David's room.

Noah faced Samuel and summed up the man who stood before him, no longer the boy from their childhood. All the bitterness and hurt he'd harbored for years was buried by the burdens of the moment. *Samuel shouldn't have to go through this.*

"Samuel, Dr. Bolton and the renal team are going to talk to you in the morning," Noah began. "I've read David's chart and talked with Dr. Bolton. Basically, you're going to have three options. And the first two don't seem feasible or practical. Option number one is for David to receive dialysis at home. That would require electricity. The bishop would likely make an exception for this." He paused. "Or David would receive dialysis three days a week here at the hospital. You would have to have rides lined up or try to seek an exception from the bishop on that as well. Both options would run in the neighborhood of ten thousand dollars per month."

Samuel's jaw dropped as he stumbled backward slightly. Noah took a step forward, but Samuel stretched his hand out, clearly keeping Noah at arm's length. Samuel sat and rested his hands on his knees, hanging his head. Noah waited while Samuel absorbed the information.

Noah knew dialysis was expensive. The federal government covered about 80 percent of all dialysis costs, and private health insurance usually picked up the balance. The problem was that Amish folks didn't accept government assistance, nor did they carry private health coverage. They self-insured, with all the members of the community contributing to a fund. Noah doubted they had the kind of money to cover a catastrophic medical expense such as ongoing dialysis.

"Samuel, you can always apply for emergency Medicare," Noah said. "However, the renal team believes the best option for David is for someone to donate one of their kidneys. There's a good success rate, and it would give David the best quality of life."

Noah couldn't imagine what his brother was feeling. Samuel had already lost a wife to cancer—and now this.

"He'll need things while he's here, no?" Samuel asked after taking a deep breath. "A toothbrush and things like that?"

Not at the top of the priority list right now, Noah thought, but obviously Samuel needed a distraction. "*Ya,* that would be *gut,*" Noah answered softly. Samuel looked perplexed at Noah's choice of wording. "I'll drive you to the farm if you want to pick up some things for David."

At first it appeared Samuel would decline the offer, but after he glanced into David's room and saw Carley holding Anna with her arm around Lillian, he reconsidered.

"Do you want to go now, while David is sleeping?" Noah asked.

Samuel nodded.

———

Noah was hoping to see the inside of Samuel's home. He waited for an invitation that didn't come. Instead, Samuel quickly exited the car and headed toward the house without saying a word. Noah waited by his car. It had been a quiet ride from the hospital.

"Samuel," Noah called after him, "you might want to get some clothes and things for you and Lillian too."

Samuel kept walking but nodded acknowledgment.

"Do you need help with anything?"

Samuel shook his head.

Noah glanced around the yard. "What about outside? Anything need to be done with the horses?"

Samuel didn't turn around as he walked up the porch steps. Again he just shook his head.

Noah wished he had something to do. Anything. Helplessness was webbing around him, suffocating him.

Samuel returned more quickly than Noah expected, toting only a small tan knapsack.

"Is that all you need?" Noah knew that at a time like this, it was easy to forget things. "What about medications or anything like that?"

"I have all we need." Samuel continued toward the passenger door.

Noah waited until they had pulled onto Lincoln Highway before he said anything. "Samuel, I'm going to help you all get through this. I'll do whatever I can to make things—"

"We don't need your help." Samuel sat taller and stared straight ahead, tightly clutching the knapsack in his lap.

Maybe this wasn't the time, or maybe it was the perfect time— either way, Noah couldn't help himself. "Samuel, we're family. No matter what. You can't change that, even if you want to. Let me help."

Samuel's blue eyes darkened, and his words pierced Noah to the core. "We are not family."

"I'm afraid, my brother, that we are." Noah knew there was too much going on to let bitterness creep in. He silently reprimanded himself and tried to make amends, something he always seemed to be doing. "I don't want to fight with you, Samuel. I just want to help."

Samuel didn't respond and continued to stare ahead. Noah didn't have the heart to push the issue. He knew Samuel was burdened with more than he could possibly understand or say grace over.

Noah assumed it would be a silent trip back to the hospital. He was surprised when Samuel spoke up. "Please stop there." He pointed to a bakery on their right.

"What for?"

"My niece Linda works there. She will get the word to the rest of the family."

"She's my niece too," Noah muttered as he turned into the parking lot.

Samuel didn't respond.

After Samuel made a quick trip into the bakery, they continued on. The ride passed as Noah expected it would—in silence.

David was sleeping, hooked up to every contraption imaginable, including a dialysis machine. The lifesaving device was five feet tall and four feet wide, with all kinds of buttons and switches and a computer screen. It featured a round filter about two feet long and as wide as a baseball. David had looked horrified when they brought the machine into the room.

Carley thought herself to be fairly hospital savvy, but she didn't even recognize some of the other gadgets surrounding the bed. Large tubes, wires, and monitors draped across David in an abstract mass of modern technology. The equipment conjured unwelcome memories that caused her to shudder. She gritted her teeth and tried not to think about it.

Carley sat beside Lillian in chairs pulled close to the bed. She watched her friend nervously rocking back and forth with Anna in her arms, and she wondered what she could do to help.

She could only think of one thing that might make Lillian feel better, despite her own reservations.

"Let's pray together." Carley offered Lillian her hand.

Lillian was too weary to even show surprise at such a suggestion coming from Carley, and she merely leaned over and rested her head on Carley's shoulder. The two women huddled together

with Anna. After a moment it became clear that Lillian was waiting for Carley to offer up the prayer. In all the years Carley had
known Lillian—they had dined out, shopped, gone to movies,
stayed up all night talking, and done all the things good friends
do—they had never prayed together. There had never been dis-
cussions about God.

"God, please bless David and this family," Carley began
slowly. "Please give them all strength through the power of Your
love. Please wrap Your arms around them all in a blanket of faith,
hope, and protection. May there never be doubts about what a
good and wonderful God You are, despite this hardship before
them. May Your grace surround all of us and heal this child."
Carley paused. She was unsure where the words were coming from,
and she felt a knot building in her throat. "And, God, I'm sorry I
haven't been around much lately. Please forgive me for—" Her
voice cracked.

"He already has, Carley," Lillian whispered. She gave Carley's
hand a comforting squeeze.

Being around Lillian and her family, and even Noah, had
awakened things long dormant in Carley. She had lost touch
with God a long time ago. When she turned to Him after the
accident, she remembered feeling unworthy to ask Him to help
her—but angry just the same when things unfolded the way
they did.

*What exactly does trusting God's will mean? And how do the Amish, and
Noah, do it with such ease?*

Lillian's head was still resting on Carley's shoulder when
Carley briefly locked eyes with Anna. Blinking back sleep, the
baby squirmed slightly in Lillian's lap, and Lillian raised her

head. She pulled the baby close to her chest, close to her heart, and whispered, "It's all right, precious."

Anna's eyes quickly slid from Carley's at the sound of her mother's voice. *What must it feel like to love like that?* Carley wondered, watching Lillian and her child. She would never know. If only the wooden spike that pierced her abdomen had gored her an inch to the left or right, maybe she would be able to have children of her own.

She watched Lillian and her daughter and recalled her relationship with her mother. Not a day went by that she didn't miss the friendship they had shared. Why was God denying her the privilege of motherhood? Somehow she needed to find peace about this.

David coughed. Carley watched Lillian tense and take a deep breath.

Why this? Why David? Surely Lillian was asking God these questions. Things had just become so good for Lillian. Carley wondered if Lillian felt cheated. Did God offer up something good, only to let something bad happen? Was He always testing?

Lillian turned her head toward Carley and smiled. "I'm so incredibly blessed."

There was no *"Why this? Why me? Why David?"* No bitterness. Just Lillian smiling. Carley attempted to smile back at her, but she was thinking about how different she was from Lillian, who appeared to always focus on the good stuff.

"I thank God for everything in my life." Lillian reached across the bed and touched David's hand.

Carley nodded in agreement. A silent lie. She hadn't been thankful for much of anything lately. Only bitter.

Maybe it was time to rethink her relationship with God. Maybe He had a different plan for her.

Anna drifted off to sleep in Lillian's lap and the women sat quietly.

Carley was trying to imagine what David must be feeling in this foreign place. All the strange machines, the IV, and tubes everywhere. It would be a lot for any thirteen-year-old to handle. But she knew it was even more frightening for an Amish boy who didn't venture to the city often,

Carley and Lillian both turned when they heard footsteps coming into the room. Samuel slowly approached his son's bedside and removed his straw hat.

Carley assumed they might like some time alone with their son, so she excused herself. Noah was sitting in a chair outside the room, his elbows resting on his knees and his head hanging low. He looked up when he heard the door close.

Carley took a seat in the chair next to him. "How did it go with Samuel earlier?"

"As I expected it would. He didn't say much. I tried not to push too much. Samuel has a lot ahead of him."

"I wonder if Lillian and Samuel will stay here tonight. I guess I could take Anna home."

"How is Lillian holding up?"

"She's weepy, as expected. Noah, I don't understand how this happened. How can someone go into full-blown kidney failure without some sort of warning?"

Noah shrugged. "David was born with dysplasia. It doesn't

present itself until puberty. With this condition, usually the only symptoms are anemia, high blood pressure, and vomiting. By the time the symptoms become apparent, the patient usually has end-stage renal disease."

"Well, there's not much for me to do here right now. I can probably be of better use if I take Anna home and see about keeping the household running."

"Some vacation, huh?" Noah frowned.

"I just want to help." She just wanted away from the hospital—the smell, the beeping of monitors, the paging of doctors, all of it. "Are you going to go in and see David?"

"No. Not now. Samuel has enough to deal with. I'll check on David when they aren't around. Plus the renal team will fill me in on everything." He paused. "Maybe I'll swing by later, if that's all right and David seems stable."

Carley nodded. "Guess I'll go see about taking Anna home, then."

It was nearing eight o'clock when Carley arrived at the farm. Anna had been sound asleep since they hit the highway in Lancaster City. She gently lifted Anna from the baby carrier and headed toward the house. As expected, both Samuel and Lillian were staying the night at the hospital. Both seemed relieved she was taking Anna home.

She entered through the kitchen, grabbed the large flashlight kept on a shelf by the door, and shined it ahead of her. Then she made her way to the couch and laid Anna on her back. She pulled the playpen from its resting place against the wall and set it up as quietly as she could. She wasn't comfortable leaving Anna alone in Samuel and Lillian's room in her crib, so she thought she'd sleep on the couch with Anna nearby in the playpen. She suspected it would be a long night, and if she set the playpen up in her room upstairs, she might not hear Noah arrive.

Carley kicked off her tennis shoes once Anna was all settled. Her white sneakers stood out against the pile of black leather shoes next to the door. She shuffled in her socks across the wooden floor and into the kitchen, where she found the box of matches Lillian kept in the cabinet. She lit two lanterns and placed one on the counter and one on the kitchen table. The aroma of freshly baked bread still permeated the room, a smell she wished she could bottle and take back to Houston with her.

Houston. Matt. She realized she'd never called her editor. She really didn't feel like making the call, but she knew she should lay the groundwork for what she felt was coming.

"Well, hello, stranger," Matt said upon hearing her voice. "I've left several messages for you. I figured you were still mad at me."

"No, not mad. Just busy."

"Busy doing what? Milking cows, riding in a buggy? Or are you baking bread and working in the garden?" He chuckled.

Not in the mood for his sarcasm, she replied, "As a matter of fact, I've been doing all those things, except for milking the cows. And I like it here."

Silence for a few seconds.

"Sorry, I'm trying to picture you baking bread and gardening," Matt joked. "So how's the story coming?"

"Slow." She hesitated. "There's a lot going on here. Lillian and

Samuel's son is sick. He's in the hospital. I'm actually at home with the baby so they can stay at the hospital with him."

"I'm sorry to hear that. Probably not the vacation you were anticipating."

"Well, I wouldn't have been on vacation if I wasn't forced to be." She thought for a moment how none of this was aiding her own emotional recovery. Then she cringed at the thought, knowing it was selfish.

"You'll come back in a couple of weeks feeling refreshed, I'm sure," Matt said. "Sometimes you just need to distance yourself from a situation for a while. You had a lot hit you all at once, Carley. Your mom, your own injuries, and Dalton."

"I don't need to be reminded, Matt. And about that couple of weeks—I don't know. I might need to stay longer to help Lillian."

"First I can't get you to go. Now I'm going to have trouble getting you to come back?" His tone was playful, but Carley knew Matt. He had said a month, figuring it would be long enough. He may not be keen on extending it.

"Well, I don't know yet," she said firmly. "I'll just have to wait and see."

Carley heard a knock at the door. "Someone's at the door, Matt. I'll have to talk to you later."

Noah looked haggard as he stood at the threshold. "Come on in," she said, opening the screen door.

When the light from the kitchen lantern shone on him, she noticed the bouquet dangling at his side.

"Do you mind if we just sit on the front porch?"

"It's more comfortable in here." She continued to hold the

door open, motioning toward the kitchen table. Her eyes drifted to the flowers at his side.

"I will walk into Samuel's house one day. But it will be because he invited me. Today isn't that day."

"Okay." She stepped onto the front porch and gently closed the screen door behind her, careful not to wake Anna.

"Oh. These are for you." Noah offered her the flowers.

In the darkness it was hard to see. Carley's hand brushed against his as she accepted the bundle then leaned toward the faint beam of light streaming from the kitchen. She took in the yellow roses and baby's breath bursting from within their green wrap. She couldn't remember the last time anyone had given her flowers.

"Thank you."

They stood there gazing into each other's eyes. It was awkward. Wonderfully awkward.

"You're welcome," Noah finally said with a tired smile.

"I'll go put these in some water." She pulled her eyes from his and headed back into the kitchen to find a vase. A large mason jar made a nice substitute when she couldn't locate a vase. She removed the green wrapper, arranged the blooms, and added water. All the while she analyzed Noah's gesture. He was a complicated man whose medical attributes she had loathed—feared—in others. But on this night, Noah was a far cry from the pushy, arrogant doctor she'd first met.

She recalled his boyish smile when he handed her the flowers and realized her fears about Noah were moving in another direction. One equally disconcerting. She'd been hurt enough. And this had nowhere to go. Noah was all about having a family, and while that was a common goal they shared, it was no longer a possibility for Carley. To speculate about a relationship was futile. If she'd learned anything from her breakup with Dalton, it was that men didn't stay with women who couldn't give them what they wanted.

She walked back outside and they each took a seat in one of the wooden porch rockers. Stars twinkled in abundance overhead, unlike in the city. Carley noticed it was a full moon. "Crazy things happen when it's a full moon," she said, searching out eyes, nose, and broad grin on the glowing orb, the way she had when she was a child. *The man on the moon.*

"Crazy things happen when it's *not* a full moon. Life is just crazy." Noah crossed an ankle over a knee, pushing the rocker slightly into motion.

"Did you hear anything else after I left?"

Noah had about two days' worth of five o'clock shadow. Stroking his stubble, he stared out at the darkness. "No."

"I'm probably going to extend my stay. I just got off the phone with my editor and put a bug in his ear. I think Lillian will need my help during all this."

Noah's eyes met Carley's. "This situation is horrible. The only bonus is that you'll be here longer than you planned."

She caught the compliment but didn't acknowledge it, glad the night hid the blush rising in her cheeks.

"Lillian and I have been friends for a long time," she said. "I'm going to help her and her family any way I can." She paused and reflected on the hardships Lillian had faced. "Lillian's had a difficult time too. She's doing great now, but she had a long journey getting here. I hate that this is happening to her family."

"I'm sure she appreciates that. Her mother showed up at the hospital right before I left."

"Oh, that's good. She and Sarah Jane are very close. They weren't always, but I'm so glad they are now. Moms aren't around forever."

"You miss your mom."

Carley crossed her arms across her chest and gave herself a heave-ho in the rocker. "Yes, I do." Cutting her eyes in his direction, she added, "And I know you miss your mother, too, Noah. That's why I have a huge problem with this whole shunning thing. Your mother is alive, and you should be allowed to have a relationship with her."

Noah started to say something but stopped short when his pocket began to vibrate. He grabbed his cell phone and glanced at the incoming number. "It's Dr. Bolton."

12

"IS EVERYTHING OKAY?" CARLEY ASKED NOAH WHEN HE hung up with Dr. Bolton.

"Ken doesn't usually call in the evenings unless it's important. He wanted to make sure I knew the renal team would be talking with the family around six thirty tomorrow morning. They're going to suggest a kidney transplant—as soon as possible."

Carley was afraid to ask the next question. "Noah, everyone keeps saying *end-stage* renal disease. What does that mean? Is he—?"

Noah finished her sentence. "Is he going to die?"

Carley's stomach twisted. If Noah's expression was any indicator, she didn't want to hear his answer.

"Noah, tell me that boy is not going to die. He's only thirteen years old."

Noah opened his mouth to speak. Instead, he shook his head.

"Noah?" she asked again.

He reached over and placed his hand on hers, as if not wanting to alarm her. But alarms were ringing about David and about his hand on hers. "The team will do everything to ensure it's a successful transplant. It's done all the time and with good success. But there are risks." He paused for a moment when she pulled her hand out from underneath his. Then went on. "Anyway, one problem can be finding a kidney. Some people are on a waiting list for years. The best option is for a family member to donate a kidney."

"Samuel?"

"Anyone who has David's blood type and whose kidney is a good match. The best match is going to come from a blood relative."

Carley took a deep breath and let it out slowly, somewhat relieved. "That sounds hopeful, then. Is there a risk to the person giving up a kidney?"

"There are risks with any type of surgery, but like I said, most of the time everything goes well. There are more risks for the person who receives the kidney. The body will automatically reject the kidney and treat it like it's a foreign object. We give the recipient immuno-suppressant medications to trick the immune system, which helps fight the natural rejection of the kidney."

"So anyone in the family who has David's blood type can donate a kidney?"

"Only if it's a good match, which is determined by running some tests. Don't get me wrong, this is major surgery. If everything goes well, living with a transplant is a lifelong process. David will have to make some lifestyle adjustments and will probably be on medication for the rest of his life." He stared at her with sympathetic eyes. "I probably need to let you get some sleep. I'm going to go back to the hospital and look at David's chart. I didn't even notice what blood type he is."

Carley stood up and watched Noah stifle a yawn. "I think you need some sleep too," she said before starting down the porch steps beside him.

"I'll call you in the morning and let you know what I find out."

"Okay." She watched him walk across the yard toward his car.

He turned once to wave, then slid into the driver's seat, turned the car around, and headed down the dirt driveway. Carley stood in the yard until he rounded the corner and was out of sight.

"The only bonus is that you'll be here longer than you planned," Noah had said.

Carley looked up toward the smiling moon and the twinkling clusters that surrounded it. It scared her to make too much of Noah's comment, but there was no denying that his words made her heart flutter.

Lillian leaned back in the reclining chair in David's room, although sleeping didn't seem to be an option. The nurse said the medications they were giving David would help him sleep. She was thankful he was resting comfortably, despite the monitors intermittently beeping to indicate one thing or another.

Lillian glanced at Samuel, who was sitting in a chair by David's bedside. It was almost one o'clock now. Her husband refused to even rest his eyes and stared intently at his son, watching every rise and fall of the boy's chest. For all the worry in her heart, she knew it couldn't compare to the fear Samuel felt. She tried to imagine how heart-wrenching it must have been for him to sit by his wife's bedside when she died in this very hospital. And now this.

"Do you miss the *boppli?*" Samuel asked after a while.

He knows me so well, Lillian thought. It was her first night away from Anna. "*Ya,* but I know Carley is taking *gut* care of her."

"She is a *gut* friend to you, no?"

"*Ya.* I'm glad she's here, although this isn't the vacation she planned."

Samuel scowled. "She vacationed with *mei bruder.*"

"Samuel," she whispered, "maybe now is the time to let go of some of your bitterness. He is your family. I know what he did was wrong, but he's trying so hard to help us."

When he didn't answer, Lillian momentarily stepped outside of her role as submissive wife, as she was known to do from time to time. "This anger you feel toward him is not right in the eyes of God, and you know that. I understand about the shunning, even though it's hard for me to accept. But, Samuel, harboring all this contempt isn't *gut.*"

"What he did was *baremlich.* All these years later, you can still walk into the Gordonville Book Store and find a copy of his book. A book filled with stories about our family and members of our district. Some *gut,* some not so *gut.* But they were all private. Not for sharing."

"I understand, Samuel. Really I do. But what about forgiveness? That is our way. We forgive, just as God forgives."

"Lillian, I forgave Noah a long time ago," he stated. "But I do not have to have him in my life. He made his choices, and he has to live with them."

"Yes, I do."

They both turned to see Noah standing in the doorway.

"And I don't know how many ways I can tell you I'm sorry, Samuel," Noah added.

"Do you have more news about David?" Lillian jumped in before Samuel could respond.

Noah shook his head. "No, only what I told you earlier. Just as I suspected, they will be recommending a kidney transplant."

"Pop?"

They all turned to David. Lillian walked to where Samuel was sitting at David's bedside. Noah stayed at the threshold, unsure whether to move forward or leave.

"*Mamm* died in a room just like this one. Am I gonna die?" David asked in a raspy voice.

"No, no, no. Of course not, sweetie." Lillian said. Her unspoken fears stabbed at her heart.

The color drained from Samuel's face, and he reached for his son's hand. "Everything will be fine."

David was unconvinced. "But I feel so bad," he whispered. "I think I might be dying." His eyes darkened with emotion. "I dreamed about *Mamm* while I was sleeping."

Samuel stood and Lillian reached for his hand. He was trembling.

Noah rounded the foot of the bed and stood on the other side of David. Lillian braced herself for Samuel's reaction. Nothing. She squeezed Samuel's hand and focused on Noah, begging him with her eyes to ease the way, to reassure all of them that everything was going to be all right.

"David, the reason you feel so bad is because your kidneys aren't working properly," Noah began. He glanced up at Samuel, as if seeking permission to go on. While Samuel wouldn't look at Noah, he didn't bark his opposition either.

Noah continued, "Plus some of the medications can make you feel strange too. But, David, we aren't going to let you die."

"I know I'm gonna have a kidney transplant," David said matter-of-factly.

No one had told David the news. Lillian looked as surprised as Noah and Samuel.

David rolled his eyes. "Sometimes I'm just resting, not sleeping."

"You have two kidneys, David," Noah said. "A donor can give you one of his or her kidneys, and the donor can live a perfectly normal life afterward. And—"

"He will take my kidney," Samuel stated. He stood a little taller, his tone firm. "My boy will have my kidney."

Noah raked his hand through his hair and turned to Samuel. "It's not that easy, Samuel. A donor must have the same blood type as David, and the kidney must be a good match. There are tests that determine who will be the best match."

"I'm his *daed*. His blood type should be the same as mine, no?"

"Not necessarily. He could have his mother's blood type." Noah turned to David. "David, we will find you a kidney. Try not to worry. I know the hospital can be a scary place."

"I'm not scared," David said boldly. Then he turned to Noah, searched his eyes. "Is this my fault?" he asked.

The question tugged at Lillian's heart. *Why is this happening? We were all so happy.*

"No, it's not your fault, David," Noah responded. "Your kidneys just never grew. You were born with this condition. It's not your fault."

David moved his eyes off of Noah and looked down. "But I . . ."

Noah touched David's arm. Lillian could feel the tension in

Samuel's hand. "You've felt sick for a while, haven't you?" Noah asked.

David nodded. "I'm sorry, Pop." He looked up at Samuel.

Samuel shook his head. "You don't need to be sorry, Son."

"But maybe I should have told you. It's just that there's so much work to be done, and I didn't want to cause hardship."

Lillian knew her own guilt probably didn't match Samuel's, but it was there amid all the questions swirling in her head. How could they not have known David was so ill? If it was anyone's fault, it was hers. She was a mother. She should have noticed.

"This is no one's fault," Noah said. He leaned down slightly toward David. Then he straightened up and glanced back and forth between Lillian and Samuel. "No one's fault," he repeated. "All of you should try to get a little sleep. There's a roomful of recliners in the ICU waiting room. The staff will provide you with some blankets and pillows. The renal team will be here at six thirty to meet with you. That's only a few hours away."

Lillian was surprised when Samuel moved toward the door. "I'll be right back," he said.

Once outside David's room, Samuel motioned for Noah to come into the hallway.

"Try to rest," Noah said as he circled around the foot of the bed and headed out the door.

Something is up. "I'm going to stretch my legs too," Lillian told David. She kissed him on the forehead before joining Samuel and Noah outside the door.

Samuel took a few steps down the hall, out of David's earshot. Lillian and Noah followed.

Samuel's questioning eyes glazed with emotion. He inhaled slowly, pursed his lips together.

"What is it, Samuel?" Noah asked.

"Samuel?" Lillian was wondering the same thing.

Lillian watched her husband look hard into Noah's eyes and painstakingly reveal what was on his mind.

"This kidney that David will get . . ."

"Yes," Noah said. "What about it?" Noah stood a little taller as if bracing himself for what Samuel was about to ask.

"How long will it last?"

Lillian had just assumed it would last forever, but the look on Noah's face said otherwise.

"Tell me."

Noah ran his hand across his brow. "Ten to fifteen years."

Lillian grabbed her chest. "In ten years, David will only be twenty-three."

She turned to Samuel. Tears were forming in the corners of his eyes.

"If all goes well, sometimes a transplant recipient can get another kidney," Noah said, reaching over to touch Samuel's arm.

Samuel jerked away and took two slow steps backward as he glanced back and forth between Lillian and Noah, his eyes reddening with each wide stride. He blinked back his emotion, lifted his chin, and spun around on one foot. He'd only taken a few steps in the other direction when Lillian saw him hang his head and lift one hand to his face, nearly bumping into oncoming traffic in the hallway.

Lillian followed.

Carley was feeding Anna when she heard buggy wheels coming up the driveway the next morning. Dawn had barely broken. She wondered who could be visiting so early. She gave Anna's mouth a gentle swipe with the towel and headed toward the kitchen door. When she opened it, she was shocked to see a line of buggies coming up the driveway.

What . . . ?

She walked onto the porch and counted the buggies as they drew closer. Twelve buggies in all. Sadie's buggy was the first in line.

"Sadie, who are all these people, and what are they doing here?" Carley asked when Sadie reached her.

"Both of Samuel's sisters, Rebecca and Mary Ellen; their daughters, Linda and Miriam; Samuel's *mamm*, Esther; Katie Ann; and several others from our community," Sadie said. "Lillian's *mamm*, Sarah Jane, got a ride to the hospital from our *Englisch* friend Barbie."

"But what is everyone doing here?"

Sadie was taken aback. She clasped her hands in front of her and straightened, then blew a loose ringlet of curly red hair from her face. "Why, we're here to help, of course."

Linda handed Carley a piece of paper. "This is a schedule of who will be bringing supper each night. Everyone in the community is pitching in—a different person's cookin' for all of you every night."

Carley studied the note. "Thank you," she whispered.

Katie Ann inched forward. "Ivan has made arrangements for the fields to be tended to," she said.

"And our sons will be here early each morning to milk the cows," Mary Ellen added.

A woman Carley hadn't seen before extended her hand. "Hello, I'm Lena Mae. I will be coming by every couple of days to pick up any laundry, ironing, and mending that needs to be done."

Carley took the woman's hand, feeling overwhelmed and incredibly touched. "Thank you," she said again, fighting back tears.

One by one, the women advised Carley about the duties they had assigned themselves. A neighboring teenager, the daughter of a woman named Suzie, offered unlimited babysitting services for Anna.

"I'm Lydia," the teenager said. "*Mei bruder*, Elam, travels down Black Horse Road every day on his way to do construction in town. Leave a note on the fence post by the mailbox. Let me know the day before what time to be here. Elam will tell me."

When Carley's cell phone blared from the pocket of her blue jeans, Mary Ellen extended her arms to take Anna. "Thank you," Carley said. She handed the baby over and fumbled for her phone.

Noah updated her about the events of the early morning and told her that the renal team had just met with Lillian, Samuel, David, and Lillian's mom. Noah advised Carley about her role.

"Samuel has already been tested, and he isn't a match. He was really upset that he can't be the one to give David a kidney. So now we need to see if any of the family has David's blood type and could be a potential donor for him. It's a very personal choice that no one should be pressured or coaxed into. If they are willing, could you round up Ivan and Rebecca and bring them to the hospital? The renal doctor will talk to them, educate them, and they can decide whether to consider being a donor. You don't have to bring Mary Ellen. Lillian said she is anemic." He paused, sighing.

Carley was trying to absorb everything.

"This whole thing is just ridiculous. I have David's blood type. I should be the one who is getting screened as a potential match." Noah said.

"I suppose that's not a possibility?" Carley knew the answer.

"Samuel won't even consider it. He's very hardheaded and unforgiving."

"I'll talk to Rebecca and I'll see if we can swing by and pick up Ivan."

She hung up with Noah and promised to see him later at the hospital, then updated the women. Rebecca didn't hesitate when Carley asked her about going to the hospital to be screened. Carley suspected Ivan would be just as willing. Carley also confirmed that Mary Ellen was anemic. Leaving Anna with the other women, Carley and Rebecca left to go pick up Ivan and head to the hospital.

Carley's stomach rolled the minute she walked through the double doors of the hospital. The smell . . . She held her breath as long as she could. When she was finally forced to inhale, she choked and nearly vomited.

"You all right?" Rebecca asked.

Carley nodded but kept her hand over her mouth. Only a few more steps and she'd be in the elevator—a brief reprieve from the repugnant odor and the painful memories resurfacing.

The bell dinged for David's floor and the elevator doors began to open. She sucked in a breath, but it was pointless. She couldn't hold her breath the entire time she was there. Nor could she resist the urge to peer into patients' rooms as she, Rebecca, and Ivan headed down the hallway to David's room. Sick people. She wondered how many of them would die in those very beds.

She pushed the morbid thought out of her head as they arrived at David's room.

Carley noticed right away that David looked much worse this morning. His skin was paler and his eyes droopy, as if he was heavily sedated. Lillian and Samuel were sitting in chairs on each side of his bed, both of them slumped over with exhaustion. Lillian's mother was also sitting in a chair nearby.

Rebecca and Ivan both greeted Lillian and Samuel with hugs. Rebecca kissed David on the forehead. Carley was hoping David didn't notice the dread on both Rebecca's and Ivan's faces.

"How's Anna?" Lillian asked Carley.

"Little Anna is fine. She's with Mary Ellen and a bunch of other ladies from the community who showed up early this morning. They have meals lined up, each one taking a turn cooking for you. One of the women will be helping with washing the clothes, mending, and ironing. The men and boys are going to take care of the fields and milk the cows. We even have an on-call babysitter for Anna. It's just amazing." Carley shook her head, wondering how differently things might have been handled in her world.

"It's our way," Sarah Jane answered when Lillian appeared too choked up to respond. Even Samuel looked down, fighting his own emotions. "The community pulls together at a time like this."

Carley stood at the foot of David's bed and looked at Lillian. "I want you to utilize me the best way possible. I'll help whenever and however you need me. I'll stay at the farm and work. I'll stay here with you. I can run errands. You tell me what you want me to do."

She drew in a breath, hoping Lillian would choose to make use of her somewhere other than in the hospital.

"Lillian," Sarah Jane interjected, "since Rebecca and Ivan are here, why don't you go stretch your legs. Go take a walk with Carley."

Carley knew what Lillian's mother was trying to do. Lillian looked like she was about to fall apart, and that wouldn't be a good thing for David to see.

Lillian nodded, and she and Carley moved toward the door.

Once they were out of David's room, Lillian doubled over at the waist and clutched Carley's arm for support. Carley walked her to a bench down the hall.

"I know he's not my son, Lillian. But he feels like my son." Lillian folded her hands tightly against her chest.

"Lillian, he *is* your son." Carley wrapped her arms around her friend. "You are his mother. You are reacting exactly the way any mother would. I know in my heart that everything is going to be fine."

"David looks so much worse this morning," Lillian cried. "If anything happens, Carley, I don't know what I'll do. And Samuel . . ."

"I know you're worried about Samuel too. I think we need to get you a cup of coffee and something to eat. You've got to keep your strength up."

"I can't eat," Lillian responded, shaking her head.

"Not even a pastry from the bakery down the street?" Carley heard Noah ask as he approached with a big white box. "No one makes a better pastry than Mary King." He handed Lillian the box, which she accepted.

"Thank you, Noah. Maybe I'll have one later." She dabbed at her eyes.

Carley suspected Noah hadn't left the hospital or slept either; he'd added another day's stubble to his chin, and the shadows had darkened under his eyes. He was dressed in the same blue jeans and white T-shirt as yesterday, and Carley knew Noah was here to be with his family and not on the clock.

"Are Rebecca and Ivan here?" Noah asked Carley.

"Yes, they're in David's room."

"I'll have one of the nurses take them to the lab to have blood drawn. I don't want to upset Samuel any further by going in there."

Lillian looked relieved, but she didn't say anything.

"How long until we know if Rebecca or Ivan is a match?" Carley asked Noah.

"We'll know right away whether or not they have a compatible blood type."

13

CARLEY FINISHED HER COFFEE OUTSIDE IN THE HOSPITAL courtyard then ventured back up to David's room. Getting out of the building for a few minutes had helped, but the red Chevy continued to lurk nearby, along with the expression on her mother's face when she'd looked at Carley for the last time.

Carley was anxious to hear if Rebecca's or Ivan's kidney was a match for David, so she tried to focus on her friend's needs. When she did, her own issues waned a tad, and she was able to endure the hospital smells and memories.

She returned to find Ivan, Rebecca, and Sarah Jane sitting in chairs and glued to the television, along with an older Amish man she'd never met. David wasn't in his bed, and Lillian and Samuel were gone.

"Where are David, Lillian, and Samuel?" she asked as Noah trailed in behind her.

"Lillian and Samuel went with David to have an echocardiogram," Rebecca said. Guilt swept across her face at being caught watching the forbidden TV. The elderly man merely commented on the woman in the toothpaste commercial.

"She's a mite too skinny," he said. "She'd be *gut* to fatten up before they put her back on the television." He pushed his straw hat up slightly and took in Carley. "You must be Carley, no?"

"Yes, sir." Carley extended her hand to him and he latched on, glancing at Noah. "And I reckon you're the wayward *bruder*?"

"Pop, stop it," Sarah Jane reprimanded. "Carley and Noah, this is my father, Jonas. Lillian's grandpa."

"Pleased to meet you, sir," Noah said. He offered his hand to Jonas.

Without hesitation, the man firmly took hold. "You don't look like such a *baremlich* man to me." He arched his brows as if waiting for confirmation from Noah.

"Depends on who you ask," Noah said as he shrugged, then glanced at his brother and sister. Ivan wouldn't look his way, and Rebecca fiddled with the string on her black apron.

"Well, I don't reckon I'd ask those two, then," Jonas said. He cut his eyes in Ivan and Rebecca's direction.

"Pop!" Lillian's mother snapped. "Stop it."

Jonas sat up a little straighter. "I think all you people need to lighten up a bit."

Sarah Jane scolded her father with her eyes. Carley stifled a smile. What a free-spirited character this man was, so unlike the Amish men she'd met so far.

"That includes you, Sarah Jane Miller," Jonas added. He lifted his chin toward his daughter, who rolled her eyes and shook her head.

"Rebecca and Ivan, did you find out your blood type?" Noah asked.

Rebecca turned toward Ivan as if seeking permission to speak to Noah.

Ivan folded his arms across his chest and said, "Rebecca and me are neither one a *gut* match to give a kidney to David."

"Oh no," Carley sighed.

Before anyone could comment, the door to David's room swung open and two doctors entered, one of whom was Dr. Bolton. He introduced the other as Dr. Lukeman.

Noah seemed to tense up when he saw Samuel and Lillian walk in behind the two doctors.

"Where's David?" Carley asked. She could feel the uneasiness in the room.

"The lab technician took him for another test," Lillian answered wearily.

"I thought this would be a good time for us all to talk," Dr. Bolton said to the group. He motioned for Lillian and Samuel to take a seat next to each other on the edge of David's bed. Noah kept his position, leaning against the far wall.

"As some of you might have already heard, neither Ivan nor Rebecca's blood type is the same as David's, which eliminates them as potential donors," Dr. Bolton said, focusing on Lillian and Samuel. "Unless there is someone else in the family who could potentially have David's blood type, I'm afraid we'll have to put David on a waiting list."

"No," Lillian said, turning to Samuel. "Samuel, please . . ."

Samuel held his chin high when he addressed Dr. Bolton. "How long before he would have a kidney?"

Carley glanced at Noah. His arms were folded across his chest and he was biting his lower lip.

"There's no way to know, Samuel," Dr. Lukeman chimed in. "It could be a week. It could be six months or even a year."

"Or I can give David a kidney now and save his life, Samuel," Noah burst out, throwing up his hands in frustration.

To Carley's surprise, Samuel didn't say anything.

"I understand Noah has the same blood type as David," Dr. Lukeman continued as he focused solely on Samuel. "Would you like for him to be screened as a possible donor?"

"Please, Samuel," Lillian whispered.

The silence was deafening.

It was Lillian's grandfather who finally spoke up. "Samuel, you are a *gut* man," he said. "You will make the right choice."

When Samuel locked eyes with Noah, it felt like the world stopped spinning.

They all waited.

Finally, Samuel nodded. "*Ya.* We will see if Noah is a match."

His tone was a mixture of gratitude and regret.

"We'll arrange for Noah to be tested," Dr. Bolton said, relief washing over his face. He turned to Noah. "Perhaps you should go home and get some sleep first. You've been up all night."

Noah shook his head. "No, I'd rather know now if my kidney is a match. It will put everyone's mind at ease."

Noah followed the two doctors out of the room.

Lillian threw her arms around Samuel and whispered something in his ear. Then she glanced around the room. "We need to pray that Noah will be a *gut* match for David," she said. "We need to pray for both David and Noah."

Carley bowed her head, along with everyone else.

It was two days before Dr. Bolton had Noah's various test results. Having a compatible blood type had only been the first step toward determining if Noah's kidney would be a good match. They'd been told that any number of things could prevent him from giving David a kidney—high blood pressure, heart problems, or health concerns Noah might not even be aware of. It had been a tense forty-eight hours, and Carley knew they were all on edge.

No sooner had Dr. Bolton gathered the family in the waiting room than he was paged for an emergency and forced to leave.

More waiting. The tension in the room heightened.

With the exception of Noah, who was on the other side of the room, the men—Samuel, Ivan, and Jonas—stood eyeing a large fish tank, busying themselves with comments about the colorful inhabitants.

"'Tis a fast little fellow," Jonas said. He pushed back his straw hat and leaned down to have a better look.

While the men might have been trying to mask their nervousness, the women were not. Lillian, Sarah Jane, Esther, Mary Ellen, and Rebecca were huddled together next to Carley. Lillian had a firm hold on her mother's hand.

Carley had yet to see Esther acknowledge Noah.

An elderly couple occupied another section of the waiting room. The woman was crying softly. Carley wished she'd stop. She felt bad about having the thought, but each sniffle from the woman seemed to grow louder in Carley's head.

Hospital stench overwhelmed her senses. She tried not to breathe.

The woman's cries grew louder and drew attention from Carley's gang.

"I feel so sorry for that woman," Lillian whispered. "Let's pray silently for her."

Carley bowed her head with the other women, but she couldn't seem to focus on anything but her own quickening pulse.

Cool ocean breeze, calming waves . . .

Her usual methods weren't working. She took a deep breath, but that only filled her senses with antiseptic and she almost choked. And meanwhile, the woman cried harder.

Slam! The red Chevy made impact. She grabbed her side.

"Excuse me," she whispered to Lillian. She stood up and headed toward the door.

"Carley?"

She heard Noah call after her, but the minute she rounded the corner she ran, weaving between doctors, nurses, wheelchairs, and gurneys. She kept running until she reached the elevators, pushed her way into one that was going down, and held her breath. She bolted from the elevator, flew through the exit door, and gulped the crisp, clean outdoor air—a welcome relief from the misleading sterile environment of the hospital.

She'd been fighting off this moment for days, wanting to be strong for Lillian. But she finally broke.

She made her way across the ER drop-off lane and sat down on the curb. When she looked up, Noah was walking briskly toward her.

"I'm fine," she said when he sat down beside her on the curb. "I just needed . . . I needed out of there."

"Did something happen? Are you sick?" The tender way Noah put his hand on her arm soothed her. Concerned eyes met hers. "Carley?"

"You need to get back, Noah. You're going to miss hearing the test results. I'm fine. Really."

"No, I'm not leaving you." He paused and removed his hand. "Besides, I already know the test results."

"You can donate a kidney to David?" The smile on his face gave it away.

"Yes."

"Thank God for that!" Carley's shaking hands were beginning to still.

"Thank God, indeed." Noah smiled again.

"Why didn't you tell your family? Why are you making them wait?"

"I thought it would be best coming from Dr. Bolton."

Samuel hadn't a notion why Carley carted herself away so fast, nor why his brother felt the need to chase after her when they were waiting on such important news. But as he watched the two of them return, he started to get an idea. Hard to miss the way Noah looked at the *Englisch* woman. Trouble was brewing.

He tossed the thought aside even though thinking about something else had been a short distraction from the worries in his heart. The thought of anything happening to David paralyzed him beyond understanding. He'd prayed hard that his brother would be able to save his son's life, despite all that had happened. And that thought he didn't toss aside. *Save my son's life, Noah.*

All eyes were on Dr. Bolton when he reentered the room.

"I'm sorry about that," Dr. Bolton began. "I know you're all anxious, so let me just go ahead and tell you: Noah is a good match for the transplant."

Samuel didn't hear or see the responses of those around him.

Not even that of his wife, whose arms had wrapped around his waist. He only saw one person. One man. His brother. The man who would save his son's life. He wanted to run to Noah, to embrace him. Instead, he stood proudly, holding his position. He'd been hurt for so long, he didn't know how to move past it.

Dr. Bolton advised them all that David would be moved by ambulance to the Children's Hospital in Philadelphia later in the week since Lancaster General was not set up to perform a kidney transplant. According to Noah, Dr. Bolton had to call in some favors to get David's transplant scheduled so quickly.

For the next few days, Carley continued to go back and forth to the hospital as needed, bringing Samuel and Lillian more clothes since neither would leave. Some days she would bring Anna for a while, since she could tell that being away from the baby was taking a toll on Lillian. She tried to get in and out as quickly as possible, but she could tell Lillian needed the company, so she forced herself to stay at the hospital longer than she wanted to.

Carley and the women in the community kept the farm running. She'd never been so busy in her life. It was exhausting, and some days she knew she was a tad cranky. But one miraculous thing was happening—no more flashbacks about the accident. Taking care of someone else was accelerating her own healing process.

It was late afternoon on the day before David's surgery when, while walking down the hall in the hospital, Carley caught a glimpse of a little girl who looked familiar. She peered through the glass windows surrounding the children's play area and watched the girl balancing some blocks atop a small table. It was Jenna, the little girl who'd thrown herself into Noah's lap at the restaurant the other evening. She recognized Carley and waved.

Carley glanced around but didn't see Noah or Jenna's sister. She decided she'd better veer over to the playroom and make sure the child was all right.

"Hi, Carley," Jenna said when Carley entered the room. "Remember me?"

"Of course I do. Hi, Jenna. Are you okay? Where's your sister and Noah?"

"Dr. Noah is in that office." She pointed to a door across the hall.

No sooner had Jenna said this than Noah came out of the office dressed in doctor's garb. He made his way over to them.

"Well, hello there," he said to Carley. "Jenna, you remember Carley, right?"

Jenna nodded her head, preoccupied with the fortress she was building.

"Working today, huh?" Carley scanned him from head to toe.

"Yeah, I decided to get a day in before the surgery. Tomorrow's the big day." He forced a smile.

For the first time, Noah seemed nervous.

Noah bent down to Jenna's level. "That's a very cool house you're building."

Jenna smiled as Noah stood back up and motioned for Carley to follow him out the door of the playroom. "You can play a few more minutes, Jenna," Noah said. "I'm going to talk to Carley."

As Jenna nodded again, they made their way out the door and

into the hallway. Once out of earshot, Noah said, "Carley, I have a huge favor to ask of you."

"What?" She couldn't imagine.

"Dana and Jenna came up here to eat an early dinner with me. I was going to run them home, but the ER is packed. Any chance you could drive them home? It's not far, about twelve miles from here."

"Sure," Carley said. She glanced toward Jenna then back at Noah. She was wondering exactly what his relationship was with Jenna and her sister.

As if reading her mind, Noah added, "Dana is raising Jenna by herself—a big responsibility for a nineteen-year-old. Their father was a good friend of mine who was killed in a car accident about a year ago. And they lost their mother just a few months ago to breast cancer."

Carley's hand landed over her mouth. She felt a sudden connection with this nineteen-year-old girl she didn't know. "That's horrible."

"Yeah, they've had a hard time."

"Where is Dana?" She glanced around the hallway.

"She's in the restroom. Ah, there she is now." Noah pointed to his left. He waited until Dana reached them. "Dana, this is Carley. She's going to drive you and Jenna home. The ER is packed."

"We can wait until you're done," Dana said to Noah. She didn't acknowledge the introduction.

"No. It could be hours, and Carley said she didn't mind." Noah opened the playroom door. "Jenna, you ready?"

Carley smiled at Dana while Noah went to get Jenna. "I was leaving anyway, so it's no trouble."

During the drive, Jenna sat in the backseat and rambled on about her school, her classmates, and how much she liked to color. She seemed like a very happy child despite all she had been through.

Dana stared out the window.

"I'm sorry to hear about your parents," Carley said when the silence grew uncomfortable.

Dana's expression was void of emotion as she glanced briefly in Carley's direction. "Thank you." She returned her gaze back to the window.

More silence.

"So how did you meet Noah?" Carley asked after a while.

"We met him in Minnesota. My dad met him on the golf course. He was already a big-time doctor. It didn't seem to make any difference to Noah that he was a doctor and lived in a big house, and we didn't. Daddy used to invite Noah to our house for dinner all the time, since Noah didn't have any family in Minnesota. When Noah moved here to be near his own family, he moved me and Jenna here too. He bought us a nice little house." She combed her hands through her hair, pulling the long tresses above her head and holding them in a ponytail with her hands. "It's too bad about his family." She sat up a little taller. "But I guess me and Jenna are his family now." For the first time since Carley met Dana, she smiled.

"It looks like you're doing a great job raising Jenna," Carley said. "That's bound to be hard for someone your age."

Carley didn't mean anything by it, but Dana's eyes narrowed. "My age? I doubt I'm much younger than you are."

In Carley's mind, nine years was quite a bit younger. "I'm twenty-eight."

"And I'm five," Jenna said from the backseat.

Carley twisted around and smiled. "I know. You're a big girl!"

It grew quiet again.

"My mother died recently too. In a car accident," Carley said. Maybe she could get on some common ground with Dana. "My father died years before that. It's hard not to have parents."

Dana kept staring out the window.

Carley kept her eyes forward.

"Noah told me you're a friend of Lillian's." Dana twisted beneath her seat belt to face Carley. "When I first saw you with Noah at the café, I thought maybe you *liked* him."

"I do like him."

"You know what I mean. I thought you guys were on a date or something, but he told me that wasn't the case, that you're just a friend of Lillian's who's helping him get things straight with Samuel."

Carley nodded.

"That's it," Dana said, pointing to a small brown house on the left.

Carley pulled into the narrow driveway. The car was barely stopped when Dana swung the passenger door open and stepped out. She opened the back door and helped Jenna get out of her seat belt.

"Bye, Carley." Jenna waved cheerfully.

What a lovely child, Carley thought as she returned the wave. Her sister, on the other hand, was another story.

As Dana was about to slam the car door, she hesitated and stared at Carley. She didn't say anything at first.

Carley waited.

"I'm sorry about your parents," Dana said. "It *is* hard not having parents."

"Thank you, Dana." Carley smiled warmly.

Jenna was skipping up the sidewalk toward the front door.

Dana evidently had more on her mind. With one hand holding the car door open, she tapped the roof of Carley's car with the other. "Noah's going through some really intense stuff."

"Yes, he is."

"And I just know he doesn't need any more complications in his life." She paused and bit her bottom lip before she went on. "Anyway, I just don't want to see him get hurt. His girlfriend will be back in town soon. She's out of the country. I feel better knowing you guys are just friends. Thanks again for the ride."

And she closed the car door.

Girlfriend?

14

SADIE WAS SITTING ON THE FRONT PORCH HOLDING ANNA when Carley pulled into the driveway.

She had missed little Anna. She couldn't imagine how hard it must be for Lillian to be away from the baby. It would be an early start tomorrow morning, but she would make sure to get there early enough for Lillian to spend a little time with Anna before the surgery.

"Sorry I'm so late getting home," Carley said to Sadie as she walked up the porch steps.

"It's no problem. I love to spend time with the *boppli.*"

Carley scooped Anna into her arms and took a seat in the rocker next to Sadie. "Well, tomorrow is the surgery."

"*Ya.*" Sadie shook her head. "This is all happenin' so fast."

"And it's the strangest situation. I mean, with Noah being the donor and everything."

Sadie just nodded. Carley had hoped a conversation would ensue. She was curious about Sadie's thoughts on the matter since she knew her to be the most outspoken of the Amish women she had met.

"Of course, I would think things might change after this," Carley pressed on. "After all, Noah will have saved David's life. Surely members of the community will be forgiving of the past."

Sadie said nothing.

Carley hesitated to continue, but if Sadie, of all people, didn't have it in her heart to lighten up on the shunning, she didn't see much hope that the rest of the community would.

"I wouldn't think Noah's family and the people in the district would continue shunning him after he gives a vital organ to save David's life." Carley turned toward Sadie.

Sadie shrugged before she stood up. "I guess I'll be headin' home, Carley. Everything's in *gut* order in the *haus.* Do you need me to be here in the early hours to watch Anna tomorrow?"

"No. I'm going to take her with me so the family can spend some time with her before David goes into surgery. I'm sure there will be lots of people there to help with Anna."

"To be sure," Sadie agreed. She headed down the steps.

Carley rose from the rocker and walked toward the kitchen door before saying, "I'm sure someone will get word to you tomorrow." She pulled the screen door open.

"Carley?"

She turned around to see Sadie facing her at the bottom of the porch steps. "Yes?"

Sadie's eyes widened with optimism. "Maybe Noah will seek forgiveness and choose to be rebaptized in our faith. Bishop Ebersol and the elders surely would think 'bout letting him renounce his ways and come back, 'specially after this."

Carley could hear the hope in Sadie's voice, an emotion other members of the community were bound to be experiencing about Noah.

"He's not sorry for becoming a doctor, Sadie, but he is sorry for writing the book. I'm assuming you know about the book?"

"*Ya.* But he can't be accepted unless he gives up all worldly ways and is rebaptized. That would include his doctoring."

"He saves lives!" Carley realized immediately her tone was entirely too sharp. She lowered her voice. "It's just that . . . that's who Noah is. He's a doctor. It's his calling from God. How can anyone deny him that? It's terribly unfair, Sadie. He should be forgiven for writing the book, and he should be accepted by his family for who he is. He's saving David's life. If exceptions can't be made for that, then . . ." She sighed, deflated. "It's just wrong."

Sadie walked toward Carley. "You really care for him, no?"

Carley turned toward the outstretched fields and watched the sun descending on the horizon. She hadn't realized how much she cared for Noah until Dana clued her in that he was off-limits. Carley was surprised at how jealous she felt. She knew she'd have to explore her feelings more once she had time to get used to this new information.

Including her frustration at him for not mentioning his girl-friend. *That was a pretty crummy thing to do, Noah. And why the flowers?*

Still, this new knowledge didn't change who Noah was. "I think what he's doing for David is amazing. And I find it incredible that David will be able to walk among you with one of Noah's kidneys inside him . . . while Noah continues to be shunned."

"God will guide our paths, Carley. Sometimes we can't under-stand His will. I know the entire community is praying—for David and for Noah."

"Well, I'm going to pray that the community accepts Noah

back into their lives after this. His clinic is so important to him. It's a way to give back to the community by providing low-cost healthcare in a quiet environment, close enough for the Amish to drive there in horse and buggy. And, Sadie, he's a good man."

Sadie watched Carley's face, most likely wondering what she was thinking. "*Ach*, I hope to find a *gut* man someday," she said.

"Me too," Carley responded. She didn't make much effort to mask her disappointment.

Sadie didn't seem to notice. Her eyes twinkled and her voice took on a hint of mischief. "I've been writing letters to an Amish man in Texas."

"Really?" Carley tried to be interested. But she couldn't stop thinking about the way Noah had looked at her, on more than one occasion—looks she clearly misread.

"*Ya*. He's coming here to meet me soon, all the way from Texas!"

Carley smiled. "That's great. When?" *Noah, you're a jerk.*

Sadie smoothed the sides of her brown dress and looked at the ground. "I'm not sure." She kicked at a blade of grass with her black shoe. "He's been sayin' he's coming for a long time."

"Texas is a long way."

"He'll be comin' on the bus." She looked up at Carley and smiled. "Whenever he does come."

Maybe he never will.

Men certainly have a way of toying with women's minds.

———

Noah fumbled through bank documents, credit card statements, unpaid bills, and the assortment of other papers stacked up on his desk and wondered how anyone would ever find anything in the event of his death. Even as a single man, he should have been more organized with his affairs. At his age, he rarely thought about death. On this night, he couldn't help but ponder the what-ifs of the situation. He eyed the mess before him and decided that organization at the eleventh hour wasn't going to happen. He sighed and walked away from it all.

Since waking up this morning, he hadn't been able to get last night's dream out of his mind. They say you never die in your own dreams, but he was living proof that was not the case. He was certain that his apprehension about being cut open had been at the root of the dream, but he still couldn't shake the vision of Carley standing over his hospital bed, crying. Was she begging him for something? He couldn't remember.

Noah did remember being cold in the dream and unable to move or speak. He could recall overhead lights that shone brightly above him. There was no fanfare, no tunnel, no angels, no God. His kidney lived on in his nephew, but he had died—and Carley was by his bedside, crying softly, pleading with him . . .

Pleading with him to do what?

He shook his head, walked to the kitchen, and poured himself a glass of water. The transplant had been scheduled so quickly. He wished he had more time. There was no reason to think he wouldn't survive the surgery and lead a perfectly normal life. Still, he couldn't seem to shake the vision of Carley's tear-streaked face bending over him.

Carley.

A cheerier picture came to mind—him sharing something more than just friendship with her.

Time seemed to be pressing down on him all of a sudden.

The odds were in his favor that everything would go well tomorrow. And as a doctor who had been involved in his share of surgeries, he had talked to enough patients to know that his own anxiety about going under the knife was to be expected. It was only normal to worry what sort of legacy he might be leaving behind if the unthinkable happened.

After two hours of wailing, Anna was finally asleep in her playpen. Poor baby could sense all the tension around her, and Carley knew she was a weak substitute for Lillian. She had found herself crying along with Anna earlier—for reasons she wasn't sure of. Frustration. Exhaustion. Noah.

She was curled up on the couch, two lanterns lit, reading the Bible. Something else she was doing for reasons she wasn't sure of, but right now it was providing her with much-needed comfort. It had been a long time since she'd read the Good Book.

"'And God blessed Noah and his sons, and said unto them, Be fruitful, and multiply, and replenish the earth.'"

The Scripture reading brought a gush of emotion. "There'll be no multiplying for me," she whispered. "And Noah can go on to replenish the earth with his *girlfriend*." She waved her hand in the air.

Instantly she regretted her flippant attitude.

She closed the book, closed her eyes, and tried to *open* her heart. "Please, God . . ."

What she wanted to say to God and what she was thinking were not coming together as one. Feelings laced with bitterness overshadowed feelings of love and peace, emotions she'd had a glimpse of lately. She wanted more of them. She needed more of them. And she suspected God was the answer. But in the end, she felt unworthy to address Him about anything related to her personally.

Anna's tiny body shifted in the playpen. Carley darted her gaze in that direction, fearful she might wake up. She knew Anna's entire schedule had been disrupted, but having to go through another crying spell would put Carley under. That she was sure of. She was exhausted. With Lillian and Samuel at the hospital, she'd been guilty on more than one occasion of sleeping later than the customary four thirty. She wasn't sure she'd ever get used to the demands on their day.

The chirp of her cell phone sent her jumping off the couch. She didn't dare take the time to see who it was for fear another ring would wake up Anna. "Hello," she whispered.

"Did I wake you?"

She had mixed feelings about hearing Noah's voice.

"No, I wasn't sleeping." Carley tiptoed through the den to the kitchen and quietly slipped onto the front porch.

Noah covered routine niceties for a couple of minutes, but she knew what was on his mind. And despite what Dana had shared with her, she felt the need to reach out to him.

"Are you nervous about tomorrow?" she asked.

"No, not really."

You sound nervous, Carley thought.

"I'm nervous for David. He's just a kid," he added. "They moved David to the hospital in Philadelphia this evening. It's too bad Lancaster General isn't set up to do the transplant. The move was a tedious process, and I could tell David was uptight and uncomfortable."

"What time do you have to be at the hospital?"

"Six o'clock tomorrow morning. A mere nine hours away."

"I'll be there. I'm going to bring Anna with me. I think Lillian, Samuel, and David will be glad to see her before the surgery."

"Oh, I meant to thank you for taking Dana and Jenna home." Before she could say anything, he went on. "And I have another favor to ask you."

"What's that?" She was hoping it didn't involve Dana. She didn't need to hear any more about Noah's *girlfriend*.

"I know you have your hands full, and I hate to even ask this, but a guy from Finley's Glass Company is supposed to be at the clinic tomorrow to replace the glass in the front. Obviously, I'm going to be in the hospital. Would you be able to go over there and let him in? The timing of all this is really bad—not that there's ever a good time for something like this. I had all kinds of people lined up to deliver equipment in the next couple of weeks too. I can cancel all that and reschedule, but . . ."

"Why? You don't have to cancel, Noah. I can go let them in or whatever you need me to do. It's on my way to the hospital. Just tell me what to do."

Seemed like a job the *girlfriend* should handle. But of course, she was out of the country.

And at a time like this.

But the clinic was Noah's passion, and she hated to see things fall apart while he was doing something so amazing for David.

"Are you sure, Carley? I mean, it's important for me to keep things rolling, but I know you'll be taking care of Lillian's family, especially Anna. She's really lucky you're here right now."

"Well, I'm glad to be able to help, though it's great the way the entire community has pitched in."

"I'd ask Dana to do it, and I know she would, but she has a new job and her hours vary from day to day. Plus she's taking a couple of classes at the community college."

"No, no. I'll do it. I don't mind. I know it's important to you."

"I'll get you a key to the place in the morning."

Carley sensed the conversation was coming to a close, and she strained to come up with a way to question Noah about his love life. The words weren't materializing.

"Hey," he said hesitantly. "I had a dream about you last night."

"Really?" *Interesting.* "What about?"

"Oh, I don't know. I don't really remember." He paused, sighed. "I mean, I do remember, but I don't. It was about you and me and . . . Oh, never mind. I guess I don't really remember."

Carley had a strange feeling he *did* remember, but he quickly ended the conversation by wishing her a good night's sleep.

The Children's Hospital of Philadelphia was quiet at five thirty in the morning. Lillian and Samuel were sitting in chairs on each side of David, watching him sleep, when Carley walked in. She suspected neither of them had gotten much sleep.

"There's my baby girl," Lillian whispered. She took Anna from Carley and coddled her.

Carley noticed David's breathing was labored, and his complexion paler than the day before. The fear in Samuel's eyes was immeasurable.

"Thank you for coming so early and bringing Anna." Lillian continued to smother Anna with kisses. Facing the baby toward Samuel, she added, "There's your *daed*."

Samuel smiled at his little one but quickly turned his attention back toward David after nodding a thank-you in Carley's direction.

"Good morning." Dr. Lukeman entered the room with Dr. Bolton alongside him. Since David was their patient at Lancaster General, they were joining the team here for the surgery. "I see our boy is still sleeping. We just came by to let you know everything is moving along according to schedule. Someone will come to get David about seven this morning and take him to the operating room. One of you will be able to go into the operating room with him."

"Samuel is going to go with David," Lillian said, glancing at her husband, who nodded.

Dr. Lukeman turned toward Carley. "One person can go in with Noah."

"Oh, I'm not a family member." Carley couldn't think of anything more horrific than walking into an operating room. She was still struggling to adjust to these back-and-forth visits.

"Well, perhaps another family member might be interested in accompanying Noah," Dr. Lukeman said. "Any questions?"

"How long is the surgery?" Carley asked even though his question had been directed to Lillian and Samuel.

"Usually three to four hours. David and Noah will be in adjoining rooms with a different team of staff members overseeing each operation. First they'll be given a general anesthetic. Once Noah's kidney has been successfully removed, I will make a small incision in David's lower abdomen. I'll attach the artery and vein from the new kidney to David's artery and vein. Once the ureter from the new kidney is connected to David's bladder, the new kidney should start making urine as soon as the blood starts flowing through it. But as I explained to Samuel and Lillian, it can take up to a few weeks before it starts working properly. Noah should only need to stay in the hospital about a week and then finish his recovery at home. David will be here about two weeks," Dr. Bolton added. "Generally, a transplant recipient starts to feel better almost immediately, once the anesthesia wears off. David will need to take medication here at the hospital and also when he goes home, to help prevent rejection of the kidney. But we'll talk about that after the surgery."

"I believe we've covered all the risks with you," Dr. Lukeman said. "But now's the time to address any other concerns or questions you may have. Most of the risks are on the recipient's end. We don't expect any issues as far as Noah is concerned." Dr. Lukeman paused. "Which brings me to another point. Noah would like to visit with David before the surgery."

Carley and Lillian both looked at Samuel.

It looked as though he might deny the request, but then he glanced at his wife. Her eyes pleaded with him, and finally, Samuel nodded.

"Noah has been admitted. He's right down the hall. Can I bring him in?" Dr. Bolton asked.

"Yes, we'll go get some coffee," Lillian said as she motioned for Samuel and Carley to follow her out the door.

Carley edged toward the door.

Samuel didn't budge. "I don't need any *kaffi*. I will stay."

"Samuel," Lillian urged. "Maybe just give Noah a minute alone with David, no?"

Sighing, Samuel glanced at Dr. Bolton, who seemed to agree with Lillian.

"Pop, please let me talk to Noah alone."

They all turned their attention to David, who spoke before he even opened his eyes. As they watched him gain focus, his gaze centered on Samuel. "Please, Pop."

Samuel slowly stood up, reaching down to grasp his son's hand. "All right, boy," he said softly. "I will be back soon."

The six of them eased out of the room, leaving David alone. Once in the corridor, Carley could see Noah down the hallway, waiting to see whether or not he'd be able to see David.

Dr. Lukeman excused himself and walked down the opposite hall.

"I'll go get Noah," Dr. Bolton said. "If you'd like to go have some coffee in the cafeteria, I'll come find you after their visit."

Samuel nodded but glanced back through the open door of his son's room.

"Come on, Samuel," Lillian coaxed.

"I'll be there in a minute," Carley said sheepishly to Lillian and Samuel.

Lillian and Samuel headed down the hallway. Carley walked alongside Dr. Bolton the short distance down the corridor to where Noah was standing.

Dr. Noah Stoltzfus. A man who took care of everyone around him—his patients, Dana, Jenna, and now David. Noah wanted to make right the wrongs he'd done and take care of his family and the community too. As Carley eyed him, standing tall and confident, she wondered, *Who takes care of you, Noah?*

The answer made her sad. That person should be here.

He smiled warmly at her when she and Dr. Bolton came within a few yards of him. But Noah wasn't fooling her. He was nervous.

"Samuel agreed to let you speak with David," Dr. Bolton said when they reached Noah. "I'll leave you two for now. See you in a while, Noah." He tipped his head in Carley's direction and was gone.

Noah deliberately stood still, waiting for Dr. Bolton to move out of sight. Then he gazed into her eyes in a way that made her uncomfortable.

"What?" she asked.

"Carley," he said softly. He tilted his head to one side and smiled.

"What?" she asked again.

Then, with no warning, Noah wrapped his arms around her, cupping the nape of her neck with one hand. She could feel the rapid beat of his heart against her ear. The moment was nice. It was tender. It was intimate, his body next to hers. It was . . .

It was *wrong!*

She pushed him away and stepped back. "You shouldn't hug me like that."

"What?" His face soured with a mixture of anger and hurt. "It was just a hug. I thought we were friends."

"We are friends, but hugs like that should be reserved for *special* friends."

"Oh, and we're not special friends?" Noah placed his hands on his hips and leaned toward her.

"Of course we're special friends." She ran her hands through her hair and blew out a hard breath. "I meant it should be reserved for a girlfriend—or a wife."

A smile stretched across Noah's face. "Are you asking to be my girlfriend or my wife? Which is it?"

"What?" Her voice was loud enough to draw attention from a few passersby. She backed away from him. "What are you talking about?"

"What are *you* talking about?"

There couldn't have been a worse time to talk about this. "You can reserve those types of hugs for your girlfriend." She knew she sounded irritated.

"Back to the same question, I guess." Noah was still grinning. "Are you asking to be my girlfriend?"

She shook her head. "I understand the position is filled." He was disgustingly handsome, challenging her with his playful remarks.

"Filled?" He wasn't smiling anymore, and confusion swept across his face. "By who?"

Carley raised her shoulders, dropped them, and sighed. "Dana told me you had a girlfriend, Noah. That's all. Hugs like that should probably be reserved for her, and I think—"

"What?" His brows shot upward. "Dana told you what?"

"You heard me. She told me you had a girlfriend but that she's out of the country right now. And, Noah, I'm sorry she's not here to be with you during all this, but—"

Noah erupted in laughter. He leaned down with his hands on his knees and shook his head, trying to catch his breath. "Carley, I don't have a girlfriend." He looked up at her. "Far from it."

"Well, then why would Dana say that?" Carley almost instantly knew the answer.

"I don't know." Noah closed in on her, his face inches from hers. "But it pleases me to know how much that bothered you."

She stepped back. "I never said it *bothered* me."

Noah chuckled. "You didn't have to." He wrapped his arms around her, again cupping the back of her neck, holding her close. And as relief rushed over her, she didn't feel the need to push him away. "You are my special friend," he said.

She felt his lips gently brush her cheek.

"You'd better go talk to David while you have the opportunity," she said softly. Noah continued to hold her. And now that the misunderstanding was behind them, she knew what that initial hug had been about. *He* needed to be held. This wasn't about her.

She returned the hug full force, staying in his arms until *he* was ready to move forward, to go talk to David, to ready himself for surgery.

To save a life.

───

Noah eased into David's room. His nephew. Such a handsome young man. His face was pale, his eyes droopy, but still, he was a good-looking kid. The resemblance to Samuel at that age was unmistakable.

"Hey, David. How are you holding up?" Noah took a seat in the chair by the bed.

David shrugged. "Pop and Lillian look so scared. They're makin' me scared."

"They're parents. They're going to worry. But, David, I know everything is going to be just fine. Do you have any questions?"

"*Ya.* What's it going to feel like when I go to sleep?"

"First the doctors will give us something to make us kind of groggy. Then once they administer the drug to make us go to sleep, it will happen fairly quickly." He paused. "That's what I've heard, anyway."

David's eyes widened. "You've never been put to sleep before?"

"Nope. This is a first for me too."

"Hmm." David hesitated then asked, "Are you *naerfich*?"

"Yes, I'm nervous."

Admitting his own fear seemed to give David comfort. And it felt good to admit it out loud.

"*Ya*, me too." David's expression grew grim. "It's going to hurt a lot when we wake up, no?"

Noah didn't want to add to the boy's fear. But he didn't want to lie to him either. "I think we're both going to be uncomfortable when we wake up. But they will give us medications to help with that. And, David, you will most likely start feeling much better than you have been within a couple of days—better than before the surgery."

"What about you?"

"I'll be fine. I have the easy part. When they take my kidney,

I'll still have one working away. Your body will have to adjust to the new kidney. That might take a little time. But you'll be back in those fields helping your pop in no time."

"Is Carley your girlfriend?"

Boom. Right out of nowhere. "No," he answered abruptly. Carley's scent still lingered with him, a mixture of baby powder from Anna and a pleasant flowery aroma. "I mean, I'm not sure."

David grinned, causing Noah to smile. "How can you not be sure?" David asked.

Glad he was temporarily diverting David's mind from the surgery, Noah said, "I thought we were just friends, but . . . I don't know." He tilted his head to one side with the realization that he honestly *didn't* know what he and Carley were. "I just don't know," he repeated, shaking his head.

"I like her."

Noah nodded. "I like her too."

After a brief silence, David said, "*Danki, Onkel* Noah, for doing this. For giving me one of your kidneys."

Noah nodded, wishing that he knew this boy who called him *uncle*. "You're very welcome, David."

More silence. They were strangers to each other yet connected in a profound way—for life. Despite the resistance from those around them, Noah knew David felt it too.

"Are you going to return to the faith, Noah?" David asked. His eyes pleaded that it would be so.

Noah pushed his hair back, wishing he'd gotten a haircut before the surgery. "No, David. I'm not. I'm a doctor. I can't imagine doing anything else."

"I know about the book." David 's comment pierced Noah to the core. "They don't know I know. Pop and Lillian."

Noah rubbed his forehead, trying to keep the guilt at a manageable distance. "I'm not proud of the book. I wish I'd never written it."

"It's a pretty *gut* book though."

"What?" Noah was shocked. "You've read it?"

David nodded guiltily. "It's in Pop's room. Please don't tell him, *Onkle* Noah. It'd be a trip to the woodshed for sure. I was lookin' for a book to read one day, and I found it in the cedar chest in Pop's room, along with a bunch of other books." He frowned. "I'm not supposed to be goin' in Pop's room. I wasn't being *schnuppich*. I just wanted to read a new book."

Getting David in trouble was the last thing he wanted to do. "I won't tell him." He cringed at the thought of David reading the book. Samuel would be beside himself with anger.

"Did you and Pop really jump off the river bridge when you were my age?"

Noah smiled as he recalled that summer so long ago. Their own pop would have blistered their behinds repeatedly if he'd ever found out they pulled that dangerous stunt. "Yes." Noah arched his brows. "But don't you ever try it."

"No, not me. I don't much like heights."

Noah realized that the day-to-day functions of Amish life that he wrote about weren't what interested David. While Samuel felt betrayed by the personal details in the book, David had never known another way of life. He hadn't even had his *rumschpringe* yet. What interested David was Samuel at his age. Noah doubted

Samuel had ever shared any of their childhood adventures with his son. Samuel was a very private man, like most of those in the Amish community.

"And you caught thirty-seven bass in Little John's pond too?"

"We did." Noah laughed. "We weren't even supposed to be at the pond that day. Pop would've had our hides."

Recalling some of the events from the book and seeing the joy in David's eyes made Noah realize that much of what he'd written were his favorite boyhood memories. But he also knew there was no excuse for the other stories recounted in the book—events he'd recorded with bitterness. Maybe David had skimmed past those parts.

"Were you mad when you wrote some parts of the book?"

Apparently David had not skimmed any of it, and Noah wondered which parts he was referring to.

"Yes, I was bitter about being shunned and cast out from my family."

"But you knew when you were baptized that it would happen if you left, no?"

Noah nodded. He knew his anger had spilled onto the pages, often in the form of poking fun at the Amish way of life. He regretted that more than anything—more than revealing private family happenings. The Amish way of life was to be cherished. Most people would go their entire lives without a sampling of what he'd been blessed with in his youth.

"I'm not feeling so good, Noah," David said, his spirited mood slipping away as he changed the subject. "I feel real tired."

"You rest, then," Noah said, standing up. "And try not to

worry." He patted David on the arm. "Remember, I'll be nearby in an adjoining room. And your pop will be there right beside you."

Noah moved toward the door, wishing he could stay.

"*Onkel* Noah?"

Noah turned around. He was sure his expression reflected how much he liked the sound of that. "Yes?"

"I guess in a while, you'll be a part of me."

If Noah's emotions weren't frighteningly close to spilling over as it was, this kid would assure it. "Yes, I guess so," he said, smiling warmly. "Forever bonded."

David kept staring in his direction, as if he had more to say. Noah waited.

"I had a *baremlich* dream last night." David squeezed his eyes shut for a moment, as if casting the thought away.

Recalling his own dream, Noah said, "I think it's common to have scary dreams when you're facing something like this. Nothing is going to happen to you. Everything is going to be fine."

David's pale face slumped with worry. "The dream wasn't about me. It was about *you*."

15

CARLEY FOLLOWED THE NURSE INTO THE OPERATING ROOM on rubbery legs. Visions of her own surgery six months earlier swirled in her head. When she saw the operating table and the large overhead lights, she felt faint. It was cold in the room, and the smell was nightmarishly familiar. But when she looked at Noah lying on the table, the visions of her past faded.

When not one family member had offered to be with Noah in the operating room, Carley knew it was the right thing to do.

"Hello," she said nervously as she approached him.

"Carley, I know how you feel about hospitals in general. You don't have to do this." Noah reached for her hand.

"I'm fine." She squeezed his hand.

"Guess this is the big moment."

Noah was trying to keep things light, but he was not fooling her.

"Yes, it is. And it's a wonderful thing you're doing," she said tenderly "By the way, where's Dana? I'm surprised she's not here."

Noah grinned, as if recalling their conversation in the hall earlier. "I made her promise not to skip class or work today. This procedure is done all the time, and I assured her I'd be fine. She'll be here this evening when she gets off work." He smiled again. "Guess I need to have a little chat with her."

Carley started to agree when she heard David call her name from the adjoining operating room.

She gently pried her hand from Noah's. "Be right back."

She walked around Noah's gurney, entered David's room, and stood beside Samuel. "Hello, Samuel." He acknowledged her greeting with a nod. "How's our boy doing?" She carefully wound her hand through the many wires and tubes running across David's bed and clutched his hand. "I know you'll be glad to get this over with."

"*Ya.*" David motioned for Carley to lean down closer. "I'm glad you're here with Noah. He really likes you."

Carley glanced at Samuel, who didn't say anything. She looked back at David. "Yeah, he's a good guy. I'd better get back over there, but I'll see you in just a little while."

David smiled, but fear was etched across his young face. *He's too young to go through all this*, Carley thought.

She eased her way back to Noah's side, wondering if the hug they'd shared earlier was weighing as heavily on his mind as it was on hers. She reached for his hand again. She intertwined his fingers with hers and stood quietly at his side, unsure of her role.

Doctors Lukeman and Bolton were nowhere in sight, just two nurses and an anesthesiologist who indicated that he was ready to begin.

"This might make you feel a little loopy at first," the anesthesiologist told Noah as he began injecting something into Noah's IV.

"Noah." It was David, and he sounded terrified.

"David, I'm right here with you, buddy. And I'll see you in recovery," Noah responded loudly. He turned his attention back to Carley, and she saw his eyes growing glassy. He smiled. "Good night, sweetheart."

She squeezed his hand.

"You are a beautiful woman. So beautiful . . ."

"Thank you." She smiled.

"Hey." He paused, grinning like a little boy. "Wanna be my girlfriend?"

It was so silly, yet so incredibly touching. She smiled more broadly. "Maybe so."

Carley could see Samuel through the open door between the two small operating rooms. He turned around to face Carley, his eyes wide with wonder. Carley shrugged but couldn't wipe the grin from her face.

"You know," Noah said, blinking his eyes. "We might just get married someday and have a bunch of little kids." The whites of his eyes became more prevalent as he strained to keep them from rolling backward.

Samuel twisted around again. When he did, she could see David smiling, which was nice. Samuel wasn't smiling. He looked confused. Carley shrugged again in his direction.

"Yeah, lots of babies." His lips were still moving as his eyes shut.

Noah's desire to have children reminded Carley that this . . . thing between her and Noah really didn't have anywhere to go. No matter what the future brought, children wouldn't be a part of it for her.

"Will he remember this?" Carley asked the nurse standing nearby, who was grinning.

"If he doesn't, we will all remind him." She giggled.

"No, no. Don't do that," Carley begged, knowing it would embarrass him. "It's just the medication."

"It's like a truth serum," the other nurse said.

"And I'm telling the truth," Noah slurred, his eyes still closed.

Carley squeezed his hand. She leaned down and kissed him on the forehead. Then smiled. "I'll see you in recovery, Noah."

She glanced over and saw that David, too, had succumbed to his own anesthesia. Samuel held his boy's hand tightly.

Dr. Bolton walked in, scrubbed up. "Hello. Are our patients ready?"

"They are," the anesthesiologist answered.

"Guess it's time for us to go, then?" Carley asked. Noah's hand went limp in hers.

"It is. The rest of the family is in the waiting room at the far end of the hall," Dr. Bolton said as Dr. Lukeman walked through the door with another doctor Carley hadn't seen before.

Carley eased her way toward the door, glanced back at Noah, then over to David's room. She watched Samuel kiss David on his forehead and whisper something in his son's ear. When she reached the door, she turned again. Samuel had exited David's room by coming through the door connecting the operating rooms. He was standing next to Noah. His hands in his pockets, his straw hat tilted back slightly, he studied Noah as if seeing him for the first time.

"Time to go, Samuel," Dr. Bolton said softly, gesturing Samuel toward the door.

Samuel moved quickly, obviously embarrassed when he saw Carley watching him.

She walked quietly with Samuel to the waiting room where the others were. Noah's words, however drug-induced, floated around her head in a confusing mix of wonderment and fear.

He liked her.

He wanted lots of babies.

Three hours into the surgery, they were all becoming antsy. All of Samuel's family was present, along with Lillian's mother, Sarah Jane, and her grandpa, Jonas. Barbie Beiler and two other non-Amish friends were also in the waiting room, having provided rides.

"They sure been in there a long time." Jonas tipped his straw hat back and rubbed his gray beard.

"They said it would take three to four hours, Grandpa." Lillian sighed and shifted Anna in her arms. The waiting had taken the worst toll on Anna, who was squirming in her mother's arms.

Samuel paced. Everyone else sat, nervously watching the clock on the wall.

"Here, let me take the *boppli* for a while," Samuel's mother offered. Esther scooped Anna into her arms and began to pace alongside her son.

"So what's this I hear about a bedside proposal?" Lillian whispered to Carley. "Samuel told me what Noah said in the operating room."

"Oh, it was definitely the medication," Carley said. "The

doctor said it would make him loopy." She grinned. "And it certainly did."

"I see." Lillian folded her hands in her lap.

Normally Lillian would have been curious, wanting to know all the details. Clearly this was not the time for such a conversation. Plus Carley knew Lillian felt pulled between her loyalty to her husband and her friendship with Carley. For Lillian to encourage any type of friendship between Carley and Noah would go against Samuel's wishes.

Carley wasn't sure what she and Noah had. His affection in the corridor earlier left her confused about where things were headed. It was a road to nowhere, Carley knew. But somehow she was on the path and couldn't seem to make herself turn back. Not now, anyway. When Noah was well, she would put on the brakes. Why set herself up for heartache? Men who wanted families didn't stick around with women who couldn't give them one. Dalton had proven that.

Carley studied all of Noah and Samuel's family, particularly Esther. No one had said, but she wondered if Esther had visited with her son at all before the surgery. She knew his sisters, Mary Ellen and Rebecca, had at least spoken briefly with Noah, as had Ivan. But what about his mother? These people were extremely private, rarely allowing their emotions to show.

Carley recalled the look on Samuel's face when they were leaving the operating room. No matter what he had said in the past about his brother, there was no doubt in Carley's mind how Samuel felt at that very moment. But he quickly hid his emotions.

It was coming up on four hours when Mary Ellen suggested they all bow their heads in prayer again. Carley was thankful Mary Ellen had included Noah, as well as David, each time they prayed. Anything less would have been unacceptable, and Carley would have spoken up.

Even though she knew her faith wasn't nearly as strong as that of the women around her, Carley still offered her most heartfelt prayers for Noah and David. She realized that praying for others came more easily to her than praying for herself.

The prayer time was interrupted when Dr. Bolton came through the door and into the waiting room. Carley knew by the smile stretched across his face that everything was all right.

"It all looks real good, folks."

Lillian leaned her head back against the wall and closed her eyes. "Thank You, God," she whispered. Carley draped an arm around her friend.

Samuel was standing near Esther, who was still toting Anna. He extended his hand to Dr. Bolton. "*Danki*, Doctor," he said with a deep sigh. Then he turned to his wife and embraced her, his eyes gleaming with relief. Carley watched Samuel and Lillian, the way they held each other, the way they gazed into each other's eyes.

Everyone began exchanging hugs. Carley, along with the rest of the women, dabbed at their eyes. The men exchanged firm handshakes with each other.

"They are both in recovery," Dr. Bolton continued. "Samuel, if you'd like to follow me, I'll take you to David."

"What about Noah?" Carley stepped forward when she wasn't included in the invite.

"Noah's not awake yet, but I'll be back to get you when he starts to rouse."

Carley nodded. She could feel everyone's eyes on her, but no one spoke.

———

Forty-five minutes passed before Dr. Bolton reappeared, his expression more serious than it had been earlier. His creased forehead caused Carley to jump from her chair and walk toward him. Lillian followed.

"What? Is something wrong?" Lillian asked. She clutched Carley's arm. "Is David all right?"

Dr. Bolton reached over and touched Lillian's shoulder. "David is fine."

Then it's Noah, Carley realized as she drew in a breath and held it.

"Noah hasn't regained consciousness yet," Dr. Bolton stated. Carley recognized the tone of his voice. It was always the same when a doctor had bad news.

"What does that mean?" Carley asked. The rest of the family gathered to hear.

"It just means he's taking longer than normal to wake up," Dr. Bolton said, clearly shaken—no matter how hard he tried to guard his emotions.

"I don't understand," Esther spoke up. "*Mei* son will wake up, no?"

"We believe so." Dr. Bolton glanced at each of them. "We aren't sure why he hasn't woken up. Would one of you like to come in and sit with him?"

As much as Carley wanted to run to Noah, this was his family—no matter how strained the relationships. She waited quietly for one of them to speak up.

Esther looked at Mary Ellen, who looked at Rebecca, who looked at Ivan. They each looked around at their spouses, at Jonas, at Sarah Jane . . . and no one spoke up. Barbie and the two other non-Amish women stood nearby, looking as surprised as Carley felt.

"What is wrong with all of you?" Unable to keep quiet any longer, Carley homed in on Esther. "He is your son." Turning to Mary Ellen, Rebecca, and Ivan, she added, "And your brother." She shook her head. "I don't understand."

Mary Ellen started to say something, but Esther waved her hand at her daughter to signal silence. She approached Carley with tears in her eyes. "He is a stranger to us. We do not know him. *Ya*, he is our blood. He is my son. I love him. When he walked away from the Lord, he walked away from us."

"But he didn't," Carley said softly. "He didn't walk away from God. He followed his heart, followed his own calling."

Esther stepped back, twisting her hands as she looked down.

Carley looked up at Dr. Bolton. "I'll go." She didn't look at any of them as she went through the double doors.

They walked down a short hallway and into a room on the left. Dr. Bolton excused himself, and Carley walked to Noah's bedside. She was surprised and touched by what she saw. A nurse was standing on one side of the bed, and on the other side stood Samuel. His hand was resting on his brother's arm. His attempts to hide his emotions this time were futile.

With one hand, she touched Samuel's arm. The fingers of her

other hand found Noah's. She squeezed. Noah's complexion was pallid, but at least he was breathing on his own.

"I'm sure he'll be waking up soon," the nurse told Carley sympathetically.

"Noah," Carley whispered. She leaned down. "Wake up, Noah."

Samuel hurried out of the room. Carley wanted to talk to him, to tell him it was okay to feel the way he was feeling—shunning or no shunning—but he went back to be with David. And Carley wanted to stay with Noah. She wanted to be there when he opened his eyes.

"Noah, please wake up," she begged. "Everybody needs you. Dana and Jenna need you." She paused, swiping at her eyes, wondering if she should include herself.

Four hours later, David was resting comfortably in the intensive care unit at the other end of the hospital. Most of the family had gone home, and Mary Ellen had taken Anna with her. Carley hadn't left Noah's side. And Noah hadn't opened his eyes.

Barbie, along with the other non-Amish visitors, made sure each family had a cell phone to take home. Carley supposed that in such a situation as this, use of the portable devices was allowed. Lillian had promised to call the other family members with any word on David or Noah. Twice Lillian had come into the recovery room and sat with Carley, reporting that David was doing well. Doctors and nurses continued to hustle in and out of the room where Noah remained. Carley thought she might blow if she heard one more time, "Medicine is not an exact science. We aren't sure why Noah isn't waking up."

Carley was holding Noah's hand, resting her head on the side of the bed, when she caught a glimpse of a brown dress and black apron out of the corner of her eye. She lifted her head and saw Esther standing in the doorway staring at Noah, but she didn't move toward the bed.

Carley knew Esther to be a woman in her midfifties, but she looked much older. She had a full head of gray hair tucked beneath her prayer covering, and the lines of time feathered outward around her eyes. As she pressed her lips firmly together, the creases across her forehead grew deeper. Slowly she walked to the other side of Noah's bed.

"Why is *mei* boy not waking?" Esther touched Noah's expressionless face gently with her palm. A tear trickled down her cheek.

"I don't know," Carley said softly, her own eyes filling with tears.

Esther's gaze stayed on Noah for quite a while before she looked over at Carley. "You must be thinkin' we are not so *gut* a family."

It was what Carley was thinking, but she shook her head no just the same.

Esther turned back and looked hard at her son, still cupping his cheek. "It is confusing for us, what Noah did." She moved her hand to Noah's shoulder and turned to Carley again. "Our ways are different from the *Englisch*. But we love. We hurt." Esther pulled her hand from Noah's shoulder, covered her face with both hands, and cried as if she'd been holding it in for years.

Carley wound around to the other side of the bed and put her arms around Esther. At first Esther did nothing but sob, her face still buried in her hands. Then, unexpectedly, she threw her arms around Carley's neck and tightly embraced her. Esther mumbled something in Pennsylvania *Deitsch* that Carley didn't understand, but her hold on Carley never lessened.

It was nearing nine o'clock that evening when Noah was moved to an ICU room down the hall from David. No one was using the word *coma*, but no one could say if or when Noah would wake up. Carley hadn't left his side. Lillian had reported that David was doing so well she was going to go home to spend the night with the baby and return in the morning. Samuel was staying in David's room in a recliner chair similar to the one in Noah's room where Carley planned to sleep.

Several times Samuel had ventured a few feet into Noah's room. Each time Carley shook her head, and Samuel backed out of the room. No words were exchanged. No words were necessary.

It was a strange feeling to be at this man's bedside. This man she'd known for less than a month. And yet she couldn't imagine being anywhere else. Still sitting in the chair next to Noah's bed, she found his hand and squeezed.

"Please wake up, Noah."

Carley heard footsteps and turned to see Dana and Jenna. She was startled, but warmly touched, when Jenna ran into her arms.

"Why hasn't Dr. Noah woke up yet?" Jenna asked as she got comfortable in Carley's lap. With her tiny little blue jeans, white cotton T-shirt, and white tennis shoes, she was dressed almost exactly like Carley. Her long blonde locks were pulled into a ponytail, and her eyes were wide and questioning.

"I don't know," Carley said. She turned her attention to Dana and prepared to lambaste the girl for her made-up tale about Noah's girlfriend, but decided it best not to broach the matter in front of Jenna. She carefully stood up and placed Jenna on the chair. "Dana, I need to talk to you for a—"

"Have they said when he might wake up?" Dana interrupted, blinking back tears and stroking Noah's arm from the other side of the bed.

Carley shook her head. "No."

She's in love with him, Carley thought. Was it love? A teenage crush? Either way, Dana's pain seemed equivalent to Carley's, and now wasn't the time to reprimand her for lying.

"I don't get it," Dana said. "People have surgery all the time. How can he just not wake up?" She dabbed at her eyes.

"I don't know."

"What if he never wakes up?" Dana's sad eyes met Carley's, and a maternal instinct kicked in for this girl almost a decade her junior.

"He will, Dana. We have to stay positive. He's breathing on his own, and the surgery went fine. He *will* wake up."

"Is someone taking care of Chloe?" Dana sniffled, tugged at the sides of her red T-shirt, and stood a little taller.

"Noah said the boy next door is feeding and walking her. He asked me to let the glass man in tomorrow to replace the glass on the clinic's front windows. I don't want to leave, though."

"What time?" Dana asked.

"At ten o'clock tomorrow morning."

Dana pulled a piece of paper and a pen out of her purse. She scribbled something on the paper and handed it to Carley. "This is my cell phone number. I'm *sure* Noah will be awake by then, but if he isn't, call me. I can go let the glass man in."

"Are you sure?" Carley knew her surprise was evident. She would have expected her to want to stay by Noah's side instead. "Don't you have work or classes to go to?"

"I'm only working part-time right now at the market, and my summer classes are over. Noah's done a lot for me and Jenna. His clinic is important to him, and I don't want to see things fall apart."

Jenna tugged on Carley's shirt. "I want Noah to wake up."

"Me too, Jenna," Carley whispered. "Me too."

Carley had gotten comfortable in the reclining chair and fallen asleep sometime after midnight. If it could be called sleep; a constant flow of doctors and nurses going in and out prevented more than a few minutes at a time. She was feeling the exhaustion when she heard footsteps around five in the morning. It was Esther.

The older woman held back near the door as if afraid to approach. "Is he—?"

"He still hasn't woken up," Carley whispered.

"An *Englisch* friend brought me in her car. I knew it would not be *gut* news when I got here. Otherwise, the portable phone would have rung in the night." Esther finally neared the bed and touched Noah's arm.

"Everything is the same." Carley hesitated. "Do you want to spend some time alone with him? I could use a break." She didn't need a break. If Noah woke up, she wanted to be there, but maybe it would be good for Noah's mother to spend some time alone with him.

Esther nodded and took a seat in the chair opposite Carley. "I will stay with *mei* son," she said, holding her head upward a tad, as if defying anyone who might say she couldn't.

"Okay." Carley stood up. She placed her hands on each side of Noah's face and kissed him on the cheek. "I'll be back," she whispered. Esther seemed shocked. Carley didn't care.

It feels good to stretch my legs, Carley thought as she exited the room—yet odd to leave Noah. She had been glued to his side. When her cell phone started ringing, she quickly snatched it out of her purse. It was Adam. She didn't feel like dealing with her brother at the moment, but she answered anyway, slipping into the waiting room. Thankfully, it was empty.

"Why are you calling me so early in the morning?" Carley glanced at her watch.

"Carley, I left you three messages," Adam said. "Thank God you're all right, but couldn't you have the courtesy to call me back?"

"I'm sorry, Adam. I really am. Sometimes my phone doesn't get reception at the farm or in the hospital. I saw where you called once yesterday, and I was going to call you back. There's just been a lot going on."

She filled Adam in about David and Noah before he could reprimand her further. His response left her cold. "I'm sorry to hear about all that, Carley. That's a terrible situation. But you have a flight to catch in a few days."

That's it? That's all he has to say? "Well, I definitely won't be coming back in a few days." She paused, planting one hand on her hip. "Actually, I don't know when I'll be coming back."

"Carley, you have a job here. Did you forget that?"

"Uh, ya know what, Adam? My job is what landed me here in the first place—my forced vacation, remember? And as it turns out, I am very much needed around here." *And not about to leave Noah.* "So I wouldn't count on me coming back any time soon."

She could hear Adam sigh on the other end of the line. "Carley, I just worry about you, that's all."

"I know you do, Adam. And I love you for it. But I'm a grown woman. I've spent the last few months with everyone worrying about me, hovering over me. I need to take care of myself. I need to heal. I *am* healing. And taking care of Noah, helping Lillian and her family—this is helping me not to focus so much on my own issues."

"So are you staying an extra week or what? How long?"

"I don't know yet. However long it takes. However long I'm needed."

"And your job? What about your job?"

"There are other jobs. Besides, it's just until things get better around here."

Adam sighed again. "Well, you know I'm here if you need anything. Even if it's just to talk. I love you, Carley."

"I know. And I love you too."

"Have you talked to Matt?"

Carley had missed several calls from Matt also. "No," she answered, "but I will."

"Well, don't expect him to hold your job if this goes on much longer. He said a month."

"I will talk to Matt."

"All right, Carley. But keep in touch with me, please."

"I will."

She tossed the phone back in her purse and headed down the hall toward David's room. As she entered, Samuel met her by the door and motioned for her to go back outside. David was sleeping, but the look on Samuel's face indicated he had something important to tell her.

"We haven't told David about Noah," he whispered.

"I can understand that. I won't say anything." She peeked into the room. "I can see he's sleeping now. Can you tell him I stopped by?"

Samuel nodded. He looked as though he wanted to ask her something, but they were interrupted by the man she recognized as Bishop Ebersol.

"Hello, Samuel," the elderly man said, his long gray beard extending the length of his chest. He firmly clutched Samuel's hand. "How is David doing today?"

The man tipped his straw hat in Carley's direction but quickly turned back toward Samuel.

"David is doing *gut* this morning," Samuel said as he released the bishop's hand. "But Noah . . ."

Bishop Ebersol leaned in toward Samuel. "I do not think it *gut* to talk of your *bruder.*"

Carley gasped in surprise, causing Bishop Ebersol to glance in her direction, but again he refocused on Samuel. "Is the boy awake?" The bishop peered into David's room.

Samuel. Be a man. Say something.

"No, David is sleeping." Samuel stroked his beard. "But Noah—"

"I will come back in the afternoon with other members of the community. We have arranged rides with our *Englisch* friends for later. Is there anything you need?"

"He needs to tell you about Noah!" Carley snapped. "He hasn't woken up from the surgery. That's what he was trying to tell you. And everyone is very worried. *Everyone.*"

To her disbelief, Bishop Ebersol did not acknowledge her.

"I will see you in the afternoon, Samuel." The bishop again extended his hand to Samuel, who reluctantly took it.

Carley threw her hands up. "Did you hear what I said?" she demanded of Bishop Ebersol. "It's okay for Noah to give up a vital organ to save a life, but you can't even acknowledge he's in a coma?"

Realizing it was the first time the word had been used, Carley blinked back her tears.

"I am sorry for your troubles," Bishop Ebersol said, nodding in Carley's direction. "I must go."

As Bishop Ebersol turned to leave, Carley fired Samuel a look she wasn't sure she'd ever directed at anyone. Her eyes blazed with anger and hurt.

Glancing back and forth between Carley and the bishop, Samuel was clearly conflicted. The bishop had almost reached the elevators when he called out. "Bishop Ebersol!"

The bishop spun around.

Samuel motioned with his hand for the bishop to come back to where they were standing. When the bishop got close enough that Samuel wouldn't have to yell, Samuel said, "Bishop Ebersol, we need to have a talk."

16

SAMUEL STOOD A LITTLE TALLER AND LOOPED HIS THUMBS under his suspenders. Carley watched the two men face off.

Bishop Ebersol's eyes narrowed as he took in Samuel's stance. "What is it, Samuel?"

"*Mei* boy is alive and doing *gut* because he has one of Noah's kidneys. If Noah wasn't able to give David a kidney, I don't know what might have happened." Samuel paused but continued when Bishop Ebersol didn't interrupt him. "I believe God would want us to care for Noah during this time, despite his errors of the past."

Bishop Ebersol appeared to be choosing his words carefully, taking his time to respond. "Samuel, this is a *hatt* situation for all to be in. Noah's shunning is not a punishment to him, but an attempt for him to right his ways in God's eyes. It is not our place to question God's will. This selfless act by Noah will be judged by God, not by us. We must follow the *Ordnung* when it comes to these matters." The bishop shook his head. "*Es dutt mir leed*, Samuel."

"I'm sorry, too, Bishop Ebersol." Samuel placed his hands on his hips and looked toward his feet. Sighed. "Do what you must, then. I am going to go be with *mei bruder*."

Samuel turned and walked away, leaving Carley with Bishop

Ebersol. The bishop looked momentarily stunned but quickly excused himself and headed toward the elevator.

When Carley reached Noah's room, Samuel had taken a seat across from Esther. While it was nice to see them coming around, she suddenly felt like an outsider. She had been the one with Noah when he went under the anesthesia. She had stayed by his side. And she wanted to be the one with him when he woke up.

She tried to clear the selfish thoughts from her mind. After all, she'd been the one pushing for compassion from Noah's family, and Noah would certainly welcome them by his side.

"One of us will stay with Noah for now, Carley. You can go to the *haus* and bathe, or just take a break for a time," Samuel offered. Esther nodded in agreement.

"But I . . ." She didn't want to leave.

"We will call you on the portable phone," Esther said in a tone that didn't leave much room for discussion.

Noah's family had been more than willing to let Carley care for Noah. But now she wasn't needed anymore? Now they were going to do the right thing? She opened her mouth to argue, stopped short, and again realized this was what she had hoped for—understanding from Noah's family.

"I've been keeping his lips moist with that wet cloth," she instructed, pointing to the white hand towel on the bedside table.

Esther reached for the towel and began to gently pat Noah's lips. "We will take care of him now." She smiled at Carley. She might as well have added, "Now be on your way."

"We will call you with any word," Samuel added.

A knot grew in her throat as Carley backed out of the room. She was almost gone when Samuel called after her. "Carley . . ."

She waited.

"*Danki,*" he said.

Her lips curled slightly, then she nodded and left the room. She wondered if he was thanking her for staying with Noah or for the look she had fired Samuel's way, which coaxed him to stand up to Bishop Ebersol. Carley had heard enough about Samuel over the past year and a half from Lillian to know he was a good man—a conflicted man, now crippled with fear for his son, torn between his family, his love for his shunned brother, and his desire to do right in the eyes of God.

After a bath and a visit with Lillian, Carley headed back to the hospital. Lillian had expressed relief that Samuel and Esther had mellowed and were tending to Noah. Carley still had mixed feelings about it. But it shouldn't matter who was there when Noah opened his eyes—as long as he opened them.

Carley decided to check on Dana at the clinic since Lillian opted to catch a ride with Barbie a bit later. It was right at ten o'clock. When she pulled in, the glass repair van was out front, along with a blue Mazda she assumed must be Dana's. Maybe today she would talk to Dana about her little lie.

She walked through the door of the clinic, wrinkled her nose, and held her breath. What was that smell?

Dana came down the hallway pinching her nose. Jenna trailed behind in the same fashion. Carley could hear noises from the back of the building.

"What is that smell?" Carley asked Dana, still clenching her nostrils together. "And where is the glass man?"

"The glass repairman is trying to be a plumber in the back.

Something died in the pipes—a mouse or snake or something. He couldn't stand to work in here, and I don't blame him. The smell is about to kill us. So he's seeing if there's anything he can do."

No sooner had she finished explaining when the man emerged from behind Dana. He entered the room and shook his head. "You're going to need a *real* plumber. I'd get someone out here pretty soon too." The balding man in a blue uniform sighed. "Guess I'll have to replace the glass while holding my breath."

"Dana, when are we going home?" Jenna asked.

"In a little while. You can go play outside if you want to."

When Jenna was outside and the repairman was busying himself, Dana asked, "Noah still hasn't woken up?"

Carley shook her head. "But his mother and Samuel wanted to spend some time with him, so I left."

Dana's eyes widened. "Really? I'm surprised."

"They seem to be slowly coming around." Carley shrugged. "I didn't want to leave, but they are his family."

"They sure haven't acted like it." Dana wrinkled her nose. "What are we going to do about this smell?"

Carley turned toward the repairman, who was carefully prying broken pieces of glass out of the windowpane. "Sir?" she asked, waiting for him to place a piece of glass in a metal trash can near the wall. "Do you know a plumber I can call?"

"Benny Friedman." The man carefully removed another section of glass and tossed it into the trash can. "His number is in the book."

"How will we pay for it?" Dana whispered to Carley.

"I don't know, but we have to do something. If it sits like this, Noah will never get the stench out of here."

Carley and Dana locked eyes, both of them thinking the same thing—what if Noah didn't wake up?

"I'm going to head to the hospital," Carley said. "I'll call information for the number and try to make arrangements for the plumber to come out here. Can you stay here until this man is done with the windows?"

"Sure. That was my plan. And if you need me to come back and meet the plumber, call me."

Dana was being sweet, but the lie was hanging over them and bugging Carley in a big way.

"Tell Benny the situation," the repairman offered as he continued to work. "He'll bill you. This guy, Noah, is a doctor. He's good for it. Or someone from his family will handle it if he doesn't—"

He stopped midsentence, but the damage was done.

"Oh, he'll make it!" Dana bellowed. Her comment reinforced Carley's earlier thoughts about Dana's feelings for Noah. She turned toward Carley. "Call me from the hospital and let me know how Noah is doing."

Carley eased her way out the door and decided again that she would forgo an unpleasant conversation with Dana.

She pulled onto the highway and decided to call Matt before calling the plumber. It amazed her the way she had distanced herself from him, from her life in Houston, from all that had been familiar.

"Do you know how long you'll be there?" Matt asked after Carley explained about Noah.

"I don't know yet." She had money saved, plus her inheritance from her mother, which would hold her over for a while if need be.

"You didn't even want to go on this vacation. I'm surprised you aren't hightailing it back to work, but I can understand you wanting to help your friends."

For once, work wasn't the only thing sustaining her. "You almost sound like you miss me."

"Carley," he said slowly, sighing. "You just needed some time to regroup and focus on you. You'll come back refreshed and ready to roll. I've got two feature stories waiting in the wings for you. Speaking of which, how's the Amish story coming? With all that's going on, I bet you've got quite a piece going."

"I haven't exactly started it." Writing was the last thing on her mind.

"Well, I'm sure it'll be a great story."

"I'll get started on it when things settle down around here."

"If this guy hasn't woken up by now, how do the doctors know he will?"

"He will. I know it." *He has to.* "I need to go, Matt. I promise I'll call you about my plans soon."

"Take care, Carley."

It had taken longer than she expected to convey all the details of recent events to Matt. She was nearing the hospital when she finally called the plumber. She listened to the recorded greeting and then left a message. Hopefully Benny would call her back soon. The situation at the clinic needed some immediate attention before things got worse.

Noah—adrift in an altered state of consciousness—struggled to open his eyes or to move at all. Even the twitch of a finger was impossible. Darkness engulfed him from the backs of his eyelids to the depths of his soul. Sluggish thought patterns briefly formed then vanished with no recollection.

The noises around him were familiar. Hospital monitors. Faint voices from outside the door. Doctors being paged. Yes, he was in the hospital. Why wasn't his body responding?

Is this a dream?

An uncomfortable feeling in his abdomen sent a rush of brain activity spiraling around in his head—aimless thoughts too groggy to formulate into any sense.

"Where is everyone?" he heard a woman say. "They said they'd stay until I got back."

Lips brushed against his forehead.

"I'm sorry I left you. Your lips are dry."

The gentle dabbing of moisture on his lips was comforting. The softness of a hand cradling his cheek was soothing.

"Please wake up, Noah. Please. I need you to wake up."

Carley?

"Samuel and your mother sat with you earlier. Everyone is so worried about you. David's kidney is functioning so well. You saved his life." She was crying. "Please wake up."

The kidney. Yes, his kidney, Noah recalled. He gave a kidney to David.

Samuel and my mother were here? Why is Carley crying? Don't cry, Carley. I'm here.

Noah could feel her breath as she whispered, "Please wake up, Noah."

I'm trying to wake up. Why can't I? His thoughts were starting to scramble. He drew a blank.

"It's Carley, Noah."

Yes. Carley. I'm glad you're here.

He fought to keep his thoughts focused and wondered why he couldn't open his mouth and tell her.

"Noah, you're going to have to wake up so we can get your clinic up and running. There are a few problems, and I need you to tell me what to do."

There was a sloshing in his head, like water lapping against the inner walls of his mind. It was growing louder.

God, what is happening to me? Am I dying? Where are You, then?

A new, deeper voice was in the room. "We left to eat some lunch."

Samuel?

He heard another woman's voice. "*Mei* boy still has not woken yet."

Mamm, is that you?

Where was he? Things weren't making sense. Desperate to see past the haze of confusion and quiet the swooshing rush in his head, he focused all that he could muster on opening his eyes. There was no light. Only darkness—darkness and . . .

Where am I going?

Any understanding drifted away. Nothingness returned.

Only a few days ago, Carley had dreaded her trips to the hospital. But now she could hardly stay away. Exhausted, busy, worried— she didn't have time or tolerance for her past to rear up and drag her down. Even the hospital stench had grown more tolerable. Her flashbacks about the accident were less frequent.

"Is there a phone book in that drawer, Samuel?" Carley asked. She pointed to the bedside table close to where Samuel was standing.

He pulled the drawer open, then shook his head. "What do you need?"

"A plumber, I guess," she answered, sighing. "There's a terrible smell coming from the back of the building at Noah's clinic. The glass repairman thinks there's a dead mouse or snake that might have crawled into the pipes somehow. He gave me the name Benny Friedman, but I left a message and he hasn't called me back. I was going to try someone else. Maybe there's a phone book down the hall." She turned to exit the room.

"Wait, Carley," Samuel said. She turned around to see Samuel's eyes locked with Esther's.

"What?" she asked.

Esther nodded her head, and Samuel glanced toward Carley. "I will go to Noah's clinic."

"Are you a plumber? And how will you get there?" Carley crossed her arms across her chest.

"I am handy in that area. And it is a Saturday, which will make it *hatt* to find help. Barbie Beiler just brought Lillian to the hospital, but she said she was heading back to Paradise soon. I will ask her to take me."

Carley took a few steps back into the room. "A friend of his, Dana, is there right now with a glass repairman. I don't know how long she'll be there." She dug in her purse for the other key to the clinic. Thankfully, Noah had given her two, one of which she had given to Dana. "Here's the key." She pushed it in his direction, skeptical that he would actually take it and go. But he did.

Once he left the room, Carley took a seat in the chair next to the bed. Esther was still standing.

"I will go sit with David a spell," Esther said. "You will call for me if there is change, no?"

"Of course."

Carley just wanted to sit quietly for a while with Noah.

The place Samuel remembered to be Stonewall Insurance now had a new glass window with the name Stoltzfus Clinic.

"I can come back in about an hour to pick you up, Samuel," Barbie offered as Samuel got out of the car. "Are you going back to the hospital tonight?"

"No. Lillian is staying tonight. I can walk home from here. *Danki*, though."

Barbie waved and left. As Samuel put the key in the lock, he couldn't help but think how convenient it would be to have a clinic so close to home. All the community could travel by buggy, and some—such as himself—were actually close enough to walk.

But it was Noah's clinic. And his mind was all messed up where Noah was concerned. He had been praying hard about it. He had harbored so much anger toward his brother over the years, it was hard to get things straight in his head.

Samuel had never gone up against the bishop before. He knew Bishop Ebersol would have words with the elders about the matter. But Noah's kidney had saved his son's life. And Noah was in a coma. It was just a terrible mess. Tonight he would look for Noah's letter again. During these troubled times, it seemed more important than ever to find it.

Samuel blew out a breath and waved his hand in front of his face. *"Schtinkich!"* Then he clamped his nose and made his way toward the horrible smell, glad to see a supply of tools in the hallway. He picked up the square box and headed to the source of the problem—the bathroom in the back of the building.

Carley was sitting by Noah's side watching the news when Lillian walked in later that afternoon.

"I miss television sometimes," Lillian said as she entered the room and glanced at the TV suspended from the wall. She took a seat in the other chair by Noah's bed. "Still nothing?"

"No," Carley whispered, watching Noah intently.

"I'm glad Samuel went to see if he can find whatever is causing the smell at Noah's clinic."

"Me too." Carley paused. "I was a little surprised he offered."

"Samuel is a *gut* man. This is all just very confusing for him. But it is right for him to go." Lillian folded her hands in her lap. "David's asking about Noah. We just keep telling him that he's sleeping. We don't want to lie. But that is the truth, no?"

"I suppose so," Carley answered. "The doctor came in earlier. They're stumped."

"Esther is as confused as Samuel about all this. Noah is her son, but when a shunning occurs—there is just no turning back unless the person shunned redeems himself by rejoining the faith." Lillian shook her head. "But these are unusual circumstances, to say the least."

"To say the least," Carley echoed, her eyes focused on Noah.

"You care about him, don't you?" Lillian smiled slightly in Carley's direction.

"I think Noah, too, is a good man." She pulled her eyes away from Noah and turned toward Lillian. "Do you know that when he moved back here a couple of months ago, he moved his friend's two daughters here with him? Their mother had been raising the girls on her own following the death of his friend. Then she was killed, leaving a nineteen-year-old and a five-year-old with no one. Noah takes care of both the girls. He even bought them a little house."

"He does sound like a *gut* man," Lillian said. "I wish things were different for him and Samuel."

"So do I. Maybe after this, things will change."

Maybe Lillian didn't think so, because she changed the subject. "Your flight is next week, no?"

"My flight is scheduled for next week, but, Lillian, if it's okay with you, I'd like to stay. I want to help you, and I don't want to leave—"

"You don't want to leave Noah," Lillian interrupted.

"I don't want to leave any of you right now." Carley rested her head between her hands. "The truth is, being here—helping you and your family, helping with Noah—seems to be helping me get past some of my own troubles. I don't think I have the kind of connection with God that you have, but I need to find some sort of peace about everything that's happened over the past six months."

Lillian's eyes shone with warmth. "Carley, I can remember feeling the way you do before I came to Lancaster County. In some ways, I think I felt unworthy to open my heart to God. I just didn't understand or have a relationship with Him. After many misguided attempts to connect, as you say, I realized I had been connected the entire time. Just like a light switch, you can turn it off or on—but the electricity is still live all the time. It's the same with God. He's always there. Does that make sense?"

"Funny you would use a comparison with electricity."

"I guess it is, but it's the best I could come up with." Lillian smiled. "Anyone can open their heart to God, accept Him and His will. The Amish don't have some secret connection with God, any more than a priest or other member of clergy. God is here for all of us. I'm so blessed to be a daughter of the promise."

"What does that mean?"

"It's when a woman takes a spiritual journey of faith, hope, and love, promising to trust in God. Then she's a daughter of the promise."

Carley pondered that for a moment. "I guess I just feel let down by God."

"Because of your mother?"

"Partly." Carley turned away from Lillian and looked toward the wall. She wasn't sure if she was ready to spill about her inability to have children. "And I . . ."

"What, Carley?" Lillian reached across Noah and touched Carley's hand, which was resting on Noah's arm.

"I care for Noah," Carley began, "but staying would never be an option for me, even if things progressed into something more than a friendship."

"Because of your job? Or maybe because your brother is in Houston?" Lillian pulled her hand away. "Or because of what's going on between Noah and Samuel? Carley, don't let that stop you from making decisions that might be best for you—"

"No, no. It's not that. I like my job, but it's just a job. And my brother has his own family. Actually, I would like to get away from there—to start fresh. After Dalton and I broke up, I toyed with the idea of moving away. My brother hovers. I love him dearly, but he drives me crazy sometimes."

"Start fresh here!" Lillian said.

"As much as I would like to, I can't. Even if Noah might have been harboring thoughts of more than a friendship with me, I just can't. Oh, Lillian. What if he doesn't wake up?"

"He will. I know he will, Carley." She smiled. "And then the two of you will see if something is happening between you."

Carley shook her head. "It will never happen, Lillian."

"Don't say that! Stay! It would be *wunderbaar gut* to have you close by."

Carley continued to shake her head. "I can't believe we're even discussing this while Noah's lying here in a coma." She raised her chin a little higher, determined not to cry. "There is nothing more important to Noah than family. He'd do just about anything to be reconciled with his. And he has mentioned on several occasions how much he wants children of his own."

"Well, it looks as though the family might be moving in the right direction as far as renewing a relationship with Noah." Lillian grinned. "Then you and Noah can get married and have lots of *boppli!*"

Carley flinched, grabbed her side, and took a deep breath.

Please stop, Lillian.

Lillian had leaned down to tie her shoe, unaware of the color draining from Carley's face. "And over time, maybe things will be better between my Samuel and Noah. Can't you just see it, Carley? Our children playing together. There's nothing more rewarding in life than motherhood." She tightened the knot on her other shoe.

Carley rose from the chair, walked across the room, and wrapped herself in a hug, keeping her face toward the wall. She stared at the textured white specks in front of her before closing her eyes tightly—as if that would prevent the images in her mind from taking shape.

"We're so sorry, Carley," she recalled the doctor saying six months ago.

"How many children do you want? Samuel and I hope to have lots of children. At least three more, and . . ."

Carley didn't hear the rest. Her head was pounding. She took a deep breath, attempted to blink back the tears threatening to spill, and grabbed her side again. With effort, she turned to face her friend.

Please, Lillian . . .

But Lillian was preoccupied with pouring herself a cup of water from the tray a nurse had brought them earlier—and still talking, her words cutting into Carley like a jagged piece of wood in her side. "I'm going to pray that you and Noah will fall in love and make a family, and—"

"Stop it! Just stop it!" Carley threw her hands to her ears and squeezed her eyes shut. "Noah and I will never have a family! It doesn't matter how much I care for him, Lillian!"

She opened her eyes, the tears spilling down her cheeks. Lillian had dropped the small white cup on the floor. Splashes of water covered the orange chair cushion nearby. Carley trembled as she stared into Lillian's eyes—eyes now glassy with questions. "I can't have children, Lillian! A family is not in my future. So it doesn't matter how Noah and I might feel about each other." Between sobs, she gasped for a breath. "I would never pin him down with someone who couldn't give him children." She buried her face in her hands. "Someone incomplete like me."

Lillian's arms wrapped around her, and Carley buried her head in Lillian's shoulder.

"Oh, Carley. I'm so sorry," Lillian soothed.

Carley heard footsteps but didn't look up. "Is everything all right in here?" She recognized the day nurse's voice.

"Everything is fine." Lillian's response was curt. Carley heard the footsteps leaving the room.

Gently Lillian eased her away, keeping hold of her arms. "Carley, sweet Carley. You've been keeping this all bottled up. You should have told me. You shouldn't have let me carry on like that. I'm so sorry." Lillian hung her head.

"No, no," Carley said, sniffling. "Don't be sorry. You didn't know. The accident did a lot of internal damage. I'll—" Her chin trembled and she fought to say the words. "I'll never know the kind of love you're talking about. And I've wanted children for as long as I can remember."

Lillian eased Carley into the chair on one side of the bed, then took a seat in her own chair on the other side of the bed, ignoring the spilled water on the cushion. She reached across Noah and grabbed Carley's hand. "Sometimes God has a plan for us that we can't foresee."

"I know, Lillian. And I'm trying to turn my bitterness about the situation into something else. I pray about it. But I would never saddle a man with an infertile wife, especially someone like

Noah who wants a family so badly." She shook her head. "Dalton already taught me a lesson about that. Love isn't enough. And I'm not saying I love Noah. I don't know what I feel. But I know that he just has to wake up. I think he has so much to offer someone." She looked down and began to cry again.

"He will wake up, Carley." Lillian squeezed her hand. "Sweetie, just because Dalton did that to you doesn't mean Noah or another man would."

"Lillian, even if things progressed past friendship, I would never deny Noah the family he longs for. That much I do know. But I want to stay as long as I can. Until he wakes up and is back on his feet."

"It's difficult to walk away from someone you care a—"

Both women jumped and pulled back their hands.

"Did you feel that?" Lillian asked.

Carley put her hands to her mouth. "I did. He moved."

17

CARLEY'S HEART RACED AS SHE WATCHED DR. BOLTON, Dr. Lukeman, and two other doctors bend over Noah. She and Lillian were standing off to one side, out of the way. Esther had joined them, opting not to call Samuel on his borrowed cell phone until the doctors determined what Noah's movement meant.

"Might have been an involuntary jerk," Dr. Bolton said. He forced Noah's eyelid open with his finger and shone a tiny light into his pupil.

"It wasn't a jerk," Carley said. "He twisted his wrist sideways."

Dr. Lukeman walked to where the two women were standing. "He might be trying to come out of it. While we were examining him, he opened his mouth slightly."

Carley put her hand to her chest. "Really?"

"I hate to get your hopes up, but his vital signs have shifted somewhat. This might mean he is slowly waking up."

"That is wonderful!" Lillian said. "Should I call Samuel?"

Esther didn't say anything, but she eased her way to Noah's side and stood beside Dr. Bolton. She rested her hand on Noah's arm.

"It's up to you if you want to call Samuel," Dr. Lukeman said. "We're not sure of anything yet."

"Everyone in the family has borrowed cell phones," Lillian said. "I will go and call everyone."

She turned to leave but bumped into Samuel on her way out the door. "What's happening?" he asked as he entered the room. "I just got back and checked on David, but he went to sleep. Is something happenin' with Noah?" He took a couple of steps toward the doctor.

"Noah moved," Lillian said. She joined Samuel as he approached Noah's bedside.

"We think he might be trying to wake up," Dr. Bolton said.

Carley held back a few feet from the bed. Samuel, Lillian, Esther, and the four doctors hovered around Noah, and she couldn't see him. She wanted to push them all out of the way, to hold Noah's hand, tell him she'd been praying for him, begging him to come back. She shifted her weight from side to side and tried to see around Samuel, who was blocking her view the most.

When she saw Esther's hands cover her mouth, she knew something was happening, but she couldn't see Noah's face. Dr. Bolton had a stethoscope against Noah's chest, Dr. Lukeman was leaning down and saying Noah's name repeatedly, and the other two doctors were standing still with their backs toward Carley. Esther, Lillian, and Samuel had moved to the end of the bed the doctors could work. Carley took a step forward, still behind the others.

"Well, hello there," Carley heard Dr. Bolton say. "Welcome back, Noah. Can you hear me?"

Samuel was in the middle, at the foot of the bed, with Esther and Lillian on each side of him, grasping his arms. Carley slowly inched closer and peered over Lillian's shoulder. Her heart fluttered when she saw Noah blinking his eyes into focus.

"Samuel?" he asked with uncertainty.

"*Ya*, Noah. We are here. *Mamm* is here too," Samuel answered.

The doctors stepped backward to make way for Esther, Samuel, and Lillian to edge forward along the side of the bed. Esther grabbed Noah's hand and began speaking in Pennsylvania *Deitsch*. Noah smiled.

Carley stood at the foot of the bed, a smile stretching across her face as a tear trickled down her cheek.

Thank You, God.

Noah's eyes shifted back and forth between Samuel and his mother as he tried to focus. Carley could tell that both mother and brother were struggling not to let their emotions spill over.

Noah's smile slipped. "Carley? Where's Carley?"

Everyone in the room looked toward Carley.

"She's here, Noah," Lillian said. She pointed toward the end of the bed where Carley was standing.

When Noah's eyes focused and connected with Carley's, his smile returned. "Carley," he whispered as Lillian grabbed Carley's hand and pulled her to Noah's side.

"I'm here, Noah," she said, taking his hand. "I'm here."

She recalled the tender moment they had shared in the hallway, which now seemed days ago. She wanted to kiss him on the forehead or the cheek, the way she had so many times while he was sleeping. But she didn't.

"I dreamed about you," he said wearily.

"I hope it was a good dream." She smiled as she chocked back pent-up emotions. She could feel everyone's eyes on her.

The doctors had convened in the hallway to discuss Noah's progress. Carley glanced at Lillian, who was smiling, then at Esther and Samuel, who both looked relieved. Carley boldly leaned forward.

"Thank God you're awake," she said then kissed him on the cheek. "We've all been so worried."

Noah was having trouble keeping his eyes open. When they closed and didn't reopen, Carley spontaneously yelled, "Noah! Wake up!"

His eyes widened. "I'm awake."

The others were all taken aback by her outburst. Doctors Bolton and Lukeman reentered the room.

"Everything all right?" Dr. Bolton asked.

Carley put her hand on her chest and tried to calm her pounding heart. "He's trying to go back to sleep."

"Carley, he is probably going to sleep on and off, but he's not in a coma anymore," Dr. Bolton said.

"A coma?" Noah asked, focusing on Dr. Bolton. "For how long?"

"Only a couple of days, Noah. You didn't wake up after the surgery. We're not sure why."

Noah crinkled his nose and cocked his head. "What is that smell?"

"It's Samuel," Lillian blurted out. She waved her hand back and forth in front of her face. "He was working on the plumbing at your clinic. Smells like it too." She cut her eyes hard toward her husband.

Noah smiled. "Really? Thank you."

"A critter had gotten into the pipes and died. Everything is *gut* now," Samuel said. His expression was closed, his voice reverting back to the distant tone he'd had before Noah slipped into the coma. "I'd best go check on David."

"Me too," Lillian added. She smiled at Noah. "So glad to see you awake."

"David?" Noah asked groggily. "How is David?"

"He is wonderful, Noah," Carley said. "Just wonderful. You saved his life."

"We'd better go, Lillian," Samuel pushed.

"I will go too," Esther said, but her feet seemed rooted to the floor.

"Mamm," Noah said tenderly. *"Danki."*

Esther nodded at her son, dabbing her eyes. And then she left.

Carley realized that the temporary suspension of the shunning had ended. Noah was going to be all right. David was doing well. Things would go back to the way they were.

———

After Noah ate a little dinner, his eyes searched Carley's. Things were different between them. She wasn't sure exactly to what extent, but they had crossed over into new territory.

He reached for her hand. "Thank you for being here. And thank you for taking care of things at the clinic." He smiled. "So Samuel is the one who took care of it?"

"He offered," Carley confirmed, hoping Noah wouldn't get his hopes up too much where his family was concerned.

"Maybe they're coming around. I hope so."

She was trying to think of a way to lower his expectations when her cell phone started ringing. She was surprised she was getting reception in the hospital and quickly reached into her purse to answer it.

"It's Dana," she whispered to Noah. And the girl was all wound up. "Dana, slow down," Carley said. "What's wrong?"

"After you called and told me that Noah was all right, I decided to head up to the hospital. On the way, I stopped at the clinic because Jenna left her doll there. When I pulled up, there were huge boxes outside, like someone delivered something and just left them here."

"Hold on, Dana." Carley turned her attention to Noah. "Dana said a bunch of boxes were delivered to the clinic. I thought they were going to be delivered on Tuesday. That would be tomorrow."

Noah took a deep breath and rolled his eyes. "Great. That's most likely all the medical equipment. You're right, it was supposed to be delivered on Tuesday."

Carley held up one finger to indicate that Dana was talking again.

"It's raining here, Carley. Everything is getting wet. I can't get these boxes in by myself. I didn't know who else to call. What should I do?"

"Can you wait for me? It will take me about an hour to get there, though."

After hanging up with Dana, Carley told Noah, "I'm going to meet Dana at the clinic, and we'll move the boxes into the waiting room for now."

"Carley, those boxes are very heavy." Noah sighed. His eyes were droopy and he looked exhausted. She knew he didn't need this type of aggravation.

"We'll figure something out." She leaned down to kiss him on the cheek.

"Carley, you look so tired." He reached up and cupped her cheek in his hand. When he did, he flinched.

"Are you okay?"

"Sore," he said, groaning before bringing his hand down and continuing. "And those delivery people should never have left those boxes outside, especially on the wrong day. There's thousands of dollars' worth of equipment in those boxes, and they are much too heavy for you and Dana. Maybe Samuel will help you."

"I'll ask him." Carley straightened up and reached for her purse on the chair. "Try to get some rest. I'll be back to see you later."

"Carley, no." He shook his head. "Go home. Get some rest. As much as I'd love for you to be here, you look exhausted. The nurse told me you've been here almost the entire time."

She sensed it was Noah who needed the rest more than she did. "Okay, but I'll be back in the morning."

Before she reached the door, Noah called her back. His face was serious. "Carley, I'm going to make this up to you. You should not have to do all this—any of it. I'm going to make it up to you somehow. And don't forget to see if Samuel can help you with those boxes. He might be ready for a ride home anyway."

She nodded and walked down the hall toward David's room. Lillian was sitting in the chair cradling Anna. No Samuel. No David.

"Can you believe David is already up and walking?" Lillian asked. "Samuel and the nurse took him down the hall. You just missed Mary Ellen, Rebecca, and Sadie," she added. "They came to see David, and they just went downstairs to get something to drink. Barbie brought them. We're so fortunate to have such nice friends to give us car rides. If they hadn't brought Anna up here for a visit, she would have already been asleep by the time I got home tonight. We're staying at home tonight since David is doing so *gut*. Annie Lapp is here with her car also."

Carley needed to get on the road, but she had a question for Lillian. "Are Mary Ellen and Rebecca going to see Noah while they're here?"

Lillian looked down. "I don't know."

"They should," Carley said impatiently, even though she knew Lillian had no control over what the women did.

"I agree, Carley. I really do. But Noah is doing *gut* now, and—"

"So now that Noah is okay, everyone's conscience is clear? Don't you think he would enjoy a visit from his sisters after everything he's been through? Or is the shunning automatically back in force now that Noah is awake?"

"Carley, I can't speak for them, but—"

"I have to go," Carley interrupted. It was clear based on what Lillian wasn't saying that the chances were slim. "There's a problem at Noah's clinic. I'll see you later at home."

She headed down the hall after deciding not to ask Samuel for help with the boxes. It suddenly seemed awkward, and she decided she would figure something out. She felt bad about the way she had spoken to Lillian, but she just couldn't grasp the on-again, off-again ways of these people. Convenient love. That was how it seemed to her.

What about unconditional love? Wasn't that what God offered

to anyone who chose to seek Him out? Forgiveness no matter what the sin? The Amish weren't God. What right did they have to shun anyone? God never turned His back on anyone, and neither should they. She was never going to understand.

Almost instantly, Lillian's explanation about the light switch and God came into her mind. Carley knew she had been guilty of an on-again, off-again relationship with God. She pondered if she had also been guilty of convenient love, only turning to God during times of trouble. Or just the opposite—turning her back on Him because she felt betrayed by Him when events became too difficult to bear. Who was she to judge anyone? Only God could do that.

Which brought her back to where she'd started, thinking about the practice of shunning and how she couldn't accept it.

She slid into her car, buckled her seat belt, and slid the key into the ignition. But before she started the motor, she took a moment to pray for Noah and his family.

It started raining about ten minutes into Carley's drive from the hospital to the clinic. Hard pellets pounded the windshield and her wipers swooshed at full capacity. She hated to drive in the rain. It had been raining the day of the accident. As her heart began to race, she realized that despite her preoccupations in Pennsylvania and her distance from Houston, the vision of the red pickup was flashing before her. She could barely see the road.

"Please, God, help me to stay focused." She drew in a deep breath. "Help me to see clearly what lies before me and not to focus on things from the past."

The rain was still pounding hard when she pulled up at the

clinic. She bolted from the car and entered the waiting room soaked. Dana was sitting on the tile floor, leaning against the wall and reading a book to Jenna.

"Carley!" Jenna jumped up and ran to her. "You're all wet. Even wetter than us."

"Yes, I am. But it won't stop me from giving you a big wet hug." She grabbed Jenna playfully and pulled her into her arms. Jenna giggled, returned the hug, and didn't seem to mind the extra moisture.

"Those boxes outside are pretty big," Carley said. "Guess we'd better see if we can carry them in."

"Wonder what's in them?" Dana asked.

"Noah said it's medical equipment."

"Thank God he's awake and doing so well. We're going to go see him when we leave here."

"I hate the hospital, Dana. Can't I go with Carley?" Jenna's bottom lip curled under in a frown.

"Jenna, don't you want to go see Noah? I know he'd want to see you."

Jenna stared down at the floor and pouted.

Dana squatted down in front of her. "But we need to go see Noah."

Jenna looked up at Carley. "Can I go home with you tonight?"

"No, Jenna. That's rude," Dana snapped.

"I don't mind, Dana," Carley answered as she smoothed back Jenna's blonde waves. "But I'll leave it up to you." It suddenly occurred to Carley that Lillian and Samuel may not appreciate her inviting Jenna to spend the night. Besides that, Carley still had a little something to discuss with Dana.

"Are you sure?" Dana asked.

Carley wasn't sure but said, "Yes, that's fine."

"Goody!" Jenna jumped up and down.

"We'd better get the stuff moved in." Carley opened the door. The rain had let up, but the dark, lingering clouds overhead hinted that more might be on the way.

Carley eyed the boxes, each of them about six feet long, then grabbed the end of one and lifted. "It's awkward, but not as heavy as I thought."

Dana lifted the other end, but with much effort.

"Are you sure you can get it?" Carley asked.

"Definitely. I don't want Noah's stuff to get ruined."

Six boxes later, they both collapsed on the floor. Carley pushed back strands of wet hair and studied the clutter. The large boxes added to the mess of smaller boxes scattered throughout the clinic, along with file cabinets, piles of papers, phones, and miscellaneous office supplies.

"How long is Noah going to be in the hospital? A week?" Dana asked.

"Yes, but his full recovery is going to take several weeks. He won't be able to organize this place for a while."

Dana rolled her eyes. "Have you seen Noah's house? He's not exactly the most organized person to begin with anyway."

"No, I haven't seen his house, but I suspected as much." Carley paused then cut her eyes sharply at Dana, just enough to let her know she was onto her. "I'm sure his *girlfriend* will help him get things organized when she gets back into the country."

"Yeah, I guess." Dana twisted her hands together while her eyes veered away from Carley's.

"You must care for him an awful lot." Carley squinted at Dana and wondered exactly how much. "It sounds like he's been very good to you and Jenna."

"Yes, he's taken good care of us." Dana curled a strand of hair around her finger and continued to avoid Carley's eyes.

Carley resisted the urge to tear into her in front of Jenna. "So when did you say his girlfriend will be back? Oh, and what's her name, by the way?"

"Uh, I'm not sure. When she'll be back, I mean."

"Dana—" Carley hesitated when Jenna's big blue eyes rose to hers. "I . . . Never mind."

Dana stood, put her hands on her hips, and took a deep breath. Then she looked hard at Carley. "You know, she's not really much of a girlfriend anyway. More of a friend."

"Really?" Carley didn't hide the sarcasm in her tone. She stood too. "Because Noah sure is going to be disappointed not to have this place ready to open when he planned." Carley glanced around at the mess. "I think he underestimated how much work there is to do. All the big stuff like painting and plumbing has been handled, but look at this mess."

Carley wasn't sure what the rush was. She doubted the Amish community would be knocking the door down with business. But it was important to Noah. She looked around and wondered if she could pull off what she was thinking.

"When Noah gets home from the hospital, he's not going to be able to do a whole lot for a while. That includes getting this place ready," Carley said. She began walking from room to room, Dana and Jenna following her.

"I know what you're thinking," Dana said. "And I'll help you. Together we can do it."

Carley looked in one of the boxes in the reception area. A fax machine. It would be a project, no doubt. She turned to Dana. "Do you have time, with your job and all?" She wasn't sure she wanted to partner with Dana on this project, but she didn't think she could do it alone either.

"I work about twenty hours a week right now, but I'd love to do this for Noah." She grinned. "Let's don't tell him. Let's make it a surprise!"

"He'll be in the hospital for a week and then probably won't be able to leave the house for another week. After that, he's going to want to at least come up here, even if he can't work."

"I can start early in the morning," Dana said. "As early as you want to get here. We'll still visit Noah at the hospital, of course. He doesn't have to know we're doing this. It would be a small way for me to repay his kindness for everything he has done for me and Jenna. I mostly work in the afternoons, and the lady next door watches Jenna. She's really old, but Jenna likes her."

Carley glanced around again at the project they were preparing to undertake. She couldn't think of anything she'd rather do. But she and Dana needed to clear the air. Although she suspected Noah would take care of that this evening.

"Six o'clock too early for you?" Carley asked.

"Yowsers! That *is* early. But I'll be here." Dana turned to Jenna and pointed a finger in her direction. "Are you going to be able to keep this a secret? You can't tell Noah what we're doing. Do you understand me?"

"Yes," Jenna answered before she turned to Carley. "Let's go to your house now."

"Well, it's not exactly *my* house, but if it's okay with Dana, I'm ready. It'll be dark soon."

"I don't have any clothes or anything for her," Dana said as Carley locked the door behind them.

"I bet Jenna can wear one of my T-shirts to bed. She'll be okay for one night," Carley said, Jenna bouncing behind her as they made their way to the car.

"It will be good to go see Noah and then have some time to myself. I don't get that too often."

Carley thought about how difficult it must be for Dana to raise Jenna on her own. She supposed it would be natural, under the circumstances, for a girl her age to have a crush on Noah.

"Be good, Jenna," Dana said.

"We'll have a good time," Carley assured Dana. She snapped Jenna's seat belt across her in the backseat.

The rain had stopped, and the sun was bearing down on the horizon when Carley turned onto the dirt driveway. Jenna was delighted, pointing to the cows grazing to her left. Then at the two buggies parked by the house.

"Have you ridden in a buggy since you've been here?" Carley asked her.

Jenna's eyes widened in anticipation. "No, never."

"Well, when things get better for Noah and David, we'll just have to see about making that happen."

Lillian and Samuel were on the front porch. Carley assumed

it had been awhile since they'd had some quiet time together away from the hospital. And now she was bringing a strange child into their home. She wasn't sure exactly how they'd feel about that.

Knowing Lillian, she should have known better than to worry.

"And who is this?" Lillian asked merrily when she met Carley and Jenna in the front yard.

"Lillian, this is Jenna. I hope you don't mind that I brought her to stay tonight. She's the little girl I was telling you about— the friend of Noah's."

"Mind?" Lillian asked. She smoothed out the wrinkles in her apron as she faced Jenna. "Of course I don't mind. And it just so happens that I have some cookies on the table inside with your name on them."

"What kind of cookies?" Jenna shyly asked.

"They're called raisin puffs. They're David's favorite. I'm taking him some to the hospital tomorrow." Lillian offered her hand to Jenna. "Want to come try one?"

Jenna nodded as she latched onto Lillian's hand. Lillian was such a natural mother. Carley worried that since she was now infertile, perhaps the mom gene had abandoned her too. "Thank you, Lillian," she whispered.

They walked up the porch steps to where Samuel was sitting in the rocker, sipping a glass of tea.

"Samuel, we have company for tonight," Lillian said. "This is Jenna, and she wants to try my raisin puffs."

Samuel smiled. "Well, hello, Jenna. You'll save me one of those cookies, no?"

Jenna's face lit up and she nodded. Carley followed her and

Lillian into the house, pleased Samuel didn't seem to have a problem with her bringing Jenna to stay.

"It's dark," Jenna said when they walked into the kitchen.

"Lillian and Samuel don't use electricity," Carley said as Lillian lit the lantern suspended above the table and another one on the counter.

"Ooh," Jenna purred. Her eyes grew wide and she seemed in awe of Lillian's kitchen. "I like this place, and it smells good."

"It always smells good in Lillian's kitchen." Carley took in the aroma of freshly baked cookies. "David will be thrilled to have some of your cookies." She motioned for Jenna to take a seat beside her on the bench at the kitchen table.

"It's amazing how quickly he's getting his appetite back," Lillian said, putting two cookies on a plate in front of Jenna. "What about you, Carley? Need a cookie?"

"Absolutely." Carley accepted one from the round platter.

As Lillian took a seat across from them at the table, they heard the screen door shut. Samuel entered the kitchen, hanging his straw hat on a stand by the door. "How are those cookies, Jenna?"

"Good," she answered with a mouthful.

"Well, you enjoy them. I'm going to say good night and bathe for bed. Been a long day, no?"

"*Ya*," Lillian answered. "I'll be upstairs soon."

"Good night, Samuel," Carley added.

As they munched on cookies, Carley filled Lillian in about the day's events and her plans for Noah's clinic.

"But, Lillian, I'm going to help around here too. Don't worry about that," Carley reassured her friend. "And I can take Anna with me and put her in a playpen, or give you rides, or whatever you need, and—"

"Carley." Lillian reached across the table to pat Carley's hand. "It's okay. Really. You see how much help we have. I have Mary Ellen and Rebecca, both their daughters, Sadie, and our three *Englisch* friends who provide rides. I have *mei mamm*, plus other members of the community are here daily to help. I don't need the help. Noah does. Now"—she paused—"where shall we have Miss Jenna sleep tonight?"

"I was going to let her sleep in my bed with me. How does that sound, Jenna?"

"Good." Jenna pushed back a strand of long blonde hair that had fallen forward.

"I have some books that were David's when he was your age," Lillian said. "When I go upstairs, I'll get them and put them on your bed. Maybe you might want Carley to read you a story?"

"Yes, yes," Jenna said.

Lillian stood up. "Well, I'm going to head upstairs, then. You enjoy your cookies, Jenna. And remind Carley to turn off the lanterns, okay?"

Jenna nodded.

"Good night, Lillian," Carley said as Lillian headed toward the stairs. Again she thought about what a natural mommy Lillian was.

And how that possibility was lost for Carley herself.

"Where's Jenna?" Noah asked Dana when she walked into the room.

"She wanted to spend the night with Carley." She sat down in the chair by the bed.

"Really?" He wasn't all that surprised. Jenna seemed to like Carley. *He* liked Carley. Which led him into a conversation he'd been dreading. He'd suspected for a long time that Dana had a crush on him, but he'd had no idea she'd go so far as to try to keep Carley away from him by creating a make-believe girlfriend.

"You must like Carley, if you let Jenna go stay with her," Noah said.

Dana shrugged. "She's okay, I guess."

Noah knew he needed to tread lightly. Dana had been through a lot. But he also wanted things to be clear in her mind. "Carley and I have become good friends." He paused. "Possibly more."

Dana turned away from him.

"Dana, look at me."

But she only shook her head.

"I love you and your sister—like I love my own sisters or even like I hope to love my daughters someday."

"I know where you're going with this!" She rose from the chair, hung her head for a moment, then looked back at him. A tear rolled down her cheek. "And I'm sorry for what I did. I just . . ."

Noah reached for her hand. "You and Jenna will always be in my life in some capacity. You know that, right?" He squeezed her hand. "There's all kinds of love, Dana."

"But things wouldn't be the same if you had a girlfriend or got married or something."

"Do you think I would abandon you and Jenna?" He gave her an incredulous look.

She pulled her hand away, covered her face, and wept. "I don't know."

"Well, it's not going to happen." He waited while she gathered herself. "I know you want me to be happy."

She nodded.

"It would make me happy to get to know Carley better." He paused. "And, Dana, it would make me happy if you and Jenna got to know Carley better too."

She nodded again. "Okay."

After helping Jenna with a bath and getting bathed herself, Carley lit lanterns on each side of the bed and pulled back the covers for Jenna to crawl underneath.

"These sheets smell good." Jenna buried her head in the pillow.

"It's because they hang them outside to dry." Carley reached for the pile of books Lillian had left on the bedside table. "Let's see. Which book should we read?"

Carley offered Jenna four books to choose from while she tucked the quilt up around their waists—the quilt Noah had bought her at the mud sale. Running her hand across the fabric, she couldn't help but wonder if he was thinking about her too. But every time she tried to imagine them as more than friends, a roadblock slammed down in front of her. He would ultimately regret a life with her.

So why was she allowing things to move forward so naturally with him?

"This one, Carley. Read this one!"

Carley accepted the book. *My Family.* "Are you sure?" She wondered if a book about family would upset Jenna, given her circumstances.

Jenna's head bobbed up and down with excitement, so Carley read the book—three times. Then Jenna rested her head in the nook of Carley's shoulder. It didn't take long for her to fall fast asleep.

Carley brought the book about family to her chest. While it seemed to give Jenna comfort, it was Carley who was upset after reading it. She missed her mother more than ever, and her regret rose to the surface at not being able to have her own children. As an onslaught of self-pity threatened to drown her, she closed her eyes, knowing she needed a new approach. There had to be some way to feel peace again, some way to move forward.

She'd prayed for David, for Noah, for Lillian and her family. Why was it so hard to ask God to guide *her?*

Samuel could hear Lillian bustling around in the kitchen and knew she'd be upstairs soon. She'd already caught him looking for the letter once and didn't seem to understand how important it was. With his son on the mend, nothing seemed more crucial than finding the missive from Noah.

Did God know he'd need this letter someday? Is that why he'd felt so strongly about opening it . . . and then kept it? He'd felt such despair after Rachel died, like he'd never stop hurting. He remembered wanting to go to the shanty to call Noah after he received the letter. But he hadn't.

He thanked God repeatedly that Noah was able to give his

boy a kidney, but he knew things couldn't change. Samuel's heart might have softened, but the ways of the community and Bishop Ebersol had not.

Still. He needed that letter.

After checking every drawer in the chest a second time, he sat down on the bed. Where could he have put it?

As Carley tried to push past her feelings of unworthiness and talk to God on her own behalf, Jenna groaned. Carley could see her neck was twisted awkwardly against Carley's shoulder. She gently nudged Jenna down onto her own pillow and reached for the bedside table. As she set down the book they had read, something fell from the back of it.

A small envelope addressed to Samuel—from Noah. Turning it over, she could see it had been opened. She recalled Noah saying that all his letters to Samuel had been returned unopened or gone unanswered. Evidently, this one Samuel had kept—and read.

She stared at the envelope, then pulled out the wrinkled piece of paper. It looked as if it had been read a hundred times. Knowing full well what she was doing was as wrong as anything she'd ever done, she unfolded the lined piece of white paper. And she read.

When she was done, she cried. She cried for Noah. She cried for Samuel. Now she knew exactly what she needed to do.

18

AFTER THEY CAUGHT A RIDE WITH BARBIE TO THE HOSPITAL the next morning, Lillian carefully broached the subject of Noah with Samuel. While they waited for the elevator, she said, "I think it's nice what Carley's doing for Noah."

"*Ya*," Samuel responded. Lillian could have sworn he smiled for a split second. "They are *in lieb*," he added, shaking his head, his expression reflective of his disapproval.

"Samuel, no one has said anything about love. But what if it were to happen?" she said enthusiastically, threading her arm through his as they entered the elevator. "Don't you remember how *wunderbaar* it is when you are first *in lieb*?" Glad the elevator was empty, she added jokingly, "It hasn't been that long for us, Samuel. Surely you haven't forgotten."

"No. And I love you even more now."

She released her hold on Samuel's arm since he wasn't fond of public affection. "I feel the same way."

The elevator doors opened. They exited and headed toward David's room. By now, Lillian was immune to the curious stares they received. She could tell they bothered Samuel, but he never said anything.

"Where's David?" Samuel asked the nurse in David's room when he saw that the bed was empty.

The woman retrieved the urine jug from the floor next to the bed and scribbled the measurement on a chart. "He went for a walk with one of the aides," she said, heading to the bathroom to pour out the contents that had been saved to evaluate David's kidney output. "We try to get the patients up and walking as much as possible."

"Thank you," Lillian said as they headed toward the hall to find David.

"He said he was going to go see his uncle," the nurse added before they were out the door.

Lillian nodded at the nurse and turned quickly to Samuel, catching a frown on his face. She decided not to comment one way or the other and quietly walked alongside Samuel to Noah's room.

Lillian was surprised to find Rebecca sitting in a chair by Noah's bed. David was standing nearby, clutching a walker, with an aide by his side steadying his portable IV. Rebecca jumped up, as if she had seen a ghost.

"Samuel, you're here so early." She smoothed the wrinkles in her apron.

"How are our patients doing this morning?" Lillian glanced back and forth between David and Noah.

"*Gut*," David said. "I came to see if *Onkel* Noah wanted to go for a walk with me down the hall."

Lillian clutched Samuel's arm, hoping her touch would remind him of his surroundings. His son was in the room.

"I told David maybe later," Noah spoke up. "I have lab people on their way to draw more blood." He winked at David. "But it is amazing how well your boy is doing."

"And we probably need to get him back in a prone position," the aide added. "David has been on his feet long enough."

Samuel and Lillian backed up and made room for David to turn the walker around. "I'll see you soon, *Onkel* Noah."

Noah saw Samuel's scowl then replied, "I'll look forward to it, David."

Samuel nodded in Noah's direction, as if to bid him farewell, and followed David and the aide out of the room.

"Where's Carley?" Noah asked Lillian as Rebecca continued to look like a child who had been caught doing something naughty.

"She's not coming until this afternoon," Lillian said. There was no mistaking the disappointment that registered on Noah's face.

"I should go," Rebecca said. She edged toward the door. "Good-bye, Noah."

Noah smiled at her. "Thank you for coming, Rebecca."

Lillian felt bad about leaving Noah abruptly, but the doctors made rounds between six and seven o'clock, and she wanted to be in David's room when they arrived.

"Noah, I'm going to go, too, so that I don't miss the doctors making their rounds," she said. "But I will be back later to check on you."

Noah nodded and forced a smile, but Lillian could still see the sadness in his eyes.

When Lillian left the room, Rebecca was standing in the hallway waiting for her.

"*Mamm* was here earlier," she said. "And Mary Ellen and Sadie got a ride from Paul Shank last night. I don't think Samuel knows, but Ivan was here yesterday, too, and—"

"Rebecca," Lillian interrupted. It was clear how distraught Rebecca was. "It's all right."

"But Samuel . . . ," she said, shaking her head. "We know how he feels. And what if Bishop Ebersol finds out?"

"Everyone is confused, Rebecca," Lillian said. "Even Samuel went up against the bishop recently. What Noah did for David is an incredible thing. We should have been here for him more than we have been. That's my opinion. Instead, we all relied on Carley, and she's not even his family. Do you know that right now she is at his clinic trying to get it ready for him? He doesn't even know about it." She paused. "So don't tell anyone. She wants to surprise him."

"I won't," Rebecca said. "Do you think they're courting, Noah and Carley?"

"I don't think so—yet. But I wouldn't be surprised if it gets to that."

Rebecca smiled. "*Gut, wunderbaar gut.* I like Carley."

Lillian suspected it would ease all their consciences if Noah found love and happiness.

Carley noticed right away that Dana's demeanor was different, quieter. She was sure Noah had talked to her, and she couldn't help but feel sorry for the girl. But after a while, Dana opened up to her, sharing her dreams for the future, how she hoped to attend college someday. Carley even found herself talking about the accident.

They were about three hours into sorting boxes in the back of the clinic when they heard buggy wheels rolling into the parking area. Jenna's ears perked up from where she was sitting on the floor coloring.

"Someone's here." Jenna headed toward the door.

"They must be Amish, whoever it is," Dana added. She followed Carley down the hallway.

Before they reached the main door into the clinic, Carley stopped and peered through the large glass windows of the waiting room. Four Amish women stepped out of a gray buggy.

"What are they doing here?" Carley recognized the women as Sadie and Rebecca, along with teenagers Linda and Miriam.

She scooted past Dana and bolted out the door. *Maybe they have news about Noah or David.*

"What's wrong?" she asked. "Is it Noah or David?"

The women looked from one to the other, but it was the spirited teenager who spoke up. "Nothing is wrong. Everything is *gut*. We are here to help," Linda reported.

"I told a few people." Rebecca shrugged apologetically. "But they won't tell anyone," she added. "Mary Ellen wanted to come, too, but she is carin' for the *boppli* today, so I brought the girls and Sadie."

Carley noticed the foursome peering over her shoulder, and she turned to see Dana and Jenna behind her.

"This is Dana and Jenna," Carley told the group. "They're friends of Noah's."

"Nice to meet you," Sadie said while the other women nodded in Dana's direction.

Jenna walked blankly past them all, homing in on the large horse in front of the buggy.

"Don't get too close, Jenna," Carley warned as Jenna continued toward the large animal.

Linda followed Jenna. "This is Whistle," Linda said. "We call 'im that 'cause he sounds like he's whistling sometimes when he snorts." She looked down at Jenna. "Wanna pet 'im?"

"Yes," Jenna cooed. But then she hesitated to move closer to the massive creature.

Linda scooped Jenna into her arms and instructed her where to scratch Whistle.

"Well, let's be gettin' started," Sadie said. "Show us where to begin."

Carley and Dana locked eyes and smiled.

They just might get this clinic ready in time after all.

———————

When Carley walked into Noah's hospital room later that afternoon, she hoped she didn't look as exhausted as she felt. She still couldn't get over the way the women had stepped up to help. They'd certainly made a huge dent in the project. All the boxes were unpacked and things sorted according to room. Even the medical equipment had been placed in each examining room. Carley was optimistic she and Dana could finish before Noah was released from the hospital in a few days.

"Hi, there," she said to Noah. He was watching TV but quickly looked her way at the sound of her voice. She sat down in the chair next to the bed and crossed her legs.

"Busy day?" He almost sounded irritated.

Maybe he was hurt that she hadn't called or been by to see him yet today. Or perhaps he was expecting a hello kiss or some offer of affection. But she knew she needed to pull back.

"Yes, it was," she answered. "How are you feeling?"

"Like I'm ready to get out of here. So I didn't hear from you. Did you and Dana get the boxes carried inside the clinic yesterday?"

"Yes, everything is inside. The boxes weren't as heavy as they looked."

Noah shook his head. "I hate that you girls had to do that. Did Samuel help you?"

"No. Dana and I were able to do it."

Noah reached for her hand and locked his fingers with hers. "Thank you for doing that, Carley," he said sincerely. "I haven't seen Dana or Jenna today either. Thank Dana if you see her." He paused. "By the way, I talked to Dana last night about the girl-friend story. I guess it took me awhile to figure out why she said that, but clearly she wanted me all to herself." He smiled. "Anyway, I think things will be fine. How is she acting around you?"

"She seems okay. She'll be here at the hospital later to see you." Carley pulled her eyes from his gaze. When she looked back, his expression had intensified.

"Carley, is something wrong?" he asked.

"No, just tired. But I wanted to see you."

He smiled slightly and shook his head.

"What?" she asked when he didn't say anything.

"Guess we're going to have to talk about it."

"Talk about what?" Her fingers nervously twitched within his.

Noah brought her hand to his lips, kissing it tenderly. "I don't want things getting weird between us. You've gone from being glued to my bedside to disappearing for almost twenty-four hours. Evidently I spooked you somehow."

"No, no. I'm not spooked. We're friends." As much as she'd like to pursue more, what was the point?

"Friends?" He sounded disappointed, but quickly smiled and added, "Okay. Friends."

She returned the smile, but his eyes darkened. "You're leaving soon, aren't you?"

His fingers were still interwoven with hers. "Actually, I extended my trip. I wanted to help Lillian for a while—and you."

"Get me back on my feet and settled in? And then you're going to leave?"

"Well, I do have a job and a life in Houston." Lies. There was no life for her there anymore.

"You want to stay, Carley. I can see it in your eyes." He arched his brows, almost daring her to argue. "This is a great place to live."

"I'm going to stay. Until you and David are better."

So many things need to be said, Noah thought. But Carley was uncomfortable, and he didn't want to push her too much. She might bolt out of the room, and he didn't want that.

Nothing felt more unmanly than lying in a hospital bed. He would wait until he was back on his feet before he pursued this any further. Besides, knowing the nurse would enforce the visitation rules, he wanted to spend as much time with Carley as possible. And he didn't want her to feel pressured. He just wanted to get to know her better.

"What are your plans for tomorrow?" He still had hold of her hand and gently entwined his fingers with hers, without much of a response.

She took a deep breath, raked her free hand through her hair, and avoided looking at him. "Lots to do tomorrow. So I probably won't be back to see you until this time tomorrow."

"Lots to do helping Lillian?"

"Uh-huh."

She wasn't telling the truth, and she looked like a woman on trial. "Carley, what's going on with you? Why are you so nervous?"

"I'm not nervous."

Why couldn't she say what was on her mind? She was back-tracking, which in turn made him think about retreating. He had always been able to keep his emotions at a manageable level when it came to women; perhaps he needed to remind himself of that.

But he knew why she was refusing to open up to him. She just wasn't ready to talk about it.

Don't push her.

"Tomorrow when I come back to the hospital, do you want me to bring you something to eat?" she asked out of the blue. "I know that hospital food can get old."

She continued to avoid eye contact, and her hand felt like a limp noodle within his.

"Sure. That'd be great," he answered, then deliberated for a moment.

He let go of her hand, cupped her cheek, and guided her face to his. She hesitated when his lips drew near, but then her eyes finally locked with his in the familiar way they had in the past. Gently he touched his lips to hers. There was no resistance, no attempt to pull away. Just him loving her, and her loving him. He could feel it.

"Carley," he said softly. She pulled back slightly, but her eyes stayed with him. "I know you don't want to leave here. I know you don't want to leave me either."

Noah watched her take another deep breath. But she didn't say anything.

"Say it, Carley. Tell me there's something more than friendship going on between us." He knew he shouldn't be pushing her, but he kept on. "Talk to me, Carley—the way you did when I was in the coma. I could hear bits and pieces, and—"

Carley pulled away from him and jumped out of the chair. "What?" *Oh no! This is terrible.*

She was consumed by embarrassment, and her heart was pounding in her chest. How much had he heard while he was in the coma? Could people really hear when they weren't fully conscious? Her mind was running amok and she was trying to recall her conversation with Lillian—the very personal moment when she'd told Lillian that she cared about Noah.

Oh no. What else did I say? Closing her eyes, she tried to remember.

She could hear him saying her name, but her mind was still traveling back to her conversation with Lillian—when she was speaking freely, assuming Noah wasn't listening.

"Carley, listen to me," Noah said as he reached out his hand to her. She backed away, out of his reach.

What else did I say?

They had talked about God, about how she felt God had let her down. They had talked about the possibility of things developing past friendship between her and Noah. She cringed as she recalled crying to Lillian about how she couldn't have children. It was all very personal. How much had he heard?

"Carley . . ." His eyes pleaded with her, but she was too embarrassed to talk about this right now. "Don't run away. Everything is fine. Come here and sit down. Please, Carley. Sweetie, just come sit down."

She backed up another step.

His gentle tone. The way he called her *sweetie. Oh, Noah, what's happening with us? I want to love you. I want you to love me.* And love might be enough in the short term, but Noah wanted a family. Had he not heard the part about her being unable to have children? Did he not understand that she was an incomplete woman?

"Don't go, Carley. I just caught some of the things that were being said around me. I heard you say you cared about me. I'm sure of that. Tell me, Carley. Tell me you feel what I'm feeling."

"You don't know everything, Noah," she cried. "You don't know everything. Otherwise, you wouldn't be telling me all this."

Her tears were threatening to spill over. She bolted out of the room.

19

CARLEY COULDN'T FACE NOAH, BUT SHE WAS GOING TO make sure the clinic was organized before she left Lancaster County. Dana and the other women were hard workers, but Carley was the one who knew how things should be set up.

After Rebecca, Sadie, and the girls left for the day, Carley and Dana decided to shirk their other responsibilities and keep working. They were fairly certain they could finish the clinic that afternoon. Carley called Lillian, who encouraged her to finish, and Dana phoned her boss at the market. While her employer was not as eager as Lillian to comply, Dana ended up getting the afternoon off.

"It's been three days, Carley," Dana said. "I don't understand how you can hurt Noah like this, not going to see him at the hospital. He told me what's going on."

Carley crawled out from underneath the receptionist's desk after plugging in the telephone and fax machine, bumping her head on the way up. "What did he tell you?"

Dana tossed a box of rubber bands onto the desk, clearly irritated. "He told me he thinks you could be the one. And that you won't even talk to him." She paused and threw Carley a look. "Why even bother with this clinic? You're leaving tomorrow."

"You're nineteen years old. What do you know about relationships?" Carley spouted at Dana, standing up to face her. How interesting that Dana was pushing this—she'd have thought the girl would be glad she was leaving.

"Noah was supposed to be released today, but his incision came open and he's going to have to stay until tomorrow." Dana eyed Carley as if she were the enemy, then added, "I might be only nineteen years old, Carley, but I've been through more than most people much older than me. And no matter what . . ." Her eyes teared up. "I want Noah to be happy. He deserves that. And if I can't be the one . . ."

Carley's heart suddenly ached for Dana, and she realized how far they'd come. She ran her hands through her hair. "Noah is a good man, and—"

"Do you love him?" Dana asked aggressively.

Carley closed her eyes. "I don't know," she whispered.

"Go talk to him, Carley."

Carley ignored her comment and attempted to change the subject. "Noah would have struggled to get everything organized and ready. Since Mary Ellen, Rebecca, Sadie, and the girls have been taking turns coming by and helping, we're going to be finished today. When Noah gets released, he'll have to rest at home, but the clinic will be ready when he is."

"So you're just going to split tomorrow without saying good-bye to Noah? That's horrible, Carley." Dana was clearly disgusted.

"Noah's family is coming around. Most of them, anyway. Hopefully Samuel will open up more to Noah. His mother, sisters, Ivan, Sadie, and other members of the community are spending some time with Noah on the sly. Mary Ellen said yesterday that Bishop Ebersol is looking the other way. For now, anyway." Carley shrugged. "So hopefully it will all work out for Noah."

"Rebecca told me at the hospital that they will still only use Noah's clinic for emergencies," Dana said as she stacked pens and pencils in a holder on the desk. "That stinks. I don't care what the bishop says. Everyone's worked so hard to get this place ready. Why would the women help like that but then not come to the clinic?" She paused then glared at Carley. Under her breath she added, "Guess it's kinda like you working so hard and then leaving."

"Dana, I'm well aware that you're angry with me, but I have a life and a job in Houston. Everyone is expecting me back. Like I said, Noah's family is around. Plus he has you and Jenna." She turned her attention to the fax machine and unwound the cord. "And I figured you'd be ready for me to go."

Dana folded her arms across her chest and raised her chin. Carley prepared herself for an attack, but Dana surprised her. "He knows you can't have children," she announced.

Her eyes widening, Carley felt her heart flutter. "What?"

"Noah said that he could hear things going on around him sometimes. He said he thought he was dreaming part of the time. But when you left so upset the other day, he asked Lillian if it was true that you couldn't have children. Lillian told him it was. He doesn't care, Carley. He cares for you and wants to see where this is going."

Lillian told him? Why hadn't her friend confessed that bit of information over supper the past few nights? After working at the clinic in the mornings, Carley had been staying at the farm in the afternoons while Lillian and Samuel went to the hospital.

Suppertime was their only time to really talk. She knew why Lillian hadn't said anything—because Lillian knew Carley was right about this, that Noah's future would never be complete if she stayed.

"So everyone has just been talking behind my back, planning out what I should do with my life?" Her eyes started to burn, and she blinked back the tears. "I know everyone is just trying to help, Dana, and find a happy ending, but Noah has said repeatedly that he wants a family, and I can't give him any children." She paused. "I'm not going to subject him to a life with me that's void of something he has always wanted. I know what it's like to want a child desperately and not be able to have one. I think about it every day. I'm not doing that to Noah. I care about him enough to let him go before things get out of hand."

Dana sat down in the chair, her eyes glued to Carley. "What about adoption?"

"Waiting lists are long for adoption. I hope that's an option for me someday. But Noah will go on to meet someone else and they will have lots of babies, I'm sure. If he settled down with me, he would eventually resent me, even if he doesn't mean to."

Dalton had promised to love her no matter what.

Just words.

"Wow. You really don't know Noah as well as you think."

Carley lowered her head. She didn't know what else to say. Didn't Dana realize her heart was breaking? It would be incredibly hard to walk away from Noah.

"Aren't you going to miss us?" Jenna asked Carley.

Carley admired their project for the last time. They were done, and it looked fantastic. With the exception of some medical equipment they were unsure how to set up, the clinic was ready. In their effort to keep things Plain, there were no pictures on the white walls and no television in the waiting room. Two potted green ivies were in the corners. There were ten functional brown chairs—five against each wall—with one coffee table in the middle of the room. Stacked in three piles were various Christian books and magazines, all of which Carley found in one of the boxes Noah had in the back.

"Of course I'm going to miss you." Carley moved toward the door, the ache in her heart growing with each step.

After locking the door behind the three of them, she scooped Jenna into her arms. "I'm going to miss you very much."

Jenna squeezed Carley's neck. "I think you should marry Dr. Noah and stay here."

"Oh, Jenna." Carley pulled her close. She glanced at Dana and then back at Jenna. "But I can write you letters and maybe even come back and visit. Would you like that?"

Carley's heart sank when Jenna's eyes filled with water. She moved toward the two cars, Jenna still in her arms. Dana shrugged when Carley looked to her for guidance.

She leaned against Dana's car, kissed Jenna on the cheek, and realized how much she cared about Dana, Jenna, and the other members of the community. She wasn't just leaving Noah—she was leaving her friends. They all felt more like family than what she had waiting for her back in Houston.

Carley blinked back her own tears and whispered, "Don't cry, Jenna. Please."

She had just buckled the sniffling girl into the car when her cell phone rang.

"If that's Noah, Carley, you need to answer it," Dana instructed. "He said he's been calling you and you won't answer."

Carley snatched the phone from the pocket of her blue jeans. "It's not Noah. It's my brother. I'll call him back. He's probably just wanting to confirm when my flight gets in tomorrow." She pushed the Mute button.

She returned her attention to comforting Jenna, who calmed down after Carley promised to call and write. She closed the car door and walked around to Dana's side of the car.

"Look, I can't talk to him, Dana," she said. "If I see him or talk to him, I'll stay, and that wouldn't be fair to him in the long run. I've listened to the messages he's left over and over again. This is hurting me, and you being angry is just making me feel worse." She hung her head as the tears finally spilled over.

Dana wrapped her arms around Carley. "I didn't like you very much at first." She paused. "And you know why. But now I think you should stay. I know I'm just a kid to you, but I'm really going to miss you. It's been fun working with you on the office."

Carley returned the hug. "You're a kid who's been through a lot and who is smarter than most at your age. I'm going to miss you too."

Carley pulled into the driveway at Lillian and Samuel's, and she knew it was going to be even more difficult to say good-bye to Lillian. Watching Dana and Jenna drive off had been tough.

She sat in the car with her head resting on the steering wheel until she heard the screen door slam. She looked up to see Lillian standing on the porch, bouncing Anna on her hip.

"You look exhausted," Lillian said when Carley trudged up the steps and onto the porch.

"But the clinic looks great. And it will be all ready for Noah when he's well enough to work."

"It's a *wunderbaar gut* thing you did, Carley."

"I had lots of help." She sat down in one of the rocking chairs on the porch as Lillian paced with Anna.

"But none of it would have happened without you. Somehow you seem to be the glue that holds everything together. And I don't mean just the clinic. You've influenced everyone around here—challenged them to rethink certain issues. Even my husband seems to be second-guessing some of his decisions."

"I don't know about all that," Carley said.

She paused and considered telling Lillian about the letter she'd found and read, but decided against it. "Oh, by the way—I put those books you gave me to read to Jenna back in your room. I laid them on the nightstand." She intentionally placed the books on the nightstand on Samuel's side of the bed—with *My Family* on the top, the letter protruding from within the pages.

"*Ya, danki.* I found them. I put them in a box with all of David's other books." Lillian shook her head. "I've been telling Samuel to store those, but they're still sitting in the corner of our bedroom."

Good! There is still hope that Samuel will find the letter, Carley thought. She moved along to another subject that was weighing on her mind. "Dana said you told Noah I couldn't have children."

"*Ya*, I did." Lillian sat down in the other rocker. "The rest of the family is still worried about Bishop Ebersol, so they keep their visits with Noah brief. But I've been checking on him, and we've talked. Carley, I understand that you think you are sparing him a life of misery by leaving, but the man is crazy *in lieb* with you. Oh, he won't admit it, but I can tell. And he's very hurt that you stopped coming to the hospital and that you won't return his calls."

Carley put her face in her hands. "Lillian, if I see him, it will be too hard for me to go. I've even prayed about this, and I'm not getting any answers." She lifted her face and looked at Lillian. "Besides, we haven't known each other that long. I'm sure that once Noah has recovered and is back on his feet, he'll realize this isn't love at all. He just needed someone. Now he has his family— at least some of the time. Trust me, Lillian. I know how important it is for a man to have a complete woman." She fought the tremble in her voice. "And I'm not complete. Dalton—"

"Carley," Lillian interrupted, "Noah is not Dalton. You don't know that he wouldn't want to be with you no matter what."

There were those words again—*no matter what*. She offered Lillian a half smile, letting her know she appreciated the effort, even though her friend was wrong in her assumptions. Carley knew better. She changed the subject.

"Has Samuel spent much time with Noah?"

"No." Lillian shook her head and sighed. "I sense that he wants to, but he's not sure how to go about it. Maybe with time . . ."

"I hope they will be close again someday. Noah loves all his siblings, but there seems to be something special between him and Samuel." She thought again of the letter.

"Let's get back to you," Lillian said. "I would not be a *gut* friend if I didn't tell you I think you're making a mistake."

"You are a good friend. And I feel terrible that I'm leaving before David gets home, and that—"

"If you're going to feel bad about anything, it should be about leaving without at least saying good-bye to Noah."

"I'm going to send Noah a long letter when I get back to Houston, a safe distance away," Carley said. "Over time we will both get on with our lives and realize this is for the best."

It was barely daybreak the next morning when Samuel stowed Carley's luggage in the trunk and helped Lillian get Anna fastened into her car seat. The hospital was on the way to the airport in Philadelphia, so Carley could drop them there before catching her eight o'clock flight.

Taking a last look at the farmhouse, Carley realized their lives would all go on without her there. They would all continue helping one another, despite the challenges, and they would all be fine. The Plain life of the Old Order district provided them with everything they needed—nourishment of faith, hope, and love.

And even though Noah had fled the Amish ways to pursue his own calling, his spiritual roots were firmly grounded. Carley knew she would never understand the practice of shunning, but in her heart, she had to believe that Noah's family would find a way to accept him into their lives. He needed them.

Why had God led her to this place? Just to tempt her with all that she could never have? A kind, loving man. A community filled with simple peace and goodwill. Real friends who came together during times of need. How could this be God's will for her? There was a hopelessness about the whole situation. When would she get her shot at happiness?

What if this is it and I'm walking away from it?

She would go back to Houston, to work and her memories, and things would be as they were before she left. Petty people backstabbing each other at work. Her brother, Adam, always treating her like a child. And no one for Carley to take care of—something she found more rewarding than anything else about her stay.

Last night she had prayed for Lillian, Noah, David, and all the family. David's body was fighting to reject Noah's kidney, but the doctors had said they expected that and, all things considered, David was doing very well. Carley wished she could stay until David returned home. She wished she could stay to see the look on Noah's face when he saw the clinic for the first time. She wished . . . so many things.

A piercing sadness burrowed deep within her as Carley forced herself to get in the car and head to the hospital.

Conversation was limited on the way to Philadelphia. Anna fussed most of the way, and Lillian tended to her. Samuel was pleasant enough, but they all seemed preoccupied.

"David is expecting you to come say good-bye, Carley," Lillian said when Carley attempted to pull into the patient drop-off lane at the hospital. "He'd be very disappointed if you didn't. You should still have plenty of time to make your flight."

Carley turned to the right and into the visitor parking area. How could she even have considered leaving without saying good-bye to David?

She knew how—for fear of running into Noah. But seeing David was the right thing to do, and as difficult as it would be, she was not going to walk down the hallway to Noah's room.

I'm a horrible person, she thought. *But I just can't.*

David was sleeping when they walked into his room. Lillian kissed him on the forehead, and he stirred.

"Carley is headed to the airport," Lillian told him. "She wanted to come tell you good-bye."

"I'm so glad you're doing well," Carley said as she approached David's bedside and clutched his hand. "I'm going to miss all you guys."

David rubbed his eyes and focused. "I thought you were gonna be stayin' longer," he said. "I thought maybe . . ."

Carley cut him off. "I have to get back to work," she said, hoping she could put together some sort of article for Matt during the three-hour plane ride. "But I'm going to write letters, and Lillian is going to keep me updated about how you're doing. And I love it here, so I'll come back to visit."

David nodded.

Carley leaned down and gave him a gentle hug. "I'm going to have to go so I don't miss my flight." She glanced at her watch, realizing she was pushing it.

She turned to Samuel and, after a slight hesitation, wrapped her arms around him. "Thank you for everything, Samuel. For opening your home to me and for being a friend. Don't worry about the article. You'll be pleased—if I ever get it written." She smiled.

Carley could hear Lillian sniffling.

"Take care, Carley," Samuel said when Carley pulled away to face Lillian.

She eased her arms around Lillian and Anna and said, "No crying," even though she felt a tear trickling down her own cheek.

"I'm going to miss you. Thank you, Carley. For everything."

Carley forced herself to pull free. "I'll write. And while you have that cell phone, call to keep me updated about David."

"I will," Lillian promised.

Carley was waving as she backed out of the room. Her heart shattered at the realization she was leaving them all.

Once in the hallway, she glanced down the corridor toward Noah's room. A few people hurried by her. It was still early, and the hospital was fairly quiet. She stood, her feet rooted to the floor. She couldn't seem to make a move.

Carley uprooted herself after a nurse accidentally bumped into her shoulder. She made her way toward the elevator and waited for the doors to open. Tears were building in the corner of each eye, and she could feel a complete meltdown coming. She drew in a deep breath and attempted to blink back the sadness. She was dabbing at her eyes as she entered the elevator. There was only one person in it.

Noah.

She instinctively looked over her shoulder to consider an escape. Too late. The doors closed behind her.

"Hello, Noah," she said, standing beside him, avoiding his eyes. He was still in a robe and slippers and waiting to be released sometime today, she assumed.

Slowly Noah moved toward the buttons on the front elevator wall. He pushed one of them. Carley felt the elevator come to a halt, but the doors didn't open.

Noah put his hands on his hips and faced her. "I'd tell you this was some sort of strange coincidence, but I don't think it's a coincidence at all. The fact that you were going to leave without saying good-bye to me, without talking to me, seeing me, or returning my phone calls—no, I don't think this is any twist of fate."

"I'm sorry, Noah," she said, wishing he would back away from her.

Instead, he drew even closer. "I'm so angry with you, Carley. If I'd had the strength to leave the hospital before today, I would have come and found you. Just getting a newspaper from downstairs took a lot of effort." He glared into her eyes. "What have you been doing for the past four days? Were you so busy that you couldn't answer your phone or return my calls?"

She leaned slightly away from him. "I have been busy, and you were doing so much better that I didn't think you needed me to—"

"Well, I do need you," he interrupted, his tone laced with bitterness.

She couldn't back up any farther. With only inches between them, she looked into Noah's hardened eyes. She deserved this. "I'm sorry, Noah."

Noah cocked his head to one side, his hands still firmly planted on his hips. His eyes began to soften. "I know you are," he said, running a hand briefly through his overgrown hair. "But you are running out on us before *us* had a chance to get off the ground." He gently clutched both of her arms, his eyes fused with hers. "Don't do this, Carley. I know we haven't known each other very long, but I know how I feel." He paused. "Give us a chance."

Carley lowered her head, only to have Noah gently lift her chin until her eyes again locked with his. His lips met tenderly with hers. "Don't go, Carley," he whispered. "Stay."

There was nothing she wanted to do more in the world. The

feel of his arms wrapped around her inspired glorious visions of what a life with Noah would be like—filled with love, safety, peacefulness, and a simpler way of life.

A life without children, she reminded herself. She pushed him away.

"I can't stay, Noah. I have my job. And my brother is in Houston, and . . . ," she rambled, hoping he would step back. He held his position a few inches away, making it more difficult for her to think.

"Stop it, Carley," he said sharply. "Let's not do this—beat around the bush. You're leaving because you think that since you're unable to have children, I could never be happy with you." He pointed a finger in her face. "And you are wrong. I want *you*."

"You say that now, Noah! But what about a year from now? Five years from now? You would resent me for not being able to give you children. I've heard you mention plenty of times over the past month how badly you want to have children."

"Do you want children, Carley?"

Her emotions spilled over in an almost hysterical outpouring of words she didn't plan for. "More than anything in the world!" she cried. "I've always wanted children. And I can't have any, ever! I've been angry at God about that, but I'm trying to accept that He has another plan for me—something other than raising a family. But, Noah, you shouldn't be deprived of a family!" She brought her hands to her face.

"Carley," Noah whispered as he wrapped his arms around her and squeezed. "Families are not measured by DNA. Families come in all shapes and sizes." He eased her away from him and smiled. "Stay with me, Carley."

"I have to go. I'm going to miss my plane."

"Good." Noah folded his arms across his chest.

"Noah," Carley began, "we've known each other for six weeks. That's not very long. We will both go on to meet other people. A month from now, you'll be running your clinic. You're starting to reestablish relationships with your family. Things are turning around for you, and you'll have the life you want."

"First of all, I don't think I can get the clinic ready to open within a month. You saw the mess."

Carley smiled inwardly in spite of the pain she was feeling,

"Stay, Carley. I guarantee that a month from now—or a year from now, or ten—I'm not going to feel different."

"How could you possibly know that?" Her heart was breaking. Noah was everything she'd ever wanted in a man.

"How do I know?" His eyes met hers. "Because I love you."

Her final conversation with Dalton rushed through her mind. *"I love you, Carley, more than anything in the world,"* Dalton had said shortly after her accident. *"But I want a son. A son of my own to carry on my legacy. I just assumed that someday we would get married and have children, and I don't think I can live without that reality."*

"But we can adopt, Dalton," she had begged.

"It's not the same," Dalton told her as he walked away from her—forever.

Carley pressed her lips firmly together, gathering false strength, and said, "I don't love you, Noah—whatever you think you feel or think you heard me say. I care about you very much, and I'm glad you're doing better, but—"

"You're lying." Noah edged closer again. "Stay, Carley." His eyes held hers. "Or go home, gather a few things, and come back.

I know you have loose ends to take care of in Houston. So how
long before you can come back?"

"I'm not coming back, Noah." She glanced at her watch. "I'm
going to miss my plane."

His pleading eyes, his handsome face—it was all getting too
difficult for her to bear. She was trembling as she gently pushed
him away, stepped to the row of buttons, and pressed the one for
the lobby. Then she slowly turned to face him and stared into
eyes that were darkening with each passing second and an expression that begged her to reconsider.

"Don't do this, Carley. Don't walk out of my life and let me
think I imagined what I know we both feel. Tell me you love me."

She couldn't take it anymore. She loved him, and she didn't
think she could contain her feelings any longer, no matter how
wrong it would be to selfishly lock him into a life with her.

"Noah—," she began.

The elevator doors slid open behind her. She took two steps
backward, clearing the doors. Their eyes were locked when the
doors closed between them.

She was afraid the look on Noah's face would haunt her forever. Tears trickling down her cheeks, she stared blankly at the
closed elevator doors in front of her.

20

DURING THE PAST MONTH, CARLEY HAD REREAD THE LETTER from Noah over a dozen times. Curled up in her bed beneath the Amish quilt he'd bought for her at the mud sale, holding the worn paper in her hands, she saw his face clearly as the day she left him standing in the elevator.

She glanced around the bedroom she'd grown up in. She had come home to the big empty house with a shattered heart and had fallen into her old life.

Matt was pleased with the Amish story she wrote on the plane ride home, publishing it the first week she returned to work. He'd given her the promised assignments, plus a few more. As before, employees bickered over who deserved the best news stories and other mundane issues.

Adam continued to hover over her like she was incapable of taking care of herself. She thought about the clinic and all she'd done to get it ready. She wished Adam could have seen the way she and the other women whipped the place into shape—lifting the heavy equipment, organizing each room, setting up a filing system, and tackling all the other tasks required to get the Stoltzfus Clinic ready. Not to mention the way Carley had tended to David and Noah, helped with the household chores, and lived without electricity or modern conveniences.

Looking back at all the events of her stay, she realized she'd been exhausted most of the time, but never happier. One thing she knew—staying busy and taking care of the needs of others had kept her own issues at bay.

She looked around her bedroom again. So many wonderful memories in this big house. But she was reminded daily that it was just that—a big empty house. She missed her mother more than ever. Her anxiety problems had resurfaced, with visions of the red truck rolling through her mind at times. Funny how her vivid recollections of the accident had all but ceased in Lancaster County. She'd reached a point while she was there when she hadn't had time to focus on herself. Now, even with her job, she had too much time to think.

Life was different in Amish Country. Despite a demanding schedule that she knew would push some city folks to hightail it home, her new friends always made time for reflection, prayer, and appreciation of each other. Those times of thanksgiving were an important part of a busy day's schedule. What she wouldn't give for one day of all that.

And everyone helped each other. The food tasted better too—all homegrown and homemade. Carley could still taste Lillian's bread, melted butter heaped atop a slice fresh from the oven. Rhubarb pie. Shoofly pie. And Lillian's famous raisin puffs.

And despite the controversy about the shunning, people in the community still managed to come to Noah's aid when he needed the love of family and friends. It was difficult for them to defy the bishop, but in the end their own good natures overcame their hesitation. There was a fellowship Carley didn't think she would find anywhere else.

Two weeks ago she'd attempted to help a colleague with a news story that was going to require a ton of research. The veteran reporter was quick to tell Carley he didn't need her help, that all she was trying to do was to get credit for the story. In the world of the Amish, not only would they have offered to help with anything—they would have declined credit for their efforts. Carley didn't want credit; she just wanted to help. She needed to do something—something that made a difference.

Lillian kept her updated about David. Just yesterday Lillian had called to tell Carley that he was doing so well at home that she was returning the borrowed cell phone—after jokingly saying she would miss that particular modern convenience.

Each time she talked to Lillian, Carley asked about Noah. Lillian said she hadn't seen much of him, but from what she had heard, he was doing well. In a polite way, Lillian always tried to coax Carley to come see for herself.

Knowing the Amish community self-insured, Carley had tactfully asked Lillian if they were all going to survive the financial hit of the transplant. She knew from her own hospital stay—and her mother's—how hard the financial aspect could bear down on a family. She suspected the cost of the transplant had been a harsh reality for the Old Order district. Carley also knew David's medications would continue to run around a thousand dollars per month. Lillian had tearfully shared with her that an anonymous person was taking care of that expense. Both women knew there was no anonymity about it.

Carley's young friend Dana, whom she'd kept in touch with, wasn't always so polite when it came to Noah. "He misses you, Carley. It's wrong for you not to be here," Dana had said during their last phone call about a week before.

She looked again at the letter. Six rough drafts later, she still hadn't mailed Noah a return missive. No words seemed to express what was in her heart. But as she unfolded the pages, she remained in awe of the way Noah was able to express himself.

She really didn't have to read the letter. She knew it by heart.

Dear Carley,

It's only been a week, and I miss you even more than I thought I would. Since you haven't returned my calls, I'm sending you this letter, and I will pray to hear from you. After my release from the hospital, Dana took me by the clinic. To say that I was shocked and touched beyond words would be an understatement. What you all did represents the unconditional love I have been searching for with my family. Unconditional love means there are no boundaries when it comes to matters of the heart.

Such is my love for you—unconditional.

Not a day goes by that I don't think of you, miss you. I regret that we didn't get to date like a regular couple. Instead, we were forced into circumstances beyond our control. It made me realize that life is short. My favorite quote: "Life is not measured by the number of breaths we take, but by the moments that take our breath away." You, Carley, take my breath away.

You think my life will be incomplete if I have no children of my own. I know in my heart that my life will be incomplete without you by my side. Let me take you in my arms and love you forever. Be my family, Carley. God will see to the rest.

I am opening the clinic for business on August 15. Dr. Bolton said I should be able to resume all activity by then. I'm a good doctor, but I'm somewhat lacking in organizational skills. I need a good person to act as my office manager. Know anyone who might be interested? Qualifications for the job are: They must be beautiful, like Carley Marek. They must be kind and put the needs of others first, like Carley Marek. They must be so unselfish that they would give up love based on what they think the other person needs, like Carley Marek.

If you know anyone who fits that description, I would welcome the opportunity to talk to that person.

Perhaps I imagined what you were feeling. I don't think so, but I must consider the possibility. If I was right—that you love me the way I love you—then please call or write.

With all my love,
Noah

"No, my love. You weren't imagining anything," Carley said aloud. She pressed the letter firmly against her chest.

She was jarred from her thoughts by the unwelcome chirp of her cell phone. She reached over and, for the first time in a month, didn't check the caller ID.

"Hello," she said. *Please be Noah.*

"Everything okay? You doing all right?"

"Adam, why wouldn't I be doing all right?" She rolled her eyes and then sighed loudly enough for him to hear.

"You just haven't seemed the same since you got back from your trip. I was just checking on you."

"I'm not the same!"

"I knew it. What's wrong?"

"Nothing is wrong, Adam. I just don't need you checking on me constantly. You act like I'm incapable of taking care of myself."

Silence.

"I'm sorry, Adam. I know you love me, but I need to take care of myself."

"You're all I've got left of my family, Carley," Adam said sadly. "And after Mom dying and everything you've been through . . ."

"I don't need to keep being reminded of that. I live with it daily. I look around this house at all the pictures of our family—of Mom and Dad, of you and me. I miss Mom, Adam. I regret that I won't have a family of my own. But please quit reminding me of everything I've been through. I'm trying to move on and—"

Suddenly it hit her. She wasn't moving on. She was exactly where she was before she went to Lancaster County.

"Okay," Adam said apologetically. "Point taken. I'll try to do better."

They chatted a moment longer, then they said good-bye.

Carley snuggled beneath the quilt again. She just wanted to read Noah's letter one more time. But before that, she closed her eyes.

Dear God . . .

August fifteenth. Noah had advertised within the Amish community, hoping to draw in patients. He knew most of the Amish would seek the services of a natural doctor first. But he planned to be second in line. Offering free immunizations for the children would be an incentive for the community, along with a huge reduction in typical medical fees. And almost all members of the district could reach him via horse and buggy. Noah was well aware of the bishop's rule about utilizing his services, but he planned to remain optimistic about the clinic.

In another optimistic gesture, he had ordered a desktop nameplate engraved with Carley's name. But it had been over a month since he mailed her the letter. No return phone call. No letter. What a foolish man he was. And at this point, his pride was seriously at stake.

Not quite optimistic enough to actually place the nameplate on the desk, he kept the thing stashed in the drawer of the receptionist's desk.

He heard Gloria come through the front door of the clinic.

"Good morning, Doctor," the plump, gray-haired woman announced. She smiled broadly in her colorful blue scrubs with cartoon animals splattered about. "It's our first day," she said excitedly.

"Good morning to you," he said, smiling.

Gloria Tice was close to retirement age and one of the friendliest nurses he had ever worked with. She had jumped at the chance to leave the hospital environment for something a little less fast paced. Although, looking at the scheduling book, he could see it was going to be more than just a little less fast-paced if they didn't get some more patients scheduled.

"I see that while you were here answering the phones last week, you scheduled a few appointments." Noah glanced down at the book. "Anything from the Amish?"

"No, Doctor. Only four appointments. And none of them were Plain. I know this because they all gave me insurance information."

"Any patients for today?" He feared her answer.

"No. Not for today. But give it some time. I'm sure you'll have a lot of new patients before you know it." The woman smiled enthusiastically.

Noah nodded. "I'll be in my office," he said before he headed down the hallway.

Mid-August brought scorching temperatures to Houston, often over a hundred degrees during the day. Carley was watering the front yard when she felt her cell phone vibrate in her pocket. It was Lillian.

"Wow!" Carley exclaimed when Lillian announced that she was pregnant again.

"We are so thrilled, Carley. We both want lots of children."

A quiet moment turned into awkward silence. Carley didn't want Lillian to feel uncomfortable about the issue of children. This was a joyous occasion. "Lillian, I'm so happy for you. You Amish don't waste any time, do you?"

"Haste is waste." Lillian giggled.

"Where are you calling me from?"

"The shanty at the Lapp farm." Lillian sighed. "I don't know why Samuel won't just install a phone in the barn. Years ago, that would have been unheard of, but now lots of Amish families have a phone in the barn. It's supposed to be used just for business and emergencies, but I know that's not always the case. But Samuel believes in following the rules."

"Has Samuel grown any closer to Noah?" Carley asked with hope in her heart.

"I'm afraid not. As a matter of fact, Bishop Ebersol held another meeting recently reminding the community that no one is to visit Noah's clinic unless it is a dire emergency. So everyone has pretty much steered clear of Noah."

"Even Mary Ellen and Rebecca?" Carley worried things were reverting back to the way they were before the transplant. "And what about you, Lillian? I'm sure the baby needs vaccinations. Are you using the clinic? Have you been to see Noah?"

Another sigh from Lillian. "Carley, try to understand. I might not always agree with everything Amish, but I have professed my commitment to live by the *Ordnung*. I try to abide by the rules the bishop sets forth."

"Has everyone forgotten what Noah did for David? What about what he is trying to do for the community?"

Lillian sidestepped the question. "Have *you* forgotten him?"

"No! Never," she answered. "I'll never forget Noah."

"But yet you don't talk to him either. What's the difference? I will never forget Noah or what he did for David. Explain the difference to me."

"I can't believe you have to ask me to explain it to you," Carley said. "Your son has Noah's kidney."

"And you have his heart," Lillian quickly responded.

"It's not the same, Lillian. You know that."

"All right, Carley," Lillian said in a defeated tone. "The truth is I lose sleep about this issue. I'd like nothing more than to have Noah at the house every Sunday for supper, to take Anna to his clinic or help him with whatever else he needs. I'm well aware of what he did for David. I just don't know what to do. I'm trying to do what I'm supposed to do."

"Well, don't add 'in the eyes of God' to that, because I don't see God approving of this type of behavior."

"What do you suggest I do? We all fear being shunned if we go against the rules, Carley. It would be devastating for any of us to face that kind of consequence."

"I just feel bad for Noah. That's all."

"I'm so sorry that things didn't work out between the two of you. I think you're making a mistake, Carley."

Carley glanced down the street. Pam Higgins was pulling her toddler in a bright red wagon. Leslie Hall's children were playing in the sprinkler. Donald Livingston was mowing the yard while his teenage son operated the weed eater. Families everywhere. And Carley had never felt more alone.

As if reading her mind, Lillian said, "Come home, Carley."

Cindy had called later that afternoon and asked Carley to come down the street to eat dinner with her and Adam that night. She wasn't hungry and didn't feel like going. Her head was abuzz with thoughts of Noah and Lancaster County, and she would have rather just curled up on the couch with a frozen dinner, lost in her memories. But she was unable to come up with an excuse on the spot, so she told her sister-in-law she would be there.

She knocked on the front door before she pushed it open. "It's me," she yelled.

"Hey." Cindy met her in the entryway with a guilty look on her face. "Now don't be mad," she whispered. "There's someone here I want you to meet."

"No, Cindy. You didn't," Carley groaned. This would be

Cindy's second attempt to fix Carley up with someone since Dalton left. Looking down at her tattered blue jeans, worn flip-flops, and ragged blue T-shirt, Carley added, "I don't want to meet anyone."

"He works with me at the insurance agency. He's a great guy. Very handsome and just a couple of years older than you," Cindy said. "It's just a casual thing. This is not a setup."

"That's exactly what it is." Carley shook her head.

"Come on, everyone's already at the table." Cindy nudged Carley toward the dining room.

Adam was at one end of the table. Four-year-old Jeremy and eleven-year-old Justin were sitting on one side, impatiently waiting to dive into food that was already on the table. And a blond-headed fellow was sitting across from the kids. He smiled in Carley's direction and stood up when she entered the room.

"Carley, this is Ronald Mason," Cindy said proudly. Then she smiled at Carley, as if she expected some grand reaction from her.

Whatever.

Ronald walked around to shake Carley's hand. "Nice to meet you, Carley."

Carley took his extended hand and forced a smile before taking the seat next to him. Cindy pulled out her own chair across from Adam at the other end of the table.

Carley bowed her head to pray before the meal, something she had continued to do after arriving home from Lancaster County. As she heard spoons clicking against china, she remembered where she was and looked up to see the boys diving into meatloaf, mashed potatoes, greens beans, and store-bought rolls.

Lillian had made the best meatloaf Carley ever tasted, and no one baked homemade bread the way Lillian did. Mouthwatering. She sure was missing the butter bread, along with the variety of homemade jellies, jams, and applesauce so plentiful at each meal. Even with all the time they spent at the hospital, someone in the community always made the extra effort to keep Lillian's pantry stocked and their meals prepared daily. All the women were fabulous cooks.

"So Cindy tells me you're a reporter," Ronald said.

Great. Here we go with the small talk. "Yes," she answered as she accepted a bowl of mashed potatoes from Ronald.

"Carley just did a great story about the Amish," Adam added. "Her editor ran it when she returned from a visit to Lancaster County."

"I read it," Ronald said and then smiled. "It was a really good story. Sounds like you learned a lot about their way of life while you were there." He shook his head. "They are different, no doubt."

Maybe it was the way he said *different.* A protective mechanism kicked in, something Carley didn't even realize she possessed. "What do you mean, *different?*"

Ronald swallowed. "No electricity, the funky clothes, and those buggies." He turned to Adam and grinned. "Can you imagine living like that in this day and age?"

"It's a great way to live." Carley glared in Ronald's direction. "And you'd be surprised how well they do without all the modern conveniences we have. They use propane for their stoves and refrigerators, and they have lanterns. And the horse and buggies are a great way to see the beautiful countryside, and—"

Ronald chuckled. "I think I'll hold on to my BMW and just

keep paying my ever-growing electric bill. This heat is almost unbearable."

"Our bill is outrageous." Adam spooned potatoes onto his plate and shook his head.

The subject quickly changed.

"The Amish don't believe in any connection to the outside world," Carley went on. "Their way of life is so simple. It's peaceful there, and all the members of the community help each other. They're kind and—"

"You wrote about how they shun members of their community." He raised his brows. "That doesn't seem kind to me."

Carley's article hadn't included anything about Noah's shunning. In fact, she'd barely mentioned the subject in general. Carley was sure Ronald knew what most outsiders knew about it—not much.

"Shunning is complicated," Carley said. "It's very hard for the Amish when someone is shunned. It's difficult for the person being shunned and for those doing the shunning as well."

"And yet they call themselves Christian." Ronald shook his head. "Doesn't seem very Christian to me."

"They are very Christian." Carley wished he would shut up about things he didn't know about. "As a matter of fact, they're the most Christian people I have ever met. They have unquestionable faith and believe that all things are the will of God."

"Guess it was the will of God when all those Amish kids got shot not too long ago?"

"Tragedy happens. Bad things happen to good people." Carley rested her fork on the edge of her plate and waited for a response from this jerk.

"True. I'll give you that." He paused. "But their kids are allowed to go wild when they turn sixteen. There was a documentary about that not too long ago. And you even had something about it in your story. That whatchamacallit you wrote about."

"Rumschpringe," Carley finished. "And their kids do not go wild. They are just allowed to experience some of the activities of the *Englisch* prior to their baptism into the faith, just to make sure that's the life they want."

"I bet half of them get out into the world and never return to that crazy life of no electricity and riding in buggies." Ronald chuckled, glancing toward Adam, who smiled and nodded.

"As a matter of fact, only about 10 percent choose to leave the Old Order district," Carley corrected. *So there, you jerk.*

"Oh, I'm sure more than that leave," Ronald said. "They probably try to keep it quiet, though."

Cindy looked uncomfortable and tried to change the subject. "So, Ronald, I hear you're building a new house on Burton Street?"

Ronald nodded. "Yes, it's going to be a—"

Carley wasn't finished. "No, really. It is a wonderful community. There's a peacefulness I've never known anywhere else. I was blessed to be able to live among them for so long. They had so many challenges while I was there. Medical issues. But the way they all helped each other was amazing. Why would anyone want to leave all that?"

Cindy shrugged. "I don't know." She made another attempt at redirecting the conversation. "So tell us about your new house," she said to Ronald.

"It's going to have four bedrooms, three and a half baths. It's two stories, and it will—"

"I'm going back," Carley interrupted, raising her voice above Ronald's.

This got everyone's attention.

"Back where?" Adam lowered his fork.

"To Lancaster County," Carley stated.

Adam's face expressed his surprise. "For another visit? When?"

Resting her elbows on the table, Carley folded her hands under her chin and smiled. "No, I'm going there to live."

21

AMAZING HOW QUICKLY A PERSON CAN OVERHAUL THEIR LIFE when they make up their mind, Carley thought, taking one last look around the big house she'd grown up in. Putting the house on the market had been tough. Even more challenging had been dealing with Adam over the past two weeks. Since her announcement that she was leaving, he had been trying constantly to convince her to stay in Houston. After a glimpse at life in Lancaster County, she knew it was where she was meant to be. In Paradise—with Noah, Lillian, and her new friends.

Back in her old, familiar surroundings, old patterns were resurfacing. When she was in Pennsylvania, she felt different. Alive. And she couldn't deny that Noah was largely responsible for that. She had given him every out she could think of. And still he had pleaded with her to come back. She still worried that her inability to give him children would cause problems down the road, but she was going to put her faith in God that she was doing the right thing.

Lillian had been thrilled when Carley left a message at the shanty. She'd immediately called back and offered their home as a place to stay until Carley found a place of her own. Carley made Lillian promise not to tell Noah she was coming.

Surprising him, though, suddenly seemed a bold and scary move. The phone calls from him had stopped after the first week, and she had never responded to his letter. It had been six weeks since she left Lancaster County. What if Noah had changed his mind?

She had played things out in her head a million times. With or without Noah, a change was in order.

She wasn't Amish, and although she'd tossed around the possibility, she had no plans to ever be Amish. She knew Lillian had adapted to the strict code of conduct the Amish practiced, and she wondered if her friend's lack of a religious background had made it easier for her to make the transition. Carley, however, could feel her Catholic roots reestablishing themselves as her relationship with God grew, and she wanted to nurture the beliefs she'd been raised with. Going to church since she returned had aided in that effort.

But the faith and the strength of the women in Paradise had shed light on the person she wanted to be—a woman of faith. A hardworking woman with a purpose. Helping at Noah's clinic would provide her with an opportunity to help make a difference—if the job was still available.

Matt said he understood but that he wished she would reconsider and stay longer at the newspaper until he could find a replacement, and until she was absolutely sure this move was the right thing. In the end, she gave a week's notice. An intern at her office bought her car when Carley offered him too sweet a deal to pass up. Driving the car from Texas would have been a long haul. She'd use the money to buy herself another car when she arrived in Lancaster County.

The whole thing was crazy, but she had never felt more optimistic about the future. She just hoped Noah's feelings ran as deeply as hers. She had done him wrong by leaving the way she did, not returning his phone calls, and not answering his letter. But at the time, she'd thought she was doing the right thing. She had certainly miscalculated when she assumed the miles between them would put distance in her heart.

As the cabdriver walked up the sidewalk, Carley began hauling her luggage toward the door—three overstuffed black suitcases and a small red one that she planned to carry on the plane with her. When the last suitcase was stowed in the car, she thanked the driver and headed back to the house to lock up for the last time.

She scanned the living room again then locked the door before venturing down the sidewalk to the cab . . . and to her new life.

Lillian had just served up some dippy eggs to Samuel and David when Samuel began to question her further about Carley's return visit.

"She is coming back to be with Noah, no?" Samuel buttered a piece of toast and topped it with the eggs.

"*Ya*, partly. Noah doesn't know she's coming back. She wants to surprise him. But, too, Carley wants a fresh start, and she likes it here."

Lillian couldn't help but worry if surprising Noah was a good idea. She hadn't talked to Noah much since the hospital. Who knew if Noah would still be receptive to Carley? Her hasty departure and failure to communicate had to have been quite a blow to him.

Lillian took a seat across from Samuel at the kitchen table. "I hope things will work out *gut* for Carley and Noah."

Samuel helped himself to a biscuit but didn't say anything.

"I like Carley," David said. "I'm glad she's coming back. I hope things work out for her and *Onkel* Noah too."

Lillian glanced up at Samuel, checking for a reaction to David's use of the word *onkel*, something he had done ever since the hospital. Lillian knew it was hard for David not to be able to spend time with Noah.

Lillian wondered what was going through both Samuel's and David's minds, but she remained quiet. Maybe the less they talked about it, the better.

"What time does her plane arrive?" Samuel asked.

Lillian swiped rhubarb jam on one of the biscuits. "Eleven o'clock this morning. She'll rent a car and drive here from the airport."

Samuel nodded. Lillian knew her husband well enough to know he had serious reservations about Carley staying with them again. It would throw Noah back into their lives. But despite the shunning, despite everything, Lillian knew Samuel needed Noah in his life. So did David. They all did.

Carley had made up her mind to drive straight to the clinic from the airport. She couldn't wait to see Noah, but she was also fearful of his reaction when he saw her. What if he had changed his mind? Had she overhauled her life just for him? Could she really stay in Lancaster County if her future didn't include him?

She faced all the arguments before she left Houston and concluded she could stay in Pennsylvania with or without him.

But as she neared the clinic, she worried whether she had been honest with herself. *Only one way to find out.*

She pulled into the dirt parking lot at the clinic, smiling at the freshly planted begonias around the building. Three cars were in the parking lot. One of them was Noah's, and one was Dana's. She didn't recognize the third car. A patient, she hoped.

Carley hadn't told Dana she was coming either. She knew Dana stayed in close contact with Noah, and she was afraid it would be too hard for Dana to keep the secret.

Her heart pounded against her chest as she exited the rental car and started toward the building. She could see through the glass panes and into the waiting room. An empty waiting room.

Just breathe. She tried to calm her nerves. When she'd lingered long enough to realize she had to either go in or leave, she finally swung the door open.

"I can't believe my eyes!" Dana yelled, standing up from behind the receptionist's desk. "Noah!" she hollered, bolting out of the small area and into the waiting room.

"No, wait," Carley whispered. She wasn't ready. Not yet.

Dana threw her arms around Carley. "I knew you would come eventually."

"I'm here." Carley returned the hug and looked over Dana's shoulder to see a nurse coming down the hallway.

"Noah is on the phone," the plump, gray-haired woman said. "What's all the fuss?"

"This is Carley," Dana said proudly before turning to face the nurse.

The short woman smiled and put her hands on her hips, studying Carley from head to toe. "So you're the one," she said.

Dana spoke up before Carley could comment. "Yes, she's the one." Dana turned back and faced Carley. "Jenna is going to be so excited! She asks about you all the time."

"Where is Jenna?" Carley stretched her neck to see around the nurse and down the hall.

"She started kindergarten. Can you believe it?" Dana glanced back at the woman in the hall. "Oh, I'm sorry. Carley, this is Gloria."

The friendly woman approached Carley and extended her hand. "Very nice to meet you," she said.

"I'm working here part-time until Noah can find someone," Dana said, then her eyes lit up. "Are you staying?"

"I'd like to," Carley answered sheepishly, again looking around Gloria and down the hall. Noah was bound to come down the hallway any second.

Gloria seemed to sense Carley's anticipation. "Let me go see if Dr. Stoltzfus is off the phone."

Dana wrapped her arms around Carley again. "I'm so glad you came."

"But will Noah be glad?" Carley asked.

Dana pulled back and eyed her sharply. "You hurt him pretty bad by not returning his phone calls and letter."

"I thought I was doing the right thing, Dana. I don't know, I just—"

Noah was coming down the hall. He was still in desperate need of a haircut. His shirt was wrinkled, his nametag on crooked. And he had never looked better. But his face was as serious as Carley had ever seen. She couldn't read his solemn expression, and she suddenly wanted to run out of the building. She deserved whatever wrath was coming. She deserved for him to yell at her, to tell her to leave—to go back to Houston. Could she take that kind of rejection?

As he strutted down the hall, he gave no indication that he was happy to see her.

"Hello," Carley said meekly.

He drew near her, slowing his pace. He didn't say anything, his eyes reflecting his disbelief that she was there. But was he happy or not? She couldn't tell, and she braced herself for a negative reaction.

He stopped right in front of her, squinted his eyes, and lifted his chin slightly.

"Noah." She looked up at him with eyes that begged for forgiveness. "Oh, Noah. I'm sorry. I'm so sorry. I'm so sorry. I just . . ." The knot in her throat closed off her air supply, and her eyes filled with tears. Every emotion she had experienced over the past few weeks rose to the surface. Seeing Noah only magnified her love for him, her need to be with him. Her need for him to love her back. He had offered all that, and she had walked out on him.

Noah stepped back and glared into her pleading eyes.

Carley waited.

His eyes hardened. After staring for what felt like an eternity, Noah finally spoke. "I've been mad at you for weeks."

Carley hung her head. In a last-ditch effort to redeem herself, she rambled. "I tried to answer your letter six times. The words just weren't coming. I didn't know what to say." A tear spilled over and trickled down her cheek.

"I thought you were a writer," he responded flatly.

She looked down and sniffled. "Not when it comes to matters of the heart."

Noah didn't move, so she went on. "It's just that I didn't want to mess up your life, and I just—"

"Are you staying?" He arched his brows. "Or did you just forget something?"

Carley slowly looked up at him, swiping away a tear. "Yes, I forgot something. I came back because I forgot something."

With a scowling expression, he shifted his weight. "And what exactly did you forget?"

His tone made her want to run away. But she'd already done that once. She was at least going to say her piece.

Gazing into his eyes, she said, "I forgot to tell you that when I'm with you, life seems full of hope. I forgot to tell you what a wonderful, kind man you are." She paused as another tear spilled over. "I forgot to tell you that I can't imagine spending the rest of my life without you. I forgot to tell you that . . . I love you."

Noah tilted his head to one side and rubbed his chin. "I don't know if I can forgive you."

Her heart broke. What did she expect? What a mistake she had made. "I understand," she whispered before she looked away.

But Noah gently cupped her chin and raised her face upward. She had no choice but to look at him. His expression was solemn, but his eyes had softened.

"I can think of only one thing that would let me to forgive you."

"Anything, Noah," she pleaded.

He drew her face close to his. She could feel his breath. "Marry me, Carley."

His lips met hers in a flurry of emotion as he pulled her close.

"I will, Noah," she responded in between kisses, tears pouring down her cheeks. "I will."

Carley and Lillian were taking clothes off the line later that afternoon when Carley told Lillian her news. After Lillian jumped for joy and embraced her friend, they began to tackle the particulars.

"I can't believe Noah proposed so quickly," Lillian exclaimed. She folded a towel and placed it in the laundry basket. "I'm so excited for you, Carley."

Carley's heart was relieved of the heaviness she had carried for so long, about so many things. "I was shocked, Lillian," she said. Then she giggled. "But I wasted no time saying yes. I really do love him. I just hope that my not being able to have children won't cause problems down the road. Family is so important to Noah. I'm going to have to trust in our love and trust in God."

"God will guide your way, Carley. You're a daughter of the promise now," Lillian said, smiling.

"But I'm not Amish."

"You don't have to be. You've taken a spiritual journey and put your life in God's hands."

Carley thought about the way she had turned her life over to God. She had stopped questioning why things happened the way they did, and instead accepted them with a belief that God had a plan for her.

"Yes, I'm a daughter of the promise." She smiled back at Lillian.

Lillian placed another towel in the basket. Instead of unclipping another one from the line, she turned to Carley. "You know, I've been thinking a lot about a way to include Noah in all our lives. Especially now that you're going to be his wife. How nice it would be if we could all interact. Even if just some of the time." She shook her head. "But Samuel doesn't want to go against the bishop, and he still seems guarded about his feelings about Noah." She wiped a bead of sweat from her forehead. "This heat is horrible."

Carley had already thought about what it would be like sleeping in the farmhouse with no air-conditioning in August. "Yes, it is," she agreed.

They resumed taking clothes off the line and folding them.

"When are you planning to get married?"

"Noah said he wants to get married as soon as possible. But it all is happening so fast." Carley was still having a hard time believing she was actually going to be Noah's wife. "Neither of us wants a lot of fanfare. Just something small. I stayed at the clinic for about two hours, and we talked about it. Dana left almost immediately after I got there." Carley chuckled. "She placed a desktop nameplate, engraved with my name, on the receptionist's desk and said she was no longer needed there. She said she couldn't stand being cooped up in the small reception area. Can you believe that Noah actually ordered a nameplate in case I came back?"

"That was some very hopeful thinking on his part." Lillian scooped up the laundry basket and headed toward the house. "Guess I'd better check on David and Anna. Dr. Bolton said last week that David is doing great, but he still can't go back to work with Samuel in the fields for another few weeks. I'm going to miss him caring for Anna, though. I've been able to get so much done."

From the kitchen, Carley could hear David playing with Anna in the next room. Lillian poked her head around to see that all was well, and then she and Carley both took a welcome break at the kitchen table. The cross-breeze from the open windows was refreshing, but not enough to stop the sweat running down the back of Carley's neck. "Lillian, don't you miss air-conditioning this time of year?"

"I did at first," Lillian answered. "But believe it or not, you get used to it." She tapped her finger against her chin. "Tomorrow is Sisters' Day. It's a large group, and we're all meeting at Rebecca's house. I'm going to talk to the others about some way we can make this work with Noah. Mary Ellen, Rebecca, Sadie, and *mei mamm* were all so glad you were coming back. It was never discussed, but I know they were all hoping you and Noah would be married. Even Esther got a gleam in her eye when she heard you were returning to Paradise. They all want Noah to be happy, and although no one says much, they wish the shunning could be toned down. Can you come to Sisters' Day tomorrow morning? I know everyone wants to see you."

"Hug everyone for me, and tell them I hope to see them all soon, but it appears I have a job." Carley smiled. "I told Noah I would be there in the morning, though patients are scarce. The location he selected for the clinic was custom picked to accommodate the Amish community. And that doesn't seem to be working out."

"I know," Lillian said regretfully. Then she smiled. "We'll see about that."

A week later, Carley was settled comfortably into her routine. Up at four thirty with Lillian, she would help with breakfast and household chores until nine o'clock in the morning. Then she headed to the clinic, which was averaging two patients per day. While the lack of patrons was disheartening, the upside was that she and Noah often spent hours talking. And unlike when she arrived in Paradise the first time, there was no longer a need for a nap and the hard work exhilarated her, as opposed to exhausting her.

As she sat twiddling her thumbs this Tuesday morning, Noah was on the phone with Dr. Bolton in his office. From what Carley could hear from down the hall, Noah was asking about David's progress and updating Dr. Bolton about his own recovery. Gloria was in the file room down the hall—a small storage room converted to hold six file cabinets, most of which remained empty. But Gloria optimistically readied file folders for use when new patients arrived.

Carley glanced at her watch. Ten thirty. They'd only had one patient this morning. A woman Gloria knew brought in her two-year-old son who had a fever. Otherwise, all had been quiet.

Until now.

As much as Carley wanted the Amish to patronize Noah's clinic, the sight of the first buggy pulling up to the building sent her heart racing with worry, which escalated as she watched Mary Ellen step out of the buggy and tie off on one of the stumps Noah had installed out front. Hoping it was nothing serious, Carley watched Mary Ellen and another Amish woman she didn't recognize draw closer. The woman was toting a baby.

Carley headed down the hallway toward Noah's office. She motioned for Noah to get off the phone. He ended the conversation and met her at the door.

"Mary Ellen is here, and she's with another Amish woman with a baby." Carley tried to mask her concern, but Noah's eyes grew reflective at the mention of Mary Ellen.

"Gloria, we have a patient," Noah said to Gloria when he met her in the hallway. Gloria nodded, and Noah and Carley headed up front.

The bell Carley had placed on the front door rang when Mary Ellen and the other woman entered.

Carley took a seat in the reception nook, and Noah stood nearby.

"Hello, Carley. Hello, Noah," Mary Ellen said nervously. "This is Lizzie Kauffman and her daughter, Naomi." Mary Ellen nodded toward Lizzie and the baby. Lizzie seemed as sheepish as Mary Ellen about being at the clinic.

"Hello," Carley responded. "Which one of you is sick?"

Lizzie stepped forward. "We have an emergency!"

Noah instantly stiffened. "What's the emergency?"

"*Mei boppli* has a . . . cough," the woman said shyly.

Noah pursed his lips. "All right," he said slowly. "And is she running a high fever?"

"No," Lizzie responded.

"Why do you think it's an emergency? Has your baby showed other symptoms besides a cough?" Noah leaned in to have a closer look at the child.

"No. It's just an emergency." Lizzie turned toward Mary Ellen. "It's an emergency, no?"

Mary Ellen swallowed hard. "*Ya*, an emergency."

Carley was fighting a smile, but Noah seemed to catch on a little late.

"Oh, an *emergency*," he finally said. "Of course. Right this way." He motioned for Lizzie to head down the hallway to a room on the right.

Mary Ellen started to follow but paused at the reception desk. "It's *gut* you are back. I have jams, jellies, bread, and a pie in the buggy for Noah when we're done." She spoke in a whisper but with a smile beaming across her face.

"Thank you, Mary Ellen," Carley responded as her sister-in-law-to-be headed down the hallway.

There were six more emergencies that afternoon. All Amish patrons. Four children were brought in by their mothers—one case of pink-eye, one deeply embedded splinter, and two sinus infections. One woman about Carley's age wandered in with an earache, and an older Amish gentlemen had pulled a muscle. In every case, the person seeking treatment began by saying, "I have an emergency."

The next few weeks brought more Amish patrons, each with an ailment they claimed was a crisis.

When they weren't working at the clinic, Carley helped Lillian at the farm. But it was Lillian who often pushed her to spend more time with Noah. So Carley and Noah took walks through the park with Chloe, hand in hand, talking and planning their future. Sometimes they would go to the river, lie on a blanket, and gaze at the stars. Noah was wise about the constellations, and he would enthusiastically educate Carley. And they laughed. They laughed a lot. They were in love. It didn't matter what they were doing, just that they were doing it together.

Carley told Noah all about Dalton, the reason he gave for their breakup, and the unworthiness she had felt to share her life with anyone because she was unable to have children. Noah constantly reassured her that he would love her always, and that if it was God's will for them to be parents, the Lord would see fit to bless them with a family.

They also talked a lot about God's will and Noah's unquestionable faith. Carley still struggled at times, but she had stopped praying only for others and had begun to pray for her own direction in life. She was learning to forgive herself for walking away from Him so long ago, learning to let go of the bitterness she'd harbored since the accident. Noah was a patient man, often listening to Carley talk for hours on end about her growing relationship with God and her admitted disappointment at not being able to be a mother. It seemed to help her to talk about it with him, and he was always a good listener.

On one of their trips to the river, they lay side by side at the water's edge, Chloe curled up nearby, bursts of twinkling clusters overhead. Carley had never seen a shooting star.

"Look! Look!" She pointed upward. "Did you see it? Oh, wow! I've never seen a falling star before!"

She glanced at Noah on her right and caught him staring at her in a way she'd never seen before, his expression filled with a mixture of wonder and contentment, so much so that she didn't know what to say.

"Carley." He took her hand in his. "I love you so much."

"I love you too." She waited. Then giggled. "Did you see it?"

Noah laughed aloud. "Yes, I did. And watching you see it was the best part of all." He turned onto his side, propped his cheek on his elbow, and faced her. "Falling stars are rare, a flash of beauty against a backdrop of infinite space and time." He took her hand, kissed the tips of her fingers. "Like you. Rare. Beautiful."

"Noah," she whispered, swirling in the magic, never more in love, never happier. She was exactly where she was meant to be.

"Marry me Saturday." He leaned forward and brushed his lips against hers. "I don't want to wait."

It was Friday when Lillian walked into the clinic with Anna. She smiled at Carley then said, "I have an emergency."

"I bet you do," Carley teased.

"Everyone wants to use the clinic," Lillian whispered. "And this is the only way." She shrugged.

"Thank you, Lillian. And what emergency do we have here?" She smiled at Anna.

"She needs her shots. And it's an emergency because I'm a week late getting them." Lillian winked at Carley. "I have a peach crisp and a loaf of butter bread for Noah in the buggy."

She leaned in closer to Carley. "So tomorrow is the big day!"

"It is." Carley grinned. "No hoopla. Just me and Noah vowing to love each other for the rest of our lives. Pastor Marsh from Noah's church will be here to marry us, and I'm wearing the simple white dress I showed you."

"I think it's *wunderbaar* that you are marrying here at the clinic. The landscaping is beautiful out back, and it's become such an important part of both your lives."

"That's what we thought too," Carley said. "It's going to be hot, but we don't care. Thank you for agreeing to come stand with me as my matron of honor. I know that's not really allowed."

Lillian shrugged. "If it was a big church wedding, I wouldn't be able to. But I think I can do this in *gut* conscience, as long as you don't mind me wearing my Plain clothes."

"Of course not."

"And you can't take any pictures of me. Is that okay?"

Carley nodded. "I completely understand. I'm just thrilled that you will be here. Two of Noah's friends from the hospital are coming—Dr. Bolton and another man I haven't met. And, of course, Dana. Jenna is our flower girl. It's going to be very small." She paused. "Is Samuel or any of the family coming?" She was pretty sure she knew the answer.

Lillian pinched her lips together and met Carley's gaze. She shook her head. "I'm sorry, Carley."

"None of them are coming?"

"I don't think so," Lillian answered. "Samuel knows I'm coming, though."

"Is it going to cause a problem for you?"

Lillian shook her head. "No. Samuel knows how much I love you."

"Dr. Bolton is going to be Noah's best man. Noah said he was sure neither Samuel nor Ivan would show up. But I think he was hoping that Mary Ellen and Rebecca might come."

"They haven't said, Carley. But I wouldn't get my hopes up."

Lillian's eyes saddened. "Samuel said he would prefer that I not bring David or Anna either."

Carley's heart was breaking for Noah. "I see." She knew the entire situation was difficult for Lillian. She forced a smile and said, "Well, I'm glad you'll be here."

Noah gazed across the table at his bride-to-be. Tomorrow he would be a married man. Married to Carley Marek. He knew he should have some reservations about proposing so quickly, and he kept waiting for doubt to rear its ugly head. But nothing came. No regret. No worries. Only anticipation of a life with Carley. He'd had plenty of time to mull over Carley's concerns about not having children, but living without her wasn't a future he wanted to face. Adoption waiting lists were long, but God would bless them with children if it was meant to be.

"I love this restaurant," Carley said. Her face was aglow as she glanced around the Italian eatery.

Noah reached across the table and placed his hand on hers. "I love you," he said. "And I'm so ready to marry you tomorrow."

He had never been more certain of anything in his life. He loved Carley. He was glad Lillian would be attending the ceremony tomorrow, and he refused to darken the day with his disappointment that none of his family would be in attendance. Particularly Samuel.

"There's Dana." Carley nodded toward the door. "She's headed this way, and it looks like something is wrong."

"Hi. Sorry to bother you at dinner," Dana said when she

reached the table. "I stopped by the farm, and Lillian told me you were eating here tonight."

"Dana, is everything okay?" Noah asked.

Dana nervously wrung her hands together. "I hope so." She took a deep breath. "I have something very important to discuss with you both."

22

GOD BLESSED THEM WITH A PERFECT DAY. THE TEMPERATURE was below average by ten degrees, and the skies were clear and blue. A gentle breeze cooled the air, and Carley's white cotton dress swirled at her knees. Delicate lace trim around the short cupped sleeves, princess neckline, and hem accentuated the simple dress. It was tasteful and elegant, but plain enough to go with her matron of honor's simple blue dress, white apron, and white prayer *Kapp*.

Noah had never looked more handsome, wearing black slacks, a tailored white shirt, and a black tie. His wavy dark hair was neatly groomed, his face clean shaven, and his clothes ironed to perfection. Carley smiled in his direction as Pastor Marsh instructed the others as to their proper places.

The *others* were few. In addition to Carley and Noah, there were Dr. Bolton, Dr. Louis Sharp, Dana, Jenna, Lillian, and Pastor Marsh. Little Jenna was picture perfect, her blonde ringlets flowing around her beautiful face. Dressed in a pastel blue frock, her attire was also simple with a touch of elegance. She held a smaller version of the bouquet Carley was carrying—yellow roses.

Dipping meadows spanned as far as Carley could see. Amish farmsteads were visible in the distance, with towering silos stretching to the heavens. Faint sounds of the country could be heard—cows mooing, birds chirping, a faraway tractor, and—

Carley perked up. *Could it be?*

They all twisted around, their eyes following the sound of horse hooves coming down the road. Spontaneously they broke formation and wound their way around to the front of the clinic to see one, two, three, four, five buggies. One by one, they watched them turn into the parking lot.

Thank You, God.

Carley recognized Mary Ellen, her husband, and their two children in the first buggy that turned into the clinic. Next were Ivan and Katie Ann. Then Rachel and her family, who also brought Esther. And Sadie was in her buggy. Lillian's mother, Sarah Jane, had brought Lillian's grandfather, Jonas.

Carley's hands had landed on her chest. She glanced at Noah, whose dumbstruck expression was a sight to see. He was clearly overwhelmed, and his eyes radiated with warmth and appreciation. Carley reached for his hand. They walked around the building and greeted each new visitor with a hug.

Finally, while Noah continued to greet his family, Carley excused herself and headed back around to where Lillian was standing. Her friend looked like she would burst into tears at any minute. Carley knew why.

"I'm sorry, Carley," Lillian said with regret. "I was hoping Samuel would change his mind. I see that all the others did."

Carley embraced Lillian. "Don't you be sorry. You can't control what Samuel does. Besides, you're responsible for getting the rest of the family here, and I know how much it means to Noah."

Carley had already tried to pull at Samuel's heart by leaving

Noah's letter to him in plain view. Even though Lillian had put the stack of books aside, surely Samuel had found the letter by now. It must not have had the impact she'd thought it would.

Several times she'd thought about telling Lillian about the letter, but then Lillian would know she had read it—something Carley wasn't proud of.

It didn't make any difference now. Whether or not he'd found the letter, Samuel wasn't coming.

Everyone began to gather again. Noah was beaming, but Carley caught him glancing down the road. They faced each other. Pastor Marsh waited until everyone was settled, his Bible in his hands.

"Dearly beloved . . ."

Lillian had just left for the wedding when Samuel edged carefully around David, who was standing in the kitchen with a scowl on his face. He knew the boy wanted to attend Noah's wedding, but Samuel just couldn't see fit to defy the bishop.

Although . . . he knew what was going on all around him, with the clinic and all. And the bishop was turning a blind eye. Maybe Bishop Ebersol would turn a blind eye if he attended Noah's wedding. Or maybe the bishop would just never know.

He'd prayed about it. But in the end, not only did it defy the *Ordnung*, but he just didn't know how to go about going. Lillian had told him repeatedly he would be welcomed with open arms. But had he really done right by Noah by continuing to practice the shunning after what Noah had done for David?

That was his struggle, his question. Was doing right by Noah doing right by God? How could he do both?

Samuel trudged up the stairs with the weight of a suffering family on his shoulders, a family that should somehow be loving both Noah and God. He shook his head and walked into his bedroom.

"Tell me what to do, Lord." He leaned into Anna's crib and stared at his precious little one.

He took a deep breath and reckoned he'd better get started on some of the chores he'd told Lillian he'd work on today—household chores too heavy for her to handle. He glanced at the box of books in the corner of the room and knew he should have moved those to the storage shed weeks ago when Lillian asked him to. They wouldn't be needing the books until Anna was of reading age.

He lifted the heavy box, thinking there must have been three dozen old books of David's inside. The boy had long outgrown such books as the one on top. *My Family* by Bernard Day. Time to put them in storage and—

Samuel drew in a long breath, walked to the bed, and set the box down. He remembered. How could he have forgotten?

The letter from Noah was wedged between the pages, hanging over the edge about three inches. He'd given up looking for it weeks ago. And he hadn't paid any mind to the box in the corner, forgetting that he'd placed the letter in his favorite childhood book.

He sat down on the bed and slowly pulled it out—the letter he'd been so desperate to find.

Carley was ready to take her vows, but once again they were interrupted. This time a car slowed at the entrance to the clinic. Carley strained to see who was pulling in. Barbie Beiler. Carley hadn't invited her—she didn't know the woman all that well— but she was a dear friend of Lillian's. Of course she was more than welcome, even if a tad late.

Everyone held formation, waiting for Barbie to come around the corner of the building.

"Sorry we're late," she said as she walked up to the group holding Anna.

Lillian walked to Barbie and joyfully accepted Anna.

But all eyes were on Samuel and David when they rounded the corner.

"Hi, *Onkel* Noah." David wrapped his arms around Noah.

Carley could tell that Noah was having a difficult time keeping his emotions under control.

Lillian began weeping so hard to Carley's left that Barbie came and retrieved the baby. Carley heard Lillian ask Barbie how she'd gotten her family to the wedding.

"I was dropping off your money from the bake sale. Samuel was dressed and readying the buggy. I offered them a ride," Barbie responded.

"So you didn't talk him into it? He was already planning to bring the children and come?" Lillian cried harder as Barbie reached down and latched onto Lillian's hand.

"Yes, Lillian. He was."

Carley hugged David when he made his way toward her, but she didn't take her eyes off Noah and Samuel, studying them over David's shoulder, wondering what their next moves would be.

Noah's expression left no doubt as to his hesitancy to move toward his brother, who stood tall before him. Slowly Noah extended his hand to Samuel, who was equally slow to latch on.

"*Danki* for coming, Samuel," Noah said cautiously while still clutching Samuel's hand.

"*Gut* to be here."

Samuel handed Noah a letter.

Carley watched as Noah slowly unfolded the paper. No one moved. No one said anything. And Noah read.

When he was through reading, Carley watched as the two brothers pulled each other into an embrace.

When they separated, there wasn't a dry eye among them all. Samuel said, "I'd like to be your best man if you'd see fit."

Noah merely nodded. Carley knew it was all he could muster up. Emotion flooded his face as he turned to Dr. Bolton, who smiled and stepped away.

"Are we ready to begin?" Pastor Marsh asked Carley and Noah.

They both nodded. And with Lillian and Samuel on each side of them, Carley and Noah professed their love for each other—with all of the family present to witness the blessed event.

Two weeks later, Carley was growing anxious, fidgeting on the couch. She looked at her watch, knowing Dana and Jenna would be there any minute. It had been with Noah's blessing that Carley had redecorated the inside of what was now *their* home. Pleased with the results, she waited.

"Are you nervous?" Noah asked, taking a seat beside her on the couch.

"A little. But in a very good way."

"Have I told you today how much I love you?" Noah kissed her on the cheek.

"I believe you have, but I never tire of hearing it."

They sat quietly for a few minutes. Carley prayed, offering thanks and asking for guidance. Her new life was a blessing on so many levels.

"This is a wonderful opportunity for Dana." Noah smiled.

"And for us."

Carley recalled the important conversation Dana had wanted to have with them the day before the wedding. She had seemed so scared, yet excited and hopeful. A full scholarship to college at New York State was something to be proud of. After everything Dana had been through, she deserved this opportunity.

"I'm nineteen years old," she tearfully told Noah and Carley when she joined them that night at the Italian eatery. "I want to live my life."

As she enthusiastically told them about the scholarship, the same thing was on everyone's mind.

Jenna.

Dana had proceeded to ask Carley and Noah if they would keep Jenna while she attended school. Carley could still vividly recall the look exchanged between her and her husband-to-be as they both felt the presence of God bestowing this miracle upon them. A child in the house.

"Jenna is my sister, and I love her," Dana had said. "But I'm not ready to be a full-time mother. If you don't want to do this, then—"

"Yes, yes, yes!" Carley and Noah had said simultaneously.

And so arrangements were made. There wasn't much time—the fall semester started this week.

———

Carley sat nervously aglow, and Noah thought she'd never looked more beautiful as her eyes glistened with anticipation. They'd only discussed keeping Jenna while Dana attended school for the next four years, but there seemed to be an unspoken understanding by all parties that Jenna would be staying with them—for good.

And regardless of their closeness in age, Carley had assumed a parental role with Dana, despite their rough beginning. They had spent the past couple of weeks running around for school supplies and clothes and leasing Dana's house, and Carley had talked to Dana at length about her decision. Noah knew it would be hard for Dana to leave Jenna and that it was a choice she struggled with, but in the end Dana said she felt like she was making the right decision for everyone.

"Oh!" Carley said. "I almost forgot. I told Dana she could take my luggage to school with her. It's in our closet. I'd better go get it."

"You sit." He patted her leg and smiled, saying, "I'll go get the luggage."

Noah walked into the bedroom he shared with Carley. He smiled at the quilt he'd bought her at the mud sale, now a permanent part of their lives, their memories. Things had certainly come full circle, in so many ways.

After he pulled the three-piece luggage set from the closet, he noticed the letter he'd written to Samuel so long ago, on the nightstand by the bed. He reached for it, the way he'd done over and over since Samuel handed it to him at the wedding. He couldn't help but wonder how many times Samuel might have read the letter before he turned it over to him.

Samuel had told him it was the only letter Noah sent him that he kept—although he'd read a few others before tossing them in the trash. When something invoked by God, and God alone, touched a man, he took it with him forever.

As was the case with this letter. Noah remembered writing it the day after he found out Samuel's wife had died. He'd written plenty of letters to Samuel prior to that. In the beginning, he'd tried to explain his choices to Samuel. But looking back, he realized those first letters resonated with bitterness about the shunning. Hearing of Rachel's passing had prompted him to try harder to reach his brother at a time when he knew Samuel needed him the most. He recalled God's voice spilling onto the pages. He'd hoped and prayed for a return letter that never came. But when Noah and Samuel needed God the most, the letter had resurfaced.

Dear Samuel,

My heart is breaking as I write this letter. I am filled with so much regret about so many things. But mostly at this moment, I am filled with sorrow about Rachel. Had I known of her passing, Samuel, I would have been there. I can only try to imagine what she must have meant to you, having never experienced that kind of love myself. I wish that I could have known her.

Perhaps my being there would only have caused you further pain. And despite my desperation to be a part of your life, I would never want to inflict more heartache. It's just that you are my brother, a part of me. Yes, there is Ivan, Mary Ellen, and Rebecca, all of whom I love and miss. But, Samuel, you and I stood out from the rest, had a bond I didn't think could ever be breached, no matter what. I was wrong.

My calling from God to become a doctor took me by surprise more than anyone. When I vowed to live by the Ordnung, I was too young to foresee what God truly had in store for me. But either way, I took vows and broke them.

Then, of course, there is the book. It pains me now more than you could know. And this is my penance, Samuel. The loss of my family.

But I want you to understand the powerful message in my calling. So I am going to tell you a story that might help you to understand my message from God, and why it couldn't be ignored, why I broke my vows.

I was sixteen. Looking back, it seems awfully young to recognize the event as my calling, but I remember knowing that it was beyond a doubt. Therein is where I made my mistake. I should have followed my heart and declined membership in the community by baptism. But breaking Mamm and Daed's heart wasn't an easy thing to face either.

My rumschpringe was in full swing, and I spent a lot of my time hanging out with a kid you didn't know. He was an Englischer, and he had a car. Remember all those times I snuck out of the house late at night? I would go hang out with Paul Simpson. He was like most Englisch kids, except for one thing. He would disappear for weeks at a time. When I finally confronted him about it, he said he was on dialysis. In case you don't know what that means, his kidneys were failing. He was going to die without a kidney transplant. He'd go through periods of good health, then decline, and I wouldn't see him for a while.

I was young and stupid, didn't understand anything about such an illness, but I tried like heck to get him to take one of my kidneys. I even went so far as to go to the hospital and find out my blood type, only to learn that it wasn't a match with Paul's. He had some rare blood type and none of his family was a match either. He was on a long list, waiting for a donor.

He died two days before his seventeenth birthday. I never said anything to you or Mamm and Daed. I'd just been baptized, and I was torn between my vows and my own strong calling from God. I was so completely distraught over not being able to save Paul's life, and the message I kept getting from God was, "But there are many lives for you to save." Maybe I couldn't give a kidney to save a life, but I knew in my heart that I was meant to be a doctor.

I tell you this now so that maybe you will understand, if only a little, why I did what I did. There is no excuse for my writing the book—selfish bitterness only, at the loss of my family, particularly you. Do you remember the fish we caught at the pond? A happy memory for me. I wanted to share some of those happy recollections with the world. Unfortunately, my mind and heart were clouded with darkness, and stories ended up in that book that should not have.

While I might not understand your grief, Samuel, I understand loss. Please accept my most sincere condolences about Rachel. Mary Ellen wrote to me that you have a son, David. I will continue to hope and pray for reconciliation between the two of us, that perhaps you might feel lenient about the shunning. I will also pray that I will be able to meet your son and somehow be a part of his life.

My brother, my friend, may God bless you during these difficult times—now and always.

Noah

Noah placed the letter back on the nightstand. He knew he'd read it again.

Things had been different since the wedding. Far from perfect, and Samuel still struggled with the shunning. But their relationship was on a new path toward healing. And shunning or no shunning, Noah and Carley had spent the past two Sundays eating Sunday supper with Samuel and his entire family. Reuniting with Samuel and his other siblings was a blessing. And getting to know David . . . well, he felt even more touched by God's goodness.

He recalled a difficult conversation a few days after the wedding. Noah and Carley opted not to take any type of honeymoon, since the clinic had become popular in the Amish community. A badly scraped knee would become an emergency, especially if it was one of his siblings' children, providing opportunities for them to get to know their uncle.

Samuel had showed up at the clinic right at closing time one evening, asking Noah to take a walk with him. An intense conversation ensued, one that Noah had known was coming. David's life expectancy hadn't been discussed since that day in the hospital when Samuel questioned how long the kidney would last. But Samuel brought the matter up again.

Noah explained to him that even though a kidney usually only lasted ten to fifteen years, there had been much success with second kidney transplants. Samuel shared his fear with Noah. He broke down and cried. And Noah cried along with his brother. The memory of Paul shot through his mind, his face as clear as the last time Noah saw him. He and Samuel had both sat down on the side of the road, and for the first time in sixteen years, they had prayed together.

Noah's thoughts were interrupted when he heard Carley

calling his name. But he knew that no matter what happened in the future, Samuel's heart had opened. Things would never be the same for either of them.

"They're here," Carley said when he rounded the corner. They both headed toward the door.

Carley's heart was pounding with hope and faith that she would be a good role model for Jenna.

"Me and Jenna have already said our good-byes," Dana said when Noah opened the door. She sniffled and dabbed at her eyes.

Carley and Noah had known this would be a huge adjustment for Jenna, and they had turned Noah's extra bedroom into a beautiful little girl's room. Noah had faced the demons in his blue box, giving the books to the library to keep or distribute as they wished. The Amish keepsakes he'd held on to no longer represented regret or bitterness, but instead hope for the future. He displayed a small box he made as a boy in his and Carley's bedroom, and a cedar birdhouse hung in the backyard.

Once the keeper of past regrets, the pink room now represented something entirely different. It would be home to Jenna, filled with the sounds of laughter, playing, bedtime stories, and love of family.

Standing in the doorway of Carley and Noah's home, Jenna looked into Carley's eyes as if for the first time. Something was very much on Jenna's mind.

Squatting down to face her, Carley's heart pounded. "What is it, Jenna?" she asked.

Jenna twisted her mouth sideways and seemed to be in heavy thought.

Carley worried whether the transition was causing Jenna to have second thoughts.

Jenna ran toward Dana, who leaned down to her level. Carley watched the little girl whisper into Dana's ear. Then Dana squatted completely down to face Jenna, cupping the child's cheeks in her hands. "It is perfectly fine with me. Maybe you should ask Carley." Dana tearfully smiled in Carley's direction.

Jenna slowly walked to where Carley was still kneeling, and Carley's heart filled with worry. Perhaps Jenna wasn't going to stay after all.

"What is it, Jenna?" Carley asked again. She gently stroked Jenna's hair.

Jenna looked away from Carley and down at the floor. "Dana said that if it's okay with you, it's okay with her if I call you Mommy."

A lightning bolt of joy hit Carley's heart. She tilted her head back, trying unsuccessfully to keep the tears from spilling over. "That would be just perfect with me," she said with a smile.

Then Jenna looked up and smiled the brightest smile Carley had ever seen. "Mommy," she began slowly, "can we go get an ice cream?"

Carley felt Noah's hand on her shoulder, and her heart overflowed with love and gratitude for her many blessings. She took Jenna into her arms, squeezing her tight. "You bet we can." She tearfully glanced toward heaven.

Thank You.

Acknowledgments

A HUGE THANK-YOU TO MY FAMILY AND FRIENDS FOR YOUR constant support and encouragement.

To my husband, Patrick, thank you for the multiple roles you play in my life—companion, best friend, and soul mate forever. You complete me, and life with you makes all things possible. I love you, sweetie.

To my sons, Eric and Cory, keep it real and follow God's plan for you. You boys mean more to me than either of you will ever know until you have little ones of your own running around. I love you both with all my heart.

Mother, I'm so proud to dedicate this book to you, and even prouder to be your daughter. You are an amazing woman, and I hope you are still whitewater canoeing well into your eighties and nineties!

Thank you to all my "sistas": Laurie, Rene, Melody, Dawn, Valarie, Sue, Carol, and Mindy. You gals rock! And to my mother-in-law, Pat, for cooking for us when the deadlines crept up on me!

Reneé Bissmeyer—as cliché as it sounds, you truly are the wind beneath my wings, pushing me to keep going even when times are tough. God has truly blessed us with this lifelong friendship.

A special thank-you to Amy Clipston and her husband, Joe, for sharing details about Joe's kidney transplant and his pending operation. I keep you both in my prayers. Amy, you are such a doll. I hope we get to meet in person soon, dear friend.

To Tamara Stephens, renal transplant coordinator, thank you for lending your expertise with regard to the hospital scenes and kidney transplant issues. Your time and efforts are very much appreciated. Take care always.

Barbie Beiler, it seemed fitting to borrow your name for the *Englisch* friend in *Plain Pursuit*, as I know you help your Amish friends the same way you have so graciously assisted me throughout the writing of this novel and the previous book. Your Amish and Mennonite background helps me to keep the stories authentic. Thanks also to Barbie's mom, Anna B. King. You offered me your experience of growing up Old Order Amish as you read the books prior to publication. Many thanks, my friends.

To my Old Order Amish friend in Lancaster County, thank you for allowing me to share your fabulous recipes and for your continued availability to answer my questions. Blessings to you.

Mary Sue Seymour, it's great to have an agent who is also a friend. Thank you for everything. Peace to you always.

Leslie Peterson, you are so much fun to work with! You make what could be a tedious round of revisions not such a scary thing.

A special thank-you to Natalie Hanemann and the entire team at Thomas Nelson. I'm very proud to be a part of this amazing family. Blessings to each and every one of you.

My most heartfelt thanks will always be to God. Without His guidance these books would not be possible. *Thank You.*

Reading Group Guide

1. At the beginning of the story, Carley is forced to take a vacation because her editor believes she hasn't come to terms with the accident and the death of her mother. Do you believe that to be true? Why or why not? What might have happened to Carley if she had continued on her current path, never going to Lancaster County?

2. Early in the story, Lillian tries to talk to Carley about God. Carley is not comfortable with the topic. Have you ever had a friend who tried to widen the scope of friendship by bringing up spiritual issues never before discussed? Did you really listen to what that person had to say? Or, if you were in Lillian's shoes, how far would you push the issue in an effort for your friend to see that having a relationship with God can make a difference?

3. When Noah approaches the subject of God with Carley, she becomes agitated. However, each time Noah veers away from the subject, Carley comes back

to it. Why do you think that is? Have you ever had a difficult time reaching out to God because you felt like He had let you down? If so, how did you resolve those feelings?

4. Carley judges Noah based, in part, on his profession. Have you ever judged someone based on his or her line of work, or the way that person looked or dressed? Were opportunities missed because of your judgment? If so, in what way?

5. The Amish believe that shunning is a way to keep the church pure. It is not intended to be a punishment, but an opportunity for the person shunned to right his or her ways in the eyes of God. Do you feel this is a fair and acceptable practice? Or do you believe it is cruel? Should exceptions be made in certain cases? Have you ever been shunned by someone you love? Have you ever shunned?

6. When Noah falls into a coma, his family members fear the possibilities, causing them to struggle between upholding the shunning and standing by their loved one. Have you ever held firmly to a belief, only to have it tested during a crisis? What if someone you had pushed away lapsed into a coma—or worse, died? What regrets would you have? Are there relationships in your life you need to take a look at while you still can?

7. Carley watches those around her put their faith in God, despite the challenges they face. In what ways did Carley's life begin to change when she opened her heart to God? When she accepted that the plan she had for herself might not be the plan God had for her? Have you struggled with accepting God's plan in your own life? In what way?

8. Why was it so important to Samuel to find the letter Noah wrote him? What do you think would have happened if he hadn't found it? Would he still have gone to the wedding? Why did he give the letter to Noah?

9. Carley finds self-healing when she focuses on the needs of others. In addition to getting the clinic ready, helping Lillian with household chores, and caring for Anna, how else did she help those around her? Did she help Samuel? Dana? Esther? What opportunities have you had to minister to yourself as you minister to others?

10. Members of the Old Order Amish community worry that they will be unequally yoked with outsiders. However, despite their beliefs, they still maintain relationships with several *English* friends in the story. Have you ever felt unequally yoked with someone? Did you disregard your beliefs to help that person in a time of need or to allow a friendship to develop?

11. Lillian has everything Carley wants—a loving husband and beautiful family. Does Carley ever show signs of being envious? Or jealous? What is the difference between the two emotions? Have you ever envied someone you felt "had it all"? What did you do about it?

12. Carley is afraid to commit to a relationship with Noah, largely due to her breakup with Dalton. Would things have played out differently if Carley hadn't been haunted by those bad memories of Dalton? Have you ever allowed events from the past to influence your decisions?

Amish Recipes

Raisin Puffs

1½   cups raisins
1   cup water

Boil raisins in water until water is gone.
Then add:

1   cup butter
1   tsp. baking soda

In another pot, heat together:

1   tsp. vanilla
2   eggs
1½   cups sugar

Add to raisin mixture and stir.

In large bowl, combine raisin mixture with 3¼ cups flour and ½ tsp. salt. Mix well.

Flour hands. Roll dough into 1-inch balls. Roll balls in cinnamon-sugar mixture.

Bake at 350 degrees for 10 minutes. Makes 3 dozen.

Homemade Bread

In a small bowl, mix together:
- ½ cup warm water
- 1 tsp. sugar
- 3 T. yeast (4¼-oz. packets)

Let sit for 5 to 10 minutes.
In large bowl, mix together:

- 1½ tsps. salt
- ¼ cup sugar
- ¼ cup vegetable oil
- 1 qt. warm water
- 4 cups flour

Add yeast mixture and mix. Add 5 more cups of flour. If mixture seems too sticky, add more flour until dough pulls from side of bowl. Knead well and let rise in bowl for 30 minutes. Then knead again and put in 5 bread pans. Let rise another 30 minutes. Bake at 350 degrees for 30 minutes.

Meatloaf

1½   lbs. ground beef

1   cup tomato juice

¾   cup quick oats

1   egg (beaten)

2   T. brown sugar

¼   cup chopped onion

1½   tsps. salt

¼   tsp. pepper

Combine all ingredients and mix well. Form into small loaves and place in baking dish.

SAUCE:

1½   cups brown sugar

½   tsp. garlic powder

1   cup water

2   T. liquid smoke

1   cup ketchup

Pour sauce over top of loaves and bake at 350 degrees for 75 minutes. Let stand for 5 minutes before serving.

Baked Corn Casserole

2	cans creamed corn
1½	T. flour
1	cup milk
1	T. sugar
½	tsp. pepper
1	tsp. salt
2	eggs (beaten)

Spray casserole dish with nonstick cooking spray. In large bowl, mix together corn, flour, milk, sugar, pepper, and salt. Then add beaten eggs. Put in casserole dish.

Bake at 350 degrees for 30 minutes. While casserole is baking, combine 4 T. butter with 1½ cups Ritz cracker crumbs (1 sleeve). Pull out casserole, sprinkle with Ritz crumbs, and bake for 15 more minutes.